STUDY GUIDE
Scott A. Bailey

PSYCHOLOGY

FOURTH EDITION

Stephen F. Davis

Joseph J. Palladino

PEARSON

Prentice
Hall

Upper Saddle River, New Jersey 07458

© 2004 by PEARSON EDUCATION, INC.
Upper Saddle River, New Jersey 07458

ISBN 0-13-049242-6

Printed in the United States of America

CONTENTS

How to Use the Study Guide

This manual was created especially for you. The format of the manual conforms exactly to your textbook, *Psychology,* Fourth Edition, by Drs. Steve Davis and Joe Palladino.

Use this manual when you study your textbook and when you prepare for exams and quizzes. The two resources go hand in hand. Each chapter of the study guide contains a skeletal outline that was taken exactly from the corresponding chapter in the textbook. To get the most from each resource and from your psychology class, find a place to study where you can spread out all your material for the course.

Here are the elements that you will find in the chapters of this manual:

1. Chapter Overview. The first page of each chapter of the manual has the brief outline from the beginning of each respective chapter of the text.

2. Outline. The second page of each chapter begins a formal outline of the corresponding chapter from the textbook. Space has been provided so that you may jot down notes or questions that occur to you as you study the text.

> **a. Maximize Use of the Text.** The *Tip* section at the end of Chapter 6 of this manual, *Getting the Most from Your Textbook,* presents several ideas that help make the process of studying text material an active one.

3. Learning Objectives. At the end of each chapter outline is a list of questions and statements that relate to the content from the chapter. Having studied the chapter, you should be able to address each of these.

4. Naming Exercises. Exercises to test your knowledge of key names, terms, and anatomical structures are presented following the learning objectives in each chapter. The correct answers to these items are presented immediately following the practice tests. Naming exercises take one of two forms:

> **a. Labeling Exercises.** In Chapters 2 and 3, you will find figures that represent brain and neuron anatomy and the organs responsible for sensory awareness.

> **b. Key Word Exercises.** For every chapter except Chapters 2 and 3, you will find fill-in-the-blank exercises to test your knowledge of key words.

5. Practice Tests. Each chapter has a multiple-choice practice test. Take each of these after you have studied all the material from the relevant chapter. Answers and explanations are presented following the answers for the naming exercises.

6. Key Vocabulary Words. After the answers to the practice tests you will find each of the key terms from the chapter, presented in the order in which they appeared in the textbook. Use the space beside each term to define the term *in your own language.* In order to define the terms in language that is comfortable for you, you will have to understand the definitions from the book and process them. This process will lead to your comprehension of the terms. In addition to writing definitions of the terms, you may wish to create flash cards that have the terms on one side and their definitions on the other. Understanding the language of psychology is important in order for you to be able to understand the concepts that are built upon the language.

The pages of this manual are perforated to make them easy to remove. When you are preparing for a test, you may find it easier to carry only the pages that correspond to the chapters for which you are responsible. Another suggestion would be to remove and combine the naming exercises and practice tests relevant to the material for a forthcoming test.

The manual has been three-hole punched so that you can easily remove and insert the pages into your binder for the class. You will find that organizing your class notes, practice tests, and materials distributed by your professor (including assignments, quizzes, and tests) will be helpful when you need to refer to them in the future.

Tips for Success Topics. In addition to the chapter-related material, a dozen *Tip for Success* sections are included in this manual. The *Tips* are presented, one per chapter, at the end of the first 12 chapters. Start with the ones that will be of most use to you. The ambitious student will skip ahead and examine each tip within the first few days of the semester. Others will review them throughout the semester. They cover a range of topics, and represent ideas and techniques that can help you to be your best.

Please Send Your Comments. This study guide should help you master the content of your psychology course. If you have suggestions for changes to the manual, ideas for exercises that would make learning the material easier, or would be willing to share any other feedback, please send it to:

Scott A. Bailey, Ph.D.
Department of Psychology
Texas Lutheran University
1000 West Court Street
Seguin, Texas 78155

Email: sbailey@tlu.edu

Good Luck! I hope that you find your introductory psychology course to be both challenging and informative. The concepts that you will learn from this course will be of great value to you for years to come.

CHAPTER 1

Psychology, Research, and You

BECOMING A PSYCHOLOGICAL DETECTIVE
Arthur Conan Doyle's Belief in Fairies
Guidelines for the Psychological Detective

RESEARCH METHODS IN PSYCHOLOGY
The Case Study
Naturalistic Observation
Correlational Research
Survey Research
The Experimental Method
Statistics and Psychologists
Research Ethics

THE ORIGINS OF MODERN PSYCHOLOGY
Wundt and Structuralism
Functionalism
Gestalt Psychology
The Behavioral Perspective
Sigmund Freud and the Psychodynamic Perspective
The Humanistic Perspective
The Evolutionary Perspective
The Physiological Perspective
The Cognitive Perspective
The Cultural and Diversity Perspective

PRESENT-DAY PSYCHOLOGY

PSYCHOLOGICAL SPECIALTIES

Do You Know?

Do you know that psychology is an academic discipline that was founded upon careful scientific research? Since the establishing of a lab in Germany by Wundt in the late 1800s to the present, psychologists have sought causal explanations of human and nonhuman animal behavioral phenomena through empirical investigations. Whether working in applied settings such as clinics and counseling centers, in field settings such as crime scenes and wildlife refuges, or in traditional laboratory settings, psychologists seek to gather high quality data that will lend insight into myriad questions concerning behavior. Thus, counter to lay views on psychology, solid grounding in empirical research is central to the work of all psychologists. As you read your textbook, consider how psychologists might go about systematically studying each of the topics you study. Recall the passion for asking *why* that two-year-olds possess; psychologists similarly engage in a ceaseless quest to learn.

Notes from Class and the Textbook

Use the space provided in this outline to record notes from the textbook as well as from class lectures and discussion. Questions related to the *Psychological Detective, Hands On, Myth or Science* and *Study Tip* sections in the text have been presented in the outline; use the associated space to respond to the questions and to record your own comments about the issues.

I. Becoming a Psychological Detective

    A. Arthur Conan Doyle's Belief in Fairies

        1. The Law of Parsimony

    B. Guidelines for the Psychological Detective

Note: When a Psychological Detective feature appears in the text, you will see an icon of a magnifying glass. The magnifying glass icon will be used in the study guide outline to alert you to an opportunity to apply your critical thinking skills.

        1. What is the statement or claim and who is making it?

        2. Is the statement or claim based on scientific observations?

        3. What do statistics reveal?

        4. Are there plausible alternative explanations for the statement or claim?

Using the Guidelines for the Psychological Detective, analyze a statement or claim made in a current newspaper or magazine. How well does the statement or claim hold up under the scrutiny of these considerations?

II. Research Methods in Psychology

    A. The Case Study

    B. Naturalistic Observation

Point your Web browser at the textbook's Web page to see Live!Psych module 1.1.

    C. Correlational Research

Point your Web browser at the textbook's Web page to see Live!Psych module 1.2.

Create a scatterplot using the times of your current classes on the vertical axis (Y-axis), and the grades you are earning in each class on the horizontal axis (X-axis). Is there a pattern in your performance that suggests a relationship between time of class and how well you do? If there is a relationship, would it be characterized as positive or negative?

List several factors that could be responsible for an association between SAT scores and grade-point averages.

D. Survey Research

Why would a report on violent crimes from the police not necessarily reflect well the amount of violence that exists in society? How might the type of survey influence the kind of information that is collected?

E. The Experimental Method

Point your Web browser at the textbook's Web page to see Live!Psych module 1.3.

Why would it have been inappropriate for Bandura and his colleagues to assign only boys to the aggressive model condition and only girls to the nonaggressive model condition?

F. Statistics and Psychologists

Why is it necessary to summarize research data before disseminating them?

1. Descriptive Statistics

How do measures of central tendency and measures of variability for a given data set help contextualize and make individual data from the set more meaningful?

        2. Inferential Statistics

    G. Research Ethics

        1. Protection from Harm

        2. Confidentiality

        3. Voluntary Participation

        4. Deception and Intimidation

Create visual aids, such as icons or pictures, to help you remember the different principles of research ethics.

        5. The Ethics of Research with Animals

III. The Origins of Modern Psychology

    A. Wundt and Structuralism

    B. Functionalism

C. Gestalt Psychology

D. The Behavioral Perspective

E. Sigmund Freud and the Psychodynamic Perspective

F. The Humanistic Perspective

G. The Physiological Perspective

H. The Evolutionary Perspective

Point your Web browser at the textbook's Web page to see Live!Psych module 1.4.

I. The Cognitive Perspective

J. The Cultural and Diversity Perspective

Summarize the history of modern psychology in a short book. Write short, straightforward, one page summaries of each perspective to include in the book.

IV. Present-Day Psychology

V. Psychological Specialties

    A. Clinical and Counseling Psychology

    B. Other Specialties

List several ways that cultural issues can affect the development and conduct of psychological research.

    C. Emerging Specialties

Learning Objectives

After you have studied the chapter, you should be able to respond to the following statements and questions to convey your understanding of the material.

1. Identify and describe several ways psychologists gather information about the problems they research.

2. List, in order as they developed, the broad, thematic approaches characteristic of early psychology.

3. How do the perspectives (e.g., physiological, cognitive) psychologists adopt influence their approaches to their discipline?

4. What steps should one take when evaluating psychological research?

5. Name several different types of jobs that are held by psychology majors with bachelor's degrees.

Key Word Exercise

Fill in the blanks in the following statements with key words and terms from the textbook. Answer as many as you can without referring to your notes or to the book. If you have blanks after thinking about each item, try using your book. The answers are presented after the practice test.

1. Psychologists strive to design experiments that are void of _____ that may unintentionally influence the data they gather.

2. When describing research results, psychologists opt for the most _____ explanations, as they are the ones that rely on the fewest assumptions.

3. A _____ control group is one that illustrates the influence of having taken *any* medication in a drug experiment, even when the medication does not contain an active ingredient.

4. A *Sesame Street* definition of *hypothesis* is: an educated guess. More specifically, hypotheses are testable ideas that are carefully derived out of organized general principles called _____.

5. Correlations are relationships between sets of two variables in which changes in the level of one variable are associated with changes in the level of the other. The degree of relationship is expressed both in terms of the statistic r, and graphically with a _____.

6. _____ _____ was noted for emphasizing that perception of a whole differs from that of individual stimuli.

7. In spite of efforts to control extraneous variables, researchers are challenged by the fact that these unwanted influences on experimental data will persist. One way to reduce their impact is to distribute them among all the groups in an experiment. However, as they are typically unknown, one must use _____ _____, a technique that is employed in many experimental designs.

8. The _____ _____ was started by Pavlov and continued by Watson as an attempt to get psychologists to focus only on that which is overtly observable.

9. Though Harvard University refused to grant her a Ph.D. because of her gender, _____ _____ _____ was still elected as the 14th president of the APA.

10. The _____ _____ to psychology is one that many psychologists adopt because they use several approaches in their work.

Practice Test

Circle the letter that corresponds to the **best** alternative for each of the following items. Read each alternative carefully. The answers are presented at the end of this study guide chapter. Be sure to learn *why* each correct alternative is better than the others.

1. Proverbs are examples of:
    a. folk wisdom.
    b. falsifiable hypotheses.
    c. positive action words; their complements are converbs.
    d. universally applicable theories derived from cross-cultural research.

2. As discussed in the text passage on Arthur Conan Doyle's belief in fairies, *mediums* are:
    a. only slightly larger than smalls.
    b. the shirt sizes Doyle's Sherlock Holmes wore.
    c. descriptive statistics that share characteristics with both the mean and the mode.
    d. people who claim they can contact the spirit world and communicate with the dead during a séance.

3. *Bias* can unintentionally:
    a. cloud our observations.
    b. influence the questions we ask.
    c. influence the methods we use and the ways we interpret data.
    d. All of the above are true.

4. Which of the following statements is most parsimonious?
    a. Well-rested participants were more accurate than sleep-deprived participants.
    b. Accuracy of responding is impaired as a function of hormone cycle variations in sleep-deprived participants.
    c. Sleep-deprived participants were too fatigued to concentrate and consequently performed poorly in comparison to well-rested participants.
    d. Hormone cycle shifts, combined with the impact of overall fatigue, impaired the accuracy of functioning in sleep-deprived participants when they were compared to well-rested participants.

5. The experimental method is a preferred means of gathering information because it:
   a. is easy to use in most research contexts.
   b. can provide the basis for cause-and-effect statements.
   c. has a name that conveys credibility, and credibility is the primary goal of psychological research.
   d. is a fairly inexpensive technique when compared with other approaches (e.g., naturalistic observation).

6. Marie's research project indicated, with statistically significant data, that among first-year college students, those who took introductory psychology scored higher on a problem-solving test than did a comparable group of students who did not enroll in introductory psychology. According to this statement:
   a. students should take psychology if they get the chance.
   b. psychology students are smarter than nonpsychology students.
   c. even though the psychology students did statistically better, they did not perform absolutely better.
   d. psychology students outperformed nonpsychology students at a level greater than would be predicted by chance alone.

7. A third-variable problem occurs when people attribute a causal link between:
   a. the second and fourth variables.
   b. experiments, but not within experiments.
   c. two variables that share a relation with another variable.
   d. administrations of the independent and dependent variables.

8. Which of the following was *not* offered in the textbook as a guideline for evaluating a claim?
   a. What do statistics reveal?
   b. In what resource are the data in question published?
   c. Is the statement or claim based on scientific observations?
   d. Are there plausible alternative explanations for the statement or claim?

9. Like all scientists, psychologists employ the scientific method to investigate phenomena. An aspect of this method involves:
   a. microscopes, beakers, and the like.
   b. summarizing findings into widely applicable laws of behavior.
   c. using theories to derive hypotheses which may be tested experimentally.
   d. challenging daily the claims made by popular press information sources.

10. Which of the following statements is true about the relationship between the case study and naturalistic observation?
    a. Data from both generalize well to other contexts.
    b. Both have limitations but are useful in developing research ideas.
    c. With both, participants are scarcely aware they are being studied.
    d. Naturalistic observation involves essentially several concurrent case studies.

11. Which of the following values is indicative of the strongest degree of relationship between two variables?
    a. $r = -0.8$
    b. $r = -0.2$
    c. $r = +0.1$
    d. $r = +0.75$

12. When conducting survey research, it is important to use a representative sample of the population of interest. In other words,
    a. it is important to survey everyone in the population.
    b. one must gather a population of participants that mirrors the population of actual interest.
    c. contacting state or national governmental representatives should yield an accurate reflection of the population.
    d. the participants should reflect the gender, cultural, and other significant attributes of the population of interest.

13. Within the context of the experimental method, the independent variable is to the dependent variable as ___ is to ___.
    a. measure; manipulate
    b. manipulate; measure
    c. experimental; control
    d. control; experimental

14. If an experiment has a comparison group that does not receive the effect of the independent variable, it may be said that the experiment has a(n):
    a. control group.
    b. extraneous variable.
    c. operational definition.
    d. representative sample.

15. A significant advantage of the experimental method over other techniques for gathering information is that the experimental method can provide the basis for making cause-and-effect statements. This is because when using the experimental method, one manipulates ___ variables, controls for ___ variables, and measures ___ variables.
    a. dependent; independent; extraneous
    b. extraneous; dependent; independent
    c. independent; extraneous; dependent
    d. dependent; extraneous; independent

16. Using the random assignment procedure is one way:
    a. to ensure a proper control group.
    b. to control for extraneous variability.
    c. to really mess up an experiment; all assignments should be nonrandom.
    d. to scramble the independent and dependent variables and to help guard against bias.

17. In Bandura's study of the effects of modeling on aggression, the dependent variable was:
    a. the population of nursery school children.
    b. whether participants were in the experimental group or not.
    c. the number of hits delivered by participants to the Bobo doll.
    d. systematic exposure to either the aggressive model or the nonaggressive model.

18. Descriptive statistics are to inferential statistics as ___ is to ___.
    a. summarize; analyze
    b. analyze; summarize
    c. central tendency; variability
    d. variability; central tendency

19. The ethical guidelines that all experiments must meet concern all but which of the following issues?
    a. protection of subjects from harm
    b. the quality of the experimental design
    c. confidentiality of participants' names and identities
    d. whether subjects are debriefed after participating in an experiment involving deception

20. Much of what we understand about behavior has been learned from experiments involving animal subjects. Partially to address concerns about the use of animal subjects in medical and psychological research, the American Psychological Association has:
    a. promoted the animal rights movement.
    b. come out strongly in favor of experiments involving animals.
    c. adopted a set of principles to consider when designing an experiment.
    d. formed a task force called the Committee on Animals in Medicine and Psychology (CAMP).

21. Modern psychology represents a sort of blending of early philosophy and physiology. The first psychology laboratory did not exist until it was established by Wilhelm Wundt in 1879. Wundt was trained as a physician, but his mission in establishing the laboratory was to:
    a. describe the contents of the mind.
    b. study the purposes of consciousness.
    c. focus the study of behavior on that which was overtly observable.
    d. challenge the notion that conscious experience could be broken down into elements.

22. Sigmund Freud had a profound influence on psychology, although it is important to note that his contributions to the field have been highly controversial. It is interesting to note that Freud's background was:
    a. in neurology.
    b. greater than the sum of its parts.
    c. in the early school of thought in psychology: behaviorism.
    d. characterized by numerous unconscious sexual urges which led him to study psychology.

23. Early psychology was characterized by schools of thought such as Structuralism, Functionalism, Gestalt Psychology, and Behaviorism. Today, psychology:
    a. is in a school of thought known as the Cognitive Movement.
    b. is comprised of two major components: the Basic Movement and the Applied Movement.
    c. bears little resemblance to its earlier forms as its focus has shifted from behavior to consciousness.
    d. is a diversified field that is made up of several specialties, a growing number of which involve providing services to clients.

24. Clinical psychologist is to ___ as psychiatrist is to ___.
    a. Ph.D.; M.D.
    b. M.D.; Ph.D.
    c. less serious problems; serious problems
    d. serious problems; less serious problems

Answers to Key Word Exercise

1. biases	2. parsimonious	3. placebo
4. theories	5. scatterplot	6. Gestalt Psychology
7. random assignment	8. behavioral perspective	9. Mary Whiton Calkins
10. eclectic approach		

Practice Test Answers and Explanations

The practice test questions largely follow the order in which the material is presented in the textbook. The answers to the questions are given below, accompanied by a brief explanation of each. To develop your understanding of a concept more fully, locate and read the paragraph(s) or page(s) corresponding to the items in the text book.

1. a. Proverbs are forms of folk wisdom—a category of information that can provide explanations for every conceivable event, but can never be proved wrong.
2. d. Mediums are people who profess special abilities to communicate with those who have passed.
3. d. Bias, or preconceptions, can unintentionally influence the behaviors of researchers and participants.
4. a. Parsimonious statements (see law of parsimony) are simple explanations that rely on few or no assumptions.
5. b. Scientists prefer the experimental method because by systematically manipulating independent variables in experiments, while also using appropriate control conditions, it becomes possible to infer causal relationships from experimental results.
6. d. Statistically significant data are those that are sufficiently different than one would predict based on chance factors alone.

7. c.   Changes in the levels of two different variables often co-occur because both share a link with a third variable, and it is the third variable that is responsible for the correlation. An additional example would be the changes that occur in language acquisition and shoe size as a function of changes in level of maturation. Maturation is responsible for the changes, rather than one of the other two causing changes in the other.

8. b.   While it is important to consider the source of information one receives, the textbook focuses on critiquing the claim rather than the source for its communication.

9. c.   The scientific method is a cyclical process that involves ever adjusting the specificity of theories by way of testing the hypotheses they generate.

10. b.   Both are useful in helping develop research questions that may be addressed with the experimental method, but both also have shortcomings with respect to the validity and generalizability of the results they generate.

11. a.   The correlation coefficient, r, may potentially assume any value between -1.0 and $+1.0$, inclusive. The *strength of association* is expressed by the value's proximity to a nonzero integer (+/-1); the *direction of the relationship* is indicated by the value's sign (+ or -).

12. d.   Participants that comprise the *sample* in a survey project should reflect the diversity of the larger population that researchers are interested in studying.

13. b.   Researchers manipulate independent variables, and measure dependent variables.

14. a.   A control group is essentially an experimental group that does not receive the effect of the independent variable. Experimental and control groups are treated similarly in all other ways.

15. c.   See explanation to #13, above. Note also that experimenters attempt to control, or hold constant, unwanted, or extraneous, variability.

16. b.   One way to control for extraneous variability is to assign participants to groups randomly; this assures that each group is equally likely to have participants with any given characteristic.

17. c.   The dependent variable is that which is *measured* in an experiment; Bandura measured hits.

18. a.   Descriptive statistics summarize data sets; inferential statistics are analytic in nature.

19. b.   Institutional review boards review proposals to determine that the potential participants will be treated ethically; IRBs are not organized to provide feedback on experimental designs.

20. c.   The APA is concerned that animals be used in experimentation only after consideration of the seven principles that are presented on page 26 in your textbook.

21. b.   Wundt's interest in establishing a laboratory was to describe the contents of the conscious mind.

22. a.   Freud was trained as a neurologist. His training facilitated his recognition that the symptoms of one of his patients were neurologically impossible, and that the patient must have had a psychological rather than a neurological disorder.

23. d.   Present-day psychology is a diverse field that is comprised of many specialties.

24. a.   One must have a Ph.D. to be a clinical psychologist; psychiatrists are medical doctors who specialize in the medical treatment of illnesses.

Key Vocabulary Terms

Use the following list to write definitions *in your own words* for each of the key terms from the chapter. Translating the terms into language that is comfortable and familiar for you will facilitate your learning. For further study of these terms, go to the companion website for the textbook where you will find electronic flash cards that you may use to test your vocabulary.

psychology

bias

law of parsimony

placebo effect

scientific method

theory

hypothesis

case study

naturalistic observation

scatterplot

correlation coefficient

survey method

representative sample

experimental method

independent variable (IV)

dependent variable (DV)

operational definition

experimental group

control group

extraneous variables

random assignment

statistics

descriptive statistics

inferential statistics

measures of central tendency

measures of variability

informed consent

debriefing

structuralism

introspection

cognitive psychology

functionalism

Gestalt psychology

behavioral perspective

psychodynamic perspective

psychoanalytic therapy

humanistic perspective

physiological perspective

evolutionary perspective

cognitive perspective

eclectic approach

clinical psychology

psychiatrist

counseling psychology

research psychologist

ethnocentrism

cross-cultural psychology

school psychologist

industrial and organizational (I/O) psychologist

consumer psychology

health psychology

forensic psychologist

sport psychologist

neuropsychologist

Tip for Success: Goal Setting

So What Is a Goal, Exactly?

Webster's dictionary defines *goal* as aim or purpose. When put in those terms, it is difficult to imagine not having goals, for to not have goals would be to have no aim or purpose. In a broader sense, a goal is anything you could do, have, or be. Goal setting helps people to live meaningful lives and to attain the careers they wish to have. Let us try breaking these ideas of what goals are into three categories: those that should be accomplished within the next few days, those that should be accomplished within the next several months, and those that you hope to accomplish in some years to come.

Note that the language associated with the first two categories indicated that the goal should be accomplished *within* some allotted time frame. Depending on the specific circumstances surrounding certain goals, you may need to be more precise with respect to when the goal will be met. Other goals, however, fall into a category of things that may be done within a range of times.   Added precision regarding when the goal will be accomplished may be helpful in ensuring that the goal is, in fact, met. The third category, on the other hand, was described with a fairly undetermined, indefinite range of time in mind. These goals are nearly always more abstract and therefore it is more difficult to schedule target completion dates for them.

In short, a goal is anything you could do, have, or be, and it may be done according to one of three time frames. For ease of reference, those time frames will be referred to as immediate, short-term, and long-term goals. Some people prefer to add another category, intermediate-term, that facilitates greater specificity for the more proximal long-range objectives. You should organize your goals in a way that is most meaningful for you.

Whose Goals?

First off, it is important that the goals you set are *your own goals*. If someone else imposes them on you, you may not have the sense of ownership you will need to proceed in striving to meet them. This issue is related to the concepts of intrinsic and extrinsic rewards. Intrinsic rewards come from within you—the positive feelings you get for doing a job well, meeting the expectations you set for yourself, and so on. Extrinsic rewards come from outside. Money and material items, praise from others, and various forms of entertainment are all forms of extrinsic rewards.

It is worth noting that behaviors that are intrinsically rewarding are far more persistent than those that rely on reward and recognition from outside.   The very act of achieving a goal you set out to meet is intrinsically rewarding. On the other hand, if others set your goals for you, you will likely depend on others to reward you when you meet them. If that reward is not forthcoming, your productivity will trail off predictably. Set your own goals and take pride in meeting them.

A Healthy Attitude Goes a Long Way

In addition to understanding *why* you should set goals, it will be helpful to consider *how* you will go about attaining your goals. A key to meeting goals is embodied in the attributes of a positive attitude. No doubt, your life experiences to date have helped you to understand that keeping your chin up, so to speak, is exceedingly helpful when you fall short of a mark. People who are able to persist in spite of their shortcomings are simply more successful at meeting their goals than those who get down on themselves when they do not succeed. The old adage, "'Can't-Do-It' never did anything," really fits here. Attitude may not be everything, but without a good attitude it is hard to do anything.

Sometimes you will fail. Setting goals that keep you working your hardest is the best way to ensure a high degree of productivity. If you fall short of your mark, take stock of what happened, re-evaluate the goals you are striving to meet, and proceed with the knowledge you gained from the experience.

Why Are Goals So Important Anyway?

Learning to set appropriate goals and to attain them is one of the most important things you can do, both in terms of making the most of your college experience and in terms of living a fulfilling life beyond your college years. However, it is not an easy task to set appropriate goals; and meeting the challenges you set for yourself can be difficult at times. In the end, though, the process of setting goals and striving to meet them is well worth doing and will put you in charge of using your time in ways that are rewarding and meaningful. Before describing some important things to consider when defining goals, it will be useful to discuss why goals are helpful.

Perhaps the most important reason to set goals is that they provide a focus for your attention and energy. If you know what you want to achieve, determining what to do at any given time is easy. On the other hand, if you lack the focus gained by setting goals, it can be hard to decide how to use available time. Unfortunately, when people have a hard time deciding how to use time, they often waste it. Eventually those wasted minutes and hours return to haunt us when we find ourselves pressed to accomplish something, such as studying for a test or writing a paper. One of the most disconcerting feelings people can have is the sense they get when they realize they are unable to produce their very best work because they did not plan appropriately. Setting goals and monitoring progress toward them is an excellent way to guard against this problem.

Another reason for setting goals has to do with the mixed blessing of independent living. Many college students find it exciting to begin living without having to report on their whereabouts to others. They feel liberated being able to come and go as they please, set their own hours, perform tasks and duties when they want to rather than as instructed by someone else. With freedom, though, comes responsibility. You will find it to be rewarding to determine, more or less, when you will do these things. You will discover also that it will be up to you to monitor your own progress and decision making. By learning to set and achieve goals, you will meet your responsibilities and be able to appreciate your freedom.

What are two good reasons for setting goals?

_____

_____

Greater Opportunities through Goal Setting

A word of clarification is appropriate here. The notion of setting goals for the reason of meeting responsibilities is only part of why you should embrace goal-setting as a way of organizing your activity. The other reason, which has been implied in the previous paragraphs, is that as you meet more goals you will gain greater opportunities. Those opportunities are extensions of the freedom you get for living responsibly—that is, for responsibly setting and meeting your goals. As a student, greater opportunities will enrich your experience and expand your choices for employment or for graduate or professional training following receipt of your bachelor's degree. Enhanced opportunities in the workplace typically mean more meaningful work and better pay. People who do not set and achieve goals simply do not have the same opportunities as those who do.

Some Specific Examples: Which Goals Go Where?

Let us illustrate these categories with more detailed descriptions. Immediate goals are those that you should list each evening for the following day. This exercise will make your mornings a little less hectic, and your memory of items from the list will allow you to begin planning for each day as you retire the preceding evening, and again as you get around the next morning. These goals constitute essentially a "to-do list." Be as specific as you can with these items; think in terms of filling 15-minute intervals. If you can learn to make use of the small chunks of time in your days, you will be more productive, and will have more discretionary time in your schedule. A failure to take advantage of the small chunks of time will likely lead to a sense of frustration with your schedule, and conflicts between your need to do academic work and your desire to engage in social activity.

Identify some Immediate Goals in the spaces below:

1. _____

2. _____

3. _____

Can you assign priorities to the items in your list?

The short-term goals you set for yourself will probably center on spending a certain amount of time preparing for classes, including writing drafts of papers and organizing notes to study for quizzes and exams. Additionally, you will want to include objectives dealing with proper rest, exercise, and opportunities to pursue extracurricular interests. It is worth noting that your college experience will be most memorable and meaningful if you can keep up with your academic responsibilities *and* participate in the life of your community, be it a residential campus, a church community, or your neighborhood. Interaction with others during your college years will constitute a significant percentage of your opportunities to grow and develop. However, be certain to keep track of the academic goals you set for yourself in this category. It is a tremendous feeling to be able to relax and go to bed early on the eve of an exam because you have prepared well along the way. By stark contrast, it is miserable and counterproductive to cram the night before an exam because you procrastinated.

What are four short-term goals you have set for yourself?

1. _____

2. _____

3. _____

4. _____

Did you list your short–term goals in order of priority?

The long-term goals you set for yourself will, in part, determine the short-term and immediate goals of days to come. If you select a given academic discipline as your major, for example, it is a long-term goal to meet the criteria for that major. That goal will influence the courses you choose, and the assignments, quizzes, and exams for the courses will in turn influence your immediate-range goals. As you progress through your academic career, your long-term goals may well change. That is all right. It is common for students to change their majors once or twice during the course of their academic careers. Just keep updating your goals and measuring progress toward them and you will be able to mark progress in your development as a scholar and as a responsible person living a meaningful life.

Identify three long-term goals:

1. _____

2. _____

3. _____

Do these reflect your range of interests?

Make Your Goals Challenging

If you have ever competed with someone who is just slightly better than you most of the time, you know how that interaction can really cause you to work your hardest and do your best. Think about how much you improve your debate, musical, athletic and other skills when you are challenged. The same principles apply to goal setting and attainment. If you set goals you can easily reach, you are bound to be bored. Set appropriately challenging goals, and you will experience significant growth and development.

Take Baby Steps

One of the most prized experiences humans have is attaining a goal. On the other hand, if you were to sit down to try to attain a long-term goal in an afternoon, say becoming a financially independent person with a meaningful career, you would throw your arms in the air before you were to get started. The real value of long-term goals is to provide focus. If you can measure the steps necessary to reach a long-term goal, and then work on each of them, one at a time, you will be less daunted concerning how to begin.

Starting Over

Maslow's hierarchy of needs, which is discussed in chapter six of your textbook (beginning on page 226), suggests that after meeting needs from basic levels, humans strive for increasingly abstract goals. These include belongingness, esteem needs, and self-actualization needs. Self-actualization refers to the need to develop one's full potential. If you are to reach your potential, it will be important for you to constantly monitor your progress on goals, adding new ones when appropriate. It is not enough to set a long-term goal—say completing graduate or professional school and establishing a career—you will need to renew your goals to help maintain your focus.

Make Your Goals Measurable

In order to make the most of the goal-setting process, you should strive to set goals that you can measure. This is easier for some categories of activity than it is for others. For example, it is easier to assess whether you achieved a goal or a particular mark on an exam or paper than it is to determine whether you improved your attitude toward your roommate. However, if you are creative, you can come up with ways to determine whether you are making desirable progress toward a given goal.

Try using an end-of-the-day log for charting progress toward goals. Such a log might include responses to the following questions:

1) What goals did I accomplish today? _____

2) Which short- and long-term goals did I make progress on today? _____

3) Which immediate goals did I not attain today? _____

4) How should I change my goals lists based on what I accomplished and did not accomplish today?

_____

Use Feedback

If the techniques you have developed for measuring progress toward your goals indicate that you are doing what you set out to do, you will surely enjoy the satisfaction of meeting your aims. If you determine that something is not going as you had hoped, this is useful too. Provided you are regularly evaluating your progress, you will be worlds ahead of where you would be if you did not attach measurable goals to your activity. Use the feedback you obtain to establish a fresh plan of action—whether that means to bear down and work harder, to punt, or to change horses.

More Remarks about Goal Setting

Goal setting is a critical component of leading a productive, satisfying life. However, it is not enough to merely set goals; you must implement activities that are targeted at meeting the goals, review whether the goals were in fact met, and constantly revise your goals in order to make the most of the process. A critical step in this process involves being able to locate the goals you set for yourself. Some people record their goals in daily organizers or calendars that they carry with them at all times. Benjamin Franklin is noted for having done this and being rather successful because of it. Others prefer to keep a notebook or computer file that can be accessed easily for regular monitoring of their progress. Do whatever works best for you. It is probably worth experimenting with a few different systems until you find a good fit for your style.

Consider the Following Goal-Related Questions

1) Why did you go to college?
2) Why did you enroll in a psychology course?
3) What about the other courses you are taking?
4) What career goal(s) have you established for yourself?
5) What kind of preparation will you need to meet your career goal?
6) What resources are available to help you answer these questions?

These questions should provide fodder for a good deal of thought. If you cannot answer each of them readily, relax and schedule some time to think about them. Make it a goal to answer these and other questions regarding your life as a student. Doing so will keep you on track to becoming the best student you can be. This is the key to gaining the most from your college experience.

Commit It to Writing

While it is helpful to simply think about goal setting, it is best to record your goals in writing. So get busy. Identify goals according to each of the timelines listed above and write them down. Tape the list to your bathroom mirror or put it on your dresser. Keep your goals list current and read it often.

CHAPTER 2

Behavioral Neuroscience

Do You Know?

Do you know that psychology has important implications for one of the fastest growing scientific disciplines—neuroscience? Neuroscience is a broad term that is used to represent any of several different academic and applied domains that are characterized as being focused in large part on the structure and function of the nervous system. Neuroscientists come from psychology, biology, biochemistry, physiology, anatomy, and medicine, to name some of the key areas. Inasmuch as important work in computer modeling of neuronal activity is being done today, it is appropriate to list computer scientists in the list of people interested in neuroscience as well. Indeed, the relationship between life science-based disciplines and computer science is reciprocal; each party benefits from the work of the other. The role for psychologists in this booming area cannot be understated. As research into the roots and causes of behavior becomes increasingly molecular, as when researchers focus on the implications of particular ion channels or transmitter substances for behavior, it is critical that the behavioral measures be carried out with the same experimental rigor and control as the more molecular components of the studies. Because psychologists are trained in the study of behavior, they bring a great deal to the interdisciplinary table of neuroscience. Without good behavioral emphasis as part of a project in neuroscience, one's capacity to make inferences about the implications for the study is severely limited.

Notes from Class and the Textbook

Use the space provided in this outline to record notes from the textbook as well as from class lectures and discussion. Questions related to the *Psychological Detective, Hands On, Myth or Science,* and *Study Tip* sections in the text have been presented in the outline; use the associated space to respond to the questions and to record your own comments about the issues.

I. Biology and Behavior

Point your Web browser at the textbook's Web page to see Live!Psych module 2.1.

II. The Nervous System

    A. The Peripheral Nervous System

        1. The Somatic Division

        2. The Autonomic Division

            a. The Sympathetic System

Suppose that your tire blows out while you are driving at a high rate of speed. Which sympathetic processes would be in operation under this circumstance? Write down the processes you think of before reading on in your text.

b. The Parasympathetic System

Make flash cards with the name of an organ and either "sympathetic" or "parasympathetic" on one side, and the organ's function in that system on the other. You may wish to use Figure 2-3, on page 45 in your textbook, to guide your creation of the cards. Then, do flash card drills with a classmate in order to learn the functions of the organs when under the influence of both systems.

    B. The Central Nervous System

        1. The Spinal Cord

III. The Endocrine System

    A. Major Endocrine Glands

        1. The Pineal Gland

        2. The Pancreas

        3. Hypothalamus

        4. The Pituitary Gland

        5. The Thyroid Gland

        6. The Gonads

        7. The Adrenal Glands

On a piece of scratch paper, work from memory only to create an outline of the major endocrine glands. Summarize the function of each gland.

IV. Neurons: The Cells of the Nervous System

    A. Components of the Neuron

        1. The Cell Membrane

        2. Dendrites

        3. The Cell Body

Point your Web browser at the textbook's Web page to see Live!Psych module 2.2.

        4. The Axon

        5. Terminal Buttons

        6. The Myelin Sheath

Consider what you have learned about the function of the myelin sheath. What do you suppose happens when the myelin sheath degenerates? Write down a few answers before reading further.

    B. The Synapse and Neurotransmitters

        1. The Synapse

        2. Neurotransmitters

Parkinson's disease appears to result from low levels of the neurotransmitter, dopamine. One potential treatment for the disease would seem to be to simply administer dopamine to patients; however, this treatment is not successful in diminishing the symptoms of the disease. Write down a few reasons why this treatment does not work.

3. Dopamine

4. Serotonin

5. Acetylcholine

Point your Web browser at the textbook's Web page to see Live!Psych module 2.3.

6. Norepinephrine

Convert Table 2-1, found on page 57 in your textbook, into a visual organizer. Use learning strategies such as a mind map or a think link format, different colored pens, or any other strategy that will help you learn about the principal neurotransmitters, their effects, location in the nervous system, and their functions within the system.

Conduct the Orientation, Memory and Concentration Test on page 58 in your textbook. The directions for the test may be found with the test. Calculate your score after you complete the test and consider it in light of the criterion for determining whether someone has dementia.

7. Clearing the Synapse

8. Neurotransmitters and Drug Action

    a. Agonists

    b. Antagonists

    c. Neuromodulators

C. The Nature of the Neural Signal

V. The Brain: A Closer Look

  A. Investigating Brain Functioning

    1. The Case Study Method

    2. Stereotaxic Surgery

    3. The Electroencephalograph

      a. Alpha Waves

      b. Beta Waves

      c. Theta Waves

      d. Delta Waves

    4. Computerized Brain Imaging

Imagine that a construction worker suffered a head injury that may have resulted in brain damage. Which of the techniques for studying brain structure and function (EEG, MEG, CT Scan, PET Scan, MRI, fMRI) would be appropriate to investigate the nature and extent of his damage? What would be the advantages and disadvantages of each technique in this situation?

B. Major Components of the Brain

1. The Hindbrain

2. The Midbrain

3. The Forebrain

Point your Web browser at the textbook's Web page to see Live!Psych module 2.4.

a. Frontal Lobes

b. Parietal Lobes

Reread the paragraphs from the bottom of page 76 and the top of page 78 concerning the myth that humans only use 10 pwecent of their brains. According to the text, what misunderstanding contributes to this myth?

c. Temporal Lobes

d. Occipital Lobes

e. Language and the Brain

C. The Plastic Brain

Can a person live with only half of a brain? What are the likely consequences of such a drastic intervention of the split brain surgical intervention? Consider this issue and write down your thoughts before proceeding.

D. The Split Brain

How would the split-brain operation influence your ability to perceive and describe a stimulus that is presented in your right visual field only? What if it were presented in the left visual field?

Point your Web browser at the textbook's Web page to see Live!Psych module 2.5.

Use the basic outline from page 40 of your textbook to create a detailed outline of the chapter. Compare your outline to the one in this study guide. Are your detailed outline and the study guide outline the same? If not, how do they differ? Consider the organization of these outlines as they relate to the material that is covered in the Behavioral Neuroscience chapter.

Learning Objectives

After you have studied the chapter, you should be able to respond to the following statements and questions to convey your understanding of the material.

1. What physiological processes are involved in sensing, processing, and responding? Which components of the nervous system are necessary for those processes to occur?

2. How are relictual (phylogenetically older) brains similar to and different from derived (more evolved) brains? Can you think of explanations other than evolution to account for the differences?

3. Imagine three neurons in a sequence: a sensory neuron, an interneuron, and a motor neuron. Describe what happens in the interneuron as it conveys information from the sensory cell to the motor neuron.

Labeling Exercises

It is helpful when learning the information from this chapter to study how some of the terms are used in the contexts of figures and tables. Having studied the chapter you should be able to fill in the missing information. The answers are given at the end of the chapter.

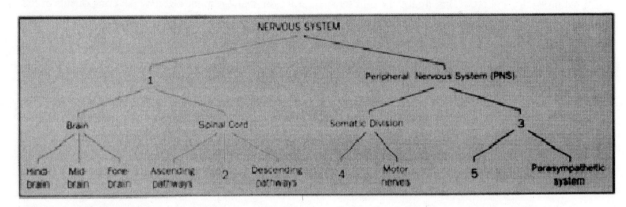

1. _____   4. _____

2. _____   5. _____

3. _____

6. _____   9. _____

7. _____   10. _____

8. _____

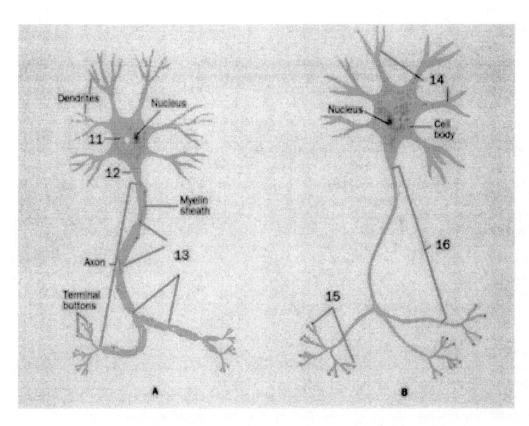

11. _____

12. _____

13. _____

14 _____

15. _____

16. _____

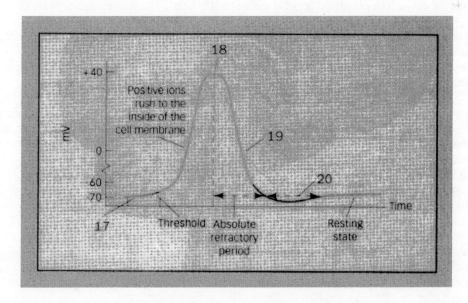

17. _____

18. _____

19. _____

20. _____

Practice Test

Circle the letter that corresponds to the *best* alternative for each of the following items. Read each alternative carefully. The answers are presented at the end of this study guide chapter. Be sure to learn *why* each correct alternative is better than the others

1. A common question asked by psychologists who adopt an evolutionary perspective is:
   a. How will I survive over generations?
   b. Why does a given behavior survive over generations?
   c. Which physiological and/or biological structures developed over generations?
   d. What role does a given structure or behavior play in survival and adaptation?

2. Which of the following is least characteristic of a behavioral neuroscientist?
   a. interested in discovering the functional contributions of each brain structure
   b. likely to come from any of several disciplines, including psychology, biology, and medicine
   c. interested in researching ways in which the brain, as well as the rest of the nervous system, is influenced by changes in diet, use of psychoactive drugs, and learning.
   d. All of the above are appropriate descriptions of behavioral neuroscientists and their interests

3. Environmental feature is to specialized cell as ___ is to ___.
   a. vision; audition
   b. space suit; toxin
   c. stimulus; receptor
   d. atmosphere; ambiance

4. An important step between the sensing of raw stimulus information and responding to it is:
   a. positioning limbs for responding.
   b. processing the information for meaning.
   c. ignoring other raw stimulus information.
   d. focusing on the raw stimulus information.

5. Quite literally, the central nervous system (CNS) is that portion of the larger nervous system that is located in the center of your body. The peripheral nervous system (PNS) constitutes the remainder of the larger system. The two major divisions of the PNS are:
   a. the brain and the spinal cord.
   b. the somatic and the autonomic.
   c. the forebrain and the hindbrain.
   d. the autonomic and the parasympathetic.

6. The autonomic nervous system may be considered as operating on a continuum as its components are antagonistic. That is, one component of the autonomic nervous system opposes the other for each function the system serves. These components are known as:
   a. extremes.
   b. neurons and glands, respectively.
   c. the left-hand, and right-hand systems.
   d. the sympathetic and parasympathetic systems.

7. Interneurons are cells:
   a. situated in the spinal cord between sensory and motor cells.
   b. that support the brain, and are technically not neurons at all.
   c. that enter neurons in order to promote more efficient activity.
   d. that die off after helping the brain turn over new cells during adolescence.

8. Psychologists are interested in the endocrine system because it impacts the nervous system. In some ways, its chemicals, ___, are analogous to neurotransmitters in that they are released from one location and influence another.
   a. hormones
   b. pheromones
   c. neuropeptides
   d. neuromodulators

9. Charles Scott Sherrington's discovery that a dog's reflex took too long:
   a. confirmed what cat lovers knew all along.
   b. was instrumental in learning about neural impulses.
   c. was exaggerated by the fact that his stopwatch was broken.
   d. occurred in the context of a brain stimulation experiment in the mid-1800s.

10. In general, signals are received by ___ and sent out by ___.
    a. axons; cell bodies.
    b. nodes of Ranvier; myelin.
    c. dendrites; terminal buttons.
    d. dendrites; nodes of Ranvier.

11. Glia cells comprise the myelin associated with about 50 percent of nerve cells. An interesting characteristic of the myelin sheath is that it has gaps, or ___, that break up the fatty covering of the axon.
    a. skips.
    b. dendrites.
    c. glia gaps.
    d. nodes of Ranvier.

12. Presynaptic cells are able to communicate with postsynaptic cells because of ___ that cross(es) the microscopic cleft that separates them.
    a. ions.
    b. myelin.
    c. anions.
    d. neurotransmitters.

13. After a signal crosses a synapse, it is important to clear the gap immediately to prepare for the next signal. This occurs in one of two ways:
    a. slashing and burning.
    b. flushing and rushing.
    c. breakdown and reuptake.
    d. All of the above are ways in which residual transmitter material is removed from the cleft.

14. Psychoactive drugs are those that impact the cells in the central nervous system. These drugs fall into two main categories: ___, that enhance the operation of a given transmitter, and ___ that block the action of a given transmitter.
    a. agonists; antagonists
    b. antagonists; agonists
    c. promoters; blockers
    d. helpers; blockers

15. Neurotransmitter is to neuromodulator as ___ is to ___.
    a. fast; local
    b. local; long
    c. widespread; fast
    d. long; widespread

16. When it is at its resting state, a nerve cell:
    a. has no charge.
    b. has a slight positive charge.
    c. has a relatively strong negative charge.
    d. None of the above; cells do not have charges, batteries do.

17. Depolarizing is to ___ as hyperpolarizing is to ___.
    a. negative; positive
    b. positive; negative
    c. less negative; more negative
    d. more negative; less negative

18. During the relative refractory period, a nerve cell is:
    a. hyperpolarized.
    b. merely depolarizing.
    c. not involved in ion exchange.
    d. at the peak in the course of its action potential.

19. If you were to suffer a closed head injury in an automobile accident, you would likely see a:
    a. Neuropsychologist
    b. Behavioral Geneticist
    c. Behavioral Neuroscientist
    d. Magnetic Neuroendocrinologist

20. The stories of "Tan" and Phineas Gage are:
    a. too poorly documented to be of lasting value.
    b. examples of the case study method for gathering information.
    c. entertaining ways of remembering some of the complex information on the brain.
    d. mere myths, but have nevertheless served to stimulate interest in brain functioning.

21. Brain structure is to brain activity as ___ is to ___.
    a. MRI; PET
    b. fMRI; MRI
    c. fMRI; CT/CAT
    d. EEG; CT/CAT

22. The hindbrain is, from an evolutionary perspective, the oldest portion of the brain. It makes sense, then, that this portion of the brain includes the structure that controls breathing, swallowing, and blood circulation. The structure that serves these functions is called the:
    a. pons.
    b. tectum.
    c. medulla.
    d. hippocampus.

23. If you accidentally drift, while driving a car, into the center section of a road or onto the shoulder of the road, you will likely be startled by the sound of your tires rolling on a different texture and making a lot of noise. The ___ is responsible for the startle response bringing you to full attention.
    a. sound of the road
    b. reticular formation
    c. ventromedial hypothalamus
    d. formation of the surface of the road

24. The limbic system regulates:
    a. the arms and legs.
    b. several branches of the PNS.
    c. heartbeat, respiration, and other vital activities.
    d. emotions and motivated behaviors including hunger, thirst, and aggression.

25. The thalamus is sometimes called a sensory switchboard because it:
    a. integrates and relays incoming information.
    b. resembles the appearance of an old time phone station.
    c. contains cells that convert raw stimulus information into neural signals.
    d. switches off and on, to conserve metabolic energy, rather than working constantly.

26. Phylogenetically newer brains are ___ than prehistoric brains.
    a. larger, in absolute terms
    b. smaller, in absolute terms
    c. the same size, in relative terms
    d. more wrinkled and crumpled on the surface

27. By selectively destroying or stimulating the tissue in living brains, researchers have:
    a. developed maps of the cortex.
    b. determined which parts we actually need.
    c. effectively discovered everything there is to know about the brain.
    d. None of the above. You cannot gain access to brain tissue without killing it.

28. Aphasia is to ___ as apraxia is to ___.
    a. vertebrate; invertebrate
    b. communication; nonverbal skills
    c. central nervous system; peripheral nervous system
    d. treatable with psychoactive drugs; incurable deficit of the brain

29. The split brain operation:
    a. was used to treat Phineas Gage after his accident.
    b. is a common procedure for treating migraine headaches.
    c. produces baffling results because brains continue to work normally in spite of tissue damage.
    d. affects dramatically the capacity for the two cerebral hemispheres to communicate with each other.

30. Which of the following is an example of functional asymmetry?
    a. Mean cell densities differ between hemispheres.
    b. The left hemisphere is more involved in speech, the right in spatial abilities.
    c. The surface anatomies of the left and right cerebral hemispheres are different.
    d. The motor strip of each respective hemisphere controls the behavior of the opposite side.

Answers to Labeling Exercises

1. Central Nervous System (CNS)
2. Interneurons
3. Autonomic Division
4. Sensory Nerves
5. Sympathetic System
6. Corpus Callosum
7. Cerebral Cortex
8. Pituitary Gland
9. Medulla
10. Cerebellum
11. Cell Body
12. Axon Hillock
13. Nodes of Ranvier
14. Dendrites
15. Terminal Buttons
16. Axon
17. Resting State
18. Action Potential
19. Positive Ions Being Pumped Out
20. Relative Refractory Period

Answers to Practice Test Questions

1. d. Psychologists are interested in behavior. Those who adopt the evolutionary perspective consider behavior as a function of the brain and biological structures that give rise to it.

2. d. Behavioral neuroscientists are interested in studying brain-behavior relationships. Work in this broad area of inquiry is done by researchers from several disciplines, and includes focus on a host of issues ranging from the effects of chemical agents on the nervous system to the ways in which the system changes as a function of learning.

3. c. The sensing process involves receiving stimulus information from the environment through receptors that have evolved to receive specific information—e.g., taste, touch.

4. b. Before any activity can transpire in response to a sensory experience, the information has to be processed.

5. b. The PNS may be further divided into the somatic and autonomic nervous systems.

6. d. The autonomic nervous system is comprised of the sympathetic and parasympathetic nervous systems.

7. a. Interneurons are located in the gray matter of the spinal cord and transfer signaling from sensory fibers to motor fibers or up the spinal cord to the brain.

8. a. Hormones are the chemicals of communication within the endocrine system.

9. b. Sherrington's discovery expanded on Ramón y Cajal's discovery of neurons being discrete units by adding that signals had to be transmitted from one cell to another for an impulse to travel through the nervous system.

10. c. Usually nerve signals are received by dendrites, processed in the cell body, and sent out through the terminal buttons.

11. d. The gaps between the glia cells that make up the myelin sheath are called nodes of Ranvier.

12. d. Neurotransmitters bridge the synaptic gaps that adjoin two neurons.

13. c. Depending on their type, neurotransmitters are either broken down or taken back into the presynaptic cells through a process called reuptake.

14. a. Agonists enhance the operation of a given transmitter, while antagonists block the action of a given transmitter.

15. b. Neurotransmitters are local, fast acting chemicals. Neuromodulators are longer lasting and cover more widespread regions.

16. c. At resting most nerve cells have net negative charges of approximately –70 millivolts.

17. c. As a cell depolarizes (becomes less polarized), it loses its negative charge. When a cell is hyperpolarized (hyper- is a prefix that means *more* or *excessive*) it has a stronger negative charge than it has when it is at its resting state.

18. a. During the relative refractory period, when it is difficult to get the neuron to fire, the cell's charge has dipped below its normal resting potential.

19. a. Neuropsychologists work primarily in human clinical settings and are trained to determine the characteristics of brain injuries and their resulting effects on adaptive behavior.

20. b. These case study examples are both key components to psychology's prehistory.

21. a. The standard MRI is used to gain structural information about the brain; PET tells researchers about the functional activity of the brain.

22. c. The medulla regulates these. Also it monitors blood chemistry and other survival promoting functions.

23. b. Before you have a chance to appraise what has happened, your reticular formation activates your brain.

24. d. The limbic system is a network of subcortical brain structures that regulates a variety of emotions and behaviors.

25. a. The thalamus receives incoming information and directs it to the cerebral cortex.

26. d. The wrinkled and crumpled appearance is the result of *convolutions* in the cortical layer of the brain. Effectively, the convolutions permit more cerebral mass to be contained within the skull. By analogy, you can put more notebook paper in a water glass if you wad it up.

27. a. The early surgical approaches to studying the brain were effective in mapping its functions.

28. b. Aphasias are deficits in communication, while apraxias are nonverbal deficits.

29. d. The split brain operation involves the severing of the corpus callosum, a bundle of fibers that connects the left and right cerebral hemispheres.

30. c. Functional asymmetry refers to differences based on what the two sides *do*. The left hemisphere is more involved in speech, the right in spatial abilities.

Key Vocabulary Terms: Use the following list to write definitions *in your own words* for each of the key terms from the chapter. Translating the terms into language that is comfortable and familiar for you will facilitate your learning. For further study of these terms, go to the companion web site for the text book where you will find electronic flash cards that you may use to test your vocabulary.

evolutionary perspective

natural selection

stimulus

receptors

central nervous system

peripheral nervous system

neurons

somatic division

afferent (sensory) nerves

efferent (motor) nerves

autonomic division

sympathetic division

parasympathetic division

homeostasis

reflex

hindbrain

medulla

pons

cerebellum

cranial nerves

midbrain

reticular formation

forebrain

corpus callosum

subcortical structures

cerebral cortex (cerebrum)

limbic system

thalamus

stroke

stereotaxic instrument

electroencephalograph (EEG)

positron emission tomography (PET)

computerized axial tomography (CT or CAT)

magnetic resonance imaging (MRI)

functional magnetic resonance imaging (fMRI)

dendrite

soma

axon

terminal buttons

myelin sheath

glia cell

nodes of Ranvier

multiple sclerosis

ataxia

synapse

neurotransmitters

synaptic vesicles

reuptake

agonist

antagonist

neuromodulators

opioid peptides

substance P

ions

resting state

depolarization

hyperpolarization

action potential

refractory period

brain asymmetries

aphasia

apraxia

endocrine system

hormones

pituitary gland

Tip for Success: Time Management

The Road Is Paved with Good Intentions

Goal setting was the topic in the first *Tip for Success* section. Another topic that is central to being successful is time management. Time management and goal setting go hand in hand. You may have noticed that the concept of time was mentioned in the section on goal setting. That was because it is not enough to have good intentions. If you want to be successful, you have to use your time to work toward achieving those intentions. Similarly, making yourself aware of time with clocks and calendars is of little value if you do not have goals. This section will focus on ways you can make the most of *your time*.

There Is Plenty of Time

That is right, there is plenty of time. Take a few moments to do the following thought exercise. Pick a task you wanted to do, but then used time as an excuse for not having done it. Now, imagine you are back in the setting for completing that task and assign a value to the task. Depending on the task, you may have to increase the value. Try setting the value at: $5...$50...$1,000...$1 Million...your life! A familiar saying goes, where there is a will, there is a way. If you want to do something badly enough, you can find the time just as you can find the resources.

The issue, then, is assigning priorities to the things you do, bearing in mind that you will need time to accomplish each of your goals, and using your time to work on your goals. You have probably heard someone say, "time is money." Consider this: there are 168 hours in a week. It does not matter which side of town people grow up on, how ambitious or lazy they are, who does their hair, or what kind of car they drive, everyone gets the same allocation of this priceless commodity. It is how people invest the commodity that determines their success.

If you require eight hours of sleep per night, then your 168 hours are down to 112. If you need more than eight hours, or like to sleep late on weekends, reduce the number accordingly. Next, subtract the number of hours you need to spend in school, preparing for classes (plan 2-4 hours outside of class for every hour spent in class) at work, eating, and so forth. How much time do you need to travel from one place to the next throughout the course of the week? Next, factor in time for exercising, reading, quiet reflection, attending to personal needs, doing laundry... The remainder is all you get for everything else you like to do: social commitments, hobbies, shopping, hanging out, or whatever. How you use *your time* is directly related to how successful you are at meeting the goals you set for yourself. Successful goal attainment will make you healthier, happier, and more likely to get exciting opportunities in the future.

Know Your Priorities

Being a student is costly. If you divide the cost of tuition at your school by the number of hours you are taking, you may be surprised at what it costs per hour for you to be enrolled. Given the costs, plus the fact that your education will determine, in part, how meaningful your life will be, it makes sense to make the most of your investment. Do not schedule appointments during your classes. If you do, you are telling yourself and others that there are things that are more important to you than planning with your future in mind. Using appointments and other excuses for missing class is a pet peeve for most professors.

Even though the hours you designate for studying are somewhat flexible, they deserve the same priority as your classes. Can you make the most of your investment in a class if you do not prepare for it? Do not allow a part-time job, your roommate's sudden need for a ride to the airport, or whatever, to prevent you from making the most of your education.

Forget About Time

Have you ever noticed what happens when you got a chance to talk with an old friend, were engrossed in a good book or movie, or got caught up in a game or working on a hobby? *Time flies.* How about the last half-hour before you get off work, when you are waiting for a call, or when you are stuck in traffic? *Time stands still.* How can both of these pearls of folk wisdom be right? The answer lies in how one's attention is focused. Time races away or stalls endlessly depending on what you are doing, and it is almost always at the wrong pace, right? Wrong. Time knows only one pace, no matter how you measure it. Worrying about time will merely serve to distract you from progress toward your goals. Focus on your goals; time will take care of itself. Now, it is usually helpful to work in designated units of time, so do not trade your watch for a sundial. But do not be a slave to your watch either.

Put Your Schedule Under a Time Microscope

It is important to study the ways you use your time. In academia there are regular opportunities to reorganize your schedule and use of time. In addition to taking advantage of the obvious opportunities at the beginning and end of each term, try to examine your efficiency at the middle of the term. You already have the resources you need to determine whether you are using your time effectively and efficiently. The table at the end of this section may be photocopied to do the exercise that is described below.

Photocopy the table at the end of this section, or make your own table. You will need enough copies to cover one week. Each cell corresponds to a 15-minute period in the day. Next, carry each day's chart with you and fill it out as accurately as possible. Write enough information in the cells that you will know how to figure out what you did at a given time. If you continue doing something through more than one block of time, simply draw an arrow to indicate continuation of the last activity. Do this for a week, then study the things you did and compare them with what you wish you had done. Assuming there is room for improvement, reread your list of goals and use your notes to plan a schedule for the next week. Carry each day's schedule with you, attending to whether the times you designated are appropriate for meeting your goals. Adjust your schedule as necessary to ensure that you are allowing for all the things you need and want to do.

If you are already fairly organized, challenge yourself by estimating how you will spend each block of time in the coming week. If you get close, congratulations! You are already aware of the advantages of keeping a schedule. If you do not get as close as you had hoped to, this exercise may help you find the stumbling blocks in your schedule. Repeat this process as often as it is helpful in getting you on track toward meeting your goals.

Threats to *Your Time*

It is important to always remember that the time you spend is yours. Sure, you have obligations, unexpected things come up, and there are occasions when you will not feel like you are in charge of how you are spending your time. Sometimes it is necessary to realize that even though you may not enjoy what you are doing, the activity may still be linked to goal attainment. Your time should always be spent in ways that are consistent with your goals, be they academic- or leisure-related. If you wonder whether you should be engaging in a given behavior, ask yourself whether you will be glad to have spent your time that way the next day...next month...in five years. It is surprising that we sometimes do things that seem really important at the moment, but thoughtful reflection would tell us to do something different.

The following list provides suggestions for combating common threats to effective use of *your time*. You may have different challenges to your schedule, or different solutions to the problems. What is important is that you give thought to making the most of every moment you get. Another adage, *time marches on*, reflects the importance of spending time wisely, for once a moment has passed, one cannot have it to spend differently.

1) **Know When You Are at Your Best.** Timing matters. Do you think more clearly after a good night's rest, or after you have been awake all day? If you are able to concentrate better in the morning, that is when you should study. If it takes 3 hours for your brain to begin working each day, you may be better off setting aside study time in the early afternoon. It is not always possible to study or work when your mind is operating at peak

efficiency. However, if you choose to study at times when you are better able to concentrate, your learning will be both more efficient and longer lasting.

2) **Save the Best for Last.** The Premack Principle, discovered by psychologist David Premack, suggests that more rewarding activities may be used to reinforce less rewarding activities (see Chapter 5, page 204 for more thorough coverage of the Premack Principle). Most people are familiar with that concept, even if they have never heard of the principle. For example, have you ever been told you can do something you want to do badly only *after* you do a household chore? It was effective, wasn't it? Use the principle on yourself for most everything you do. If you have a long list of things to study, start with the homework you are *least* excited about. If you need some incentive to make it through a set of responsibilities, establish a reward structure for yourself that will encourage you to work.

3) **Use Idle Time.** At any moment you may have to wait on someone or something for an undetermined amount of time. Waiting to meet with someone for an appointment, when your transportation plans are unexpectedly delayed, at a busy restaurant or cafeteria, or in a number of other circumstances is annoying. What is more, it chips away at your precious time. Take charge of how you use time by having something to do at any given moment. You will want to prepare according to how far from home base you will be. Bring a book (or more) with you when you travel in case your travel arrangements are altered. If you are headed to meet with an advisor, or your dentist, bring something that you can start and stop working on easily.

4) **Just Say No.** This is much easier said than done. However, if you consider each decision you make in terms of the goals you are striving to meet, it should be clear whether it is in your best interest to do something someone else asks of you. While they may be disappointed, most people will respect your need to protect time for working on your goals. The more clearly defined your goals are, the better able you will be to help others understand why you cannot always take on additional responsibilities.

5) **Be Clear About How You Use Your Time.** Sometimes the most respectful people will accidentally interrupt your activity because they do not realize *when* you are busy. Good communication can go a long way toward helping protect your time against disruptions, even if those disruptions are things that you would welcome at other times. Let people know when you are studying, whether by telling them which times are off limits, by hanging a "Do Not Disturb" sign on your door, or by donning a hat or jacket that acts as a signal.

6) **Monitor Your Effectiveness.** Sometimes in spite of good planning, you are unable to be as productive as you need to be. Sometimes you are plenty able to be productive, but allow yourself to get lazy. What would you pay yourself for the efforts you are exerting? Can you remember what you just read a few minutes ago? If the answer is no, you may want to refer to your goals list for something else you can do more effectively until you are better focused.

7) **Monitor Your Efficiency.** Perhaps you are plenty effective, but are not working as efficiently as you could be. Are you taking shortcuts where and when you should? Are you bogging yourself down by focusing too much on the details? In addition to asking yourself these few questions periodically, try this idea. Time yourself when reading a page from your textbook. As you read subsequent pages, check every once in a while to make sure you are not slowing down.

8) **Take One More Step.** Often when you are finishing a work session you have the necessary focus and additional energy to do a little more. Just as making one extra payment annually on a home loan will greatly reduce the cost of the mortgage, so too will taking one more step toward your goals when you have reached a targeted stopping point.

9) **Keep Your Word.** Some very important deals are sealed with nothing other than a handshake and a promise. Promises should be taken seriously, and should not be violated. Make promises to yourself and others as appropriate, and keep them. Do not let yourself or others down by failing to keep your word. If you adopt this attitude when making promises, they will serve as powerful motivators for striving toward your goals.

10) Don't Take Any Excuses. It is bad enough when someone else makes a promise and then fails to keep her or his word. If there is anything that is worse, it is when one lets oneself down. If you stick to your schedule as if it were a promise, you will surely be more productive and feel good about it.

Not a Paradox

It may seem contradictory that filling your schedule is the key to having enough time for relaxing, or whatever else you like to do. Many people find at the end of an evening, long weekend, or semester break, that somehow they failed to do all the work they had intended to do *and* they did not do all the other activities they had planned either. The fact is that if we do not have our time scheduled, it is easy to put off getting started on anything. As a result, too many hours get whiled away. By scheduling in everything that is important to you, you can be sure to have time for doing it. Whether its writing two pages on a term paper, playing tennis, listening to music, or propping your feet up in front of the TV, scheduling time for it and sticking to your schedule is the only way you will get it done.

Poor Time Management Is Linked to Stress

When we run out of time for completing responsibilities, we experience stress. While some stress may be helpful in motivating activity, too much stress can inhibit your ability to perform your very best. Often the sources of stress are linked to poor time management. It is clear to see that if you do not manage time effectively and experience stress as a result, it will become increasingly difficult to meet your goals, which, in turn, will create more stress. This cycle can negatively impact your attitude, behavior, and physical wellness. It is remarkable that poor time management can have such profound effects on these central issues in your life. If you desire to be happy, productive, and healthy, you will want to learn to take control of your time.

You Are Not Alone

Survey a group of successful people about the keys to their successes. Whether they are leaders in the student body, college professors, local business people, clergy, or others you may define as successful, each of them will identify the need to manage time wisely. Issues surrounding the ways that people use time are pervasive in our society. The company we keep and the people we look up to will influence us. Songs, books and plays, special seminars for business employees, and sections in bookstores are a few examples of places and ways we are exposed to comments on the usage of time.

Model your lifestyle after those who fit your definition of success. If you aspire to be a leader, but are acting like someone who is destined for a life of minimum wage jobs, something is awry. Do whatever it takes to learn to make the most of your time.

Time Microscope

Day:		Date:	
AM		PM	
Midnight		**Noon**	
12:15		12:15	
12:30		12:30	
12:45		12:45	
1:00		1:00	
1:15		1:15	
1:30		1:30	
1:45		1:45	
2:00		2:00	
2:15		2:15	
2:30		2:30	
2:45		2:45	
3:00		3:00	
3:15		3:15	
3:30		3:30	
3:45		3:45	
4:00		4:00	
4:15		4:15	
4:30		4:30	
4:45		4:45	
5:00		5:00	
5:15		5:15	
5:30		5:30	
5:45		5:45	
6:00		6:00	
6:15		6:15	
6:30		6:30	
6:45		6:45	
7:00		7:00	
7:15		7:15	
7:30		7:30	
7:45		7:45	
8:00		8:00	
8:15		8:15	
8:30		8:30	
8:45		8:45	
9:00		9:00	
9:15		9:15	
9:30		9:30	
9:45		9:45	
10:00		10:00	
10:15		10:15	
10:30		10:30	
10:45		10:45	
11:00		11:00	
11:15		11:15	
11:30		11:30	
11:45		11:45	

CHAPTER 3

Sensation and Perception

Do You Know?

Do you know that the subtractive color process is the one with which painters work when blending paints to create subtle hue differences in the objects of their attention? Because of this, subtractive color primaries are sometimes referred to as pigment or artists' primaries. Interestingly, subtractive colors can be used in combination with the Gestalt principle of closure to create the perception of continuous, blended color images using a field of small ink dots. A well-known example of this combination was created by French Neo-Impressionist painter Georges Seurat (1859-1891).

Seurat's famous painting, "A Sunday on La Grande Jatte-1884," created a dramatic effect on a canvas that now hangs in the Chicago Art Institute's gallery. You can view a reproduction of the painting over the Internet by linking to the Art Institute's Website (http://www.artic.edu/AA_Impressionist/pages/IMP_7.shtml). You are familiar with the effect, however, even if you have not seen the painting or a reproduction of it. The phenomenon Seurat pioneered by placing small dots of color on canvas is the same phenomenon that gives rise to the perception of whole images one experiences when viewing a video screen (e.g., television or computer) or reproduced images in books, magazines, and posters. Indeed, the pigment primaries, cyan, magenta, and yellow, plus black are used in the same way by common desktop printers to create the same effect. The concept of graphic resolution concerns the number of dots represented per standard unit (i.e., dots per inch, or dpi), whether in the form of pixels on a monitor or as specs of ink on paper. Examine mass-printed images with a magnifying glass and you'll see for yourself how subtractive color and the principle of closure interact to create images that appear convincingly uninterrupted.

Notes from Class and the Textbook

Use the space provided in this outline to record notes from the textbook as well as from class lectures and discussion. Questions related to the *Psychological Detective, Hands On, Myth or Science,* and *Study Tip* sections in the text have been presented in the outline; use the associated space to respond to the questions and to record your own comments about the issues.

Make flash cards of all the marginal definitions in the chapter (or book for that matter). Test yourself frequently on how well you can recall the definitions of key terms.

I. Sensation, Perception, and Psychophysics

    A. Sensation and Perception

    B. Psychophysics

    C. Thresholds

II. Sensory Systems

    A. Vision

Why is a 'red' rose everything but red?

Point your Web browser at the textbook's Web page to see Live!Psych module 3.1

    1.   How We See: The Visual System

Why are people not constantly distracted by the flashing on and off of their visual worlds when they blink?

    2.   The Visual Pathway

    3.   The Visual Receptors

Why should you expect your visual acuity to suffer when an item of interest is not in the center of your field of vision?

    4. Theories of Color Vision

How could you determine whether an animal can differentiate colors?

     5. Color Deficiencies

  B. Audition (Hearing)

     1. What We Hear: The Auditory Stimulus

     2. How We Hear: The Auditory System

Point your Web browser at the textbook's Web page to see Live!Psych module 3.2

     3. Hearing Disorders

  C. The Chemical Senses: Taste and Smell

     1. Taste (Gustation)

       a. What We Taste: The Gustatory Stimulus

       b. How We Taste: The Gustatory System

How, using only four basic tastes, can we explain the wide variety of tastes we are able to experience?

2. Smell (Olfaction)

    a. What We Smell: The Olfactory Stimulus

    b. How We Smell: The Olfactory System

Is there a relationship between the quality of smell in a work environment and the degree to which workers are productive?

3. The Interaction of Smell and Taste

D. Somatosensory Systems

    1. Vestibular Sense

    2. Kinesthetic Sense

    3. The Cutaneous Senses

        a. Pain

Work with four other students, with each member of the group being assigned to one of the five senses. Provide brief overviews for one another on the senses.

III. Perception

    A. Motivation and Attention

        1.   Motivational Influences

        2.   Attention

Enlist two friends to create a dichotic listening task for you by situating themselves on each side of you and reading different passages of text at the same time. After 20-30 seconds of the task, write down as much as you can recall from what both people read. Study your pattern of recall; did you recall content mainly from one passage, the other, or a mixture of both? Rotate positions with your friends and repeat the experience until each of you has participated in the task. How do your patterns of recall compare with one another?

    B. Basic Perceptual Abilities: Patterns and Constancies

        1.   Pattern Perception

        2.   Perceptual Constancies

            a.   Shape Constancy

            b.   Size Constancy

        3. Depth Perception

4. Binocular Cues

Point your Web browser at the textbook's Web page to see Live!Psych module 3.3

5. Monocular Cues

C. Gestalt Principles of Perceptual Organization

Point your Web browser at the textbook's Web page to see Live!Psych module 3.4

1. Figure and Ground

2. Principles of Grouping

Draw your own pictures to represent the Gestalt principles of grouping.

D. Perception of Movement

Create a circumstance to experience the autokinetic effect. How long did it take to experience the phenomenon? Did the light appear to move as was anticipated in your textbook? How would you explain the effect to someone who has not studied the physiology of the eye?

E. Perceptual Hypotheses and Illusions

Explain why the grass really appears greener on the other side of the fence.

Point your Web browser at the textbook's Web page to see Live!Psych module 3.5

Create an outline summary of the basic perceptual abilities (patterns and constancies).

F. Contemporary Issues and Findings in Perception Research

    1.   Parallel Processing, Visual Search, and the Application of Basic Perceptual Research

    2.   Perception is Affected by Social Context

What do contextual stimuli contribute to our perceptual experiences?

IV. Paranormal Phenomena

    A. Skeptical Scientists

    B. A Believing Public

      1. A Final Word

Learning Objectives

After you have studied the chapter, you should be able to respond to the following statements and questions to convey your understanding of the material.

1. Describe the systems that receive sensory information about vision, hearing, taste, smell, body position, and movement. What do these systems have in common? How are they different?

2. How are the processes of sensation and perception related? What does each process contribute to one's ability to interact with the world?

3. How is perception affected by influences such as motivation and attention?

4. What roles do coincidences and chance occurrences play in beliefs about the paranormal?

Labeling Exercises

It is helpful when learning the information from this chapter to study how some of the terms are used in the contexts of figures. Having studied the chapter you should be able to fill in the missing information. The answers are given at the end of the chapter.

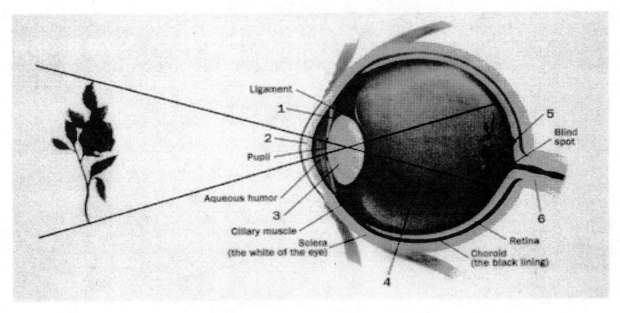

1. _____   4. _____

2. _____   5. _____

3. _____   6. _____

7. _____   8. _____

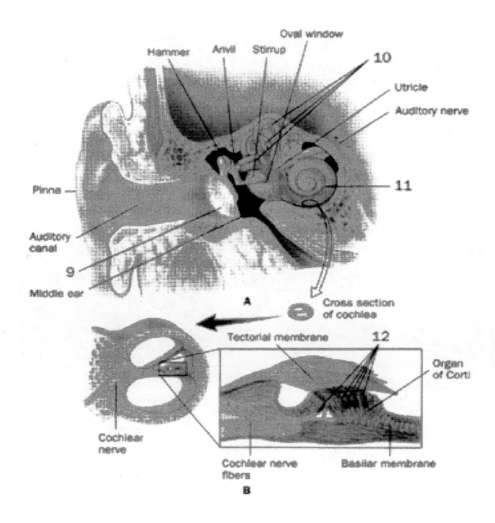

9. _____   11. _____

10. _____   12. _____

Practice Test

Circle the letter that corresponds to the ***best*** alternative for each of the following items.   Read each alternative carefully. The answers are presented at the end of this study guide chapter.   Be sure to learn *why* each correct alternative is better than the others

1. Sensation is to perception as ___ is to ___.
    a. left brain; right brain
    b. right brain; left brain
    c. seeing something red; identifying something as an apple
    d. identifying something as an apple; seeing something red

2. A common feature of the basic sensory processes in that they:
    a. involve transduction.
    b. all work the same way.
    c. were each evolved from a common process.
    d. are all involved in sensing stimuli at a distance.

3. Frank is unaware that he is wearing too much cologne. His lack of awareness is probably due to:
   a. adaptation.
   b. transduction.
   c. Weber's law.
   d. the just noticeable difference (jnd) for olfaction.

4. An absolute threshold is:
   a. a dangerous level of sensory stimulation.
   b. the largest amount of stimulation a person can perceive.
   c. the minimum amount of energy required for conscious recognition.
   d. the smallest amount of stimulation that must be added or subtracted to be able to notice the difference 50 percent of the time.

5. ___ suggests that the threshold varies with the nature of the stimulus (signal) and background stimulation.
   a. Weber
   b. The jnd
   c. Experience
   d. Signal detection theory

6. Wavelength is to ___ as amplitude is to ___.
   a. brightness; color
   b. color; brightness
   c. saturation; purity
   d. brightness; intensity

7. The color of a car occurs as a function of:
   a. amplitude.
   b. saturation.
   c. radiant light.
   d. reflected light.

8. Chris is a theater technician. Her job involves manipulating the gels that go between light bulbs and the objects they illuminate on stage. A psychologist might say her job is:
   a. boring.
   b. dangerous.
   c. to manipulate radiant light.
   d. to attend to sources of reflected light.

9. When you mix primary paints together you yield a dark, yucky color. Mixing light primaries, however, produces white light. The processes underlying these differences are called ___ and ___, respectively.
   a. additive; subtractive
   b. subtractive; additive
   c. visual art; performing art
   d. performing art; visual art

10. Paintings by Ruby reveal:
    a. that elephants can see in color.
    b. that people well into their 80s can learn to mix paints and match colors on a canvas.
    c. radiant vistas typically involving sunsets and either rocky terrain or bodies of water.
    d. All of the above may be inferred or supported directly based on Ruby's paintings.

11. The photoreceptor cells, rods and cones, are:
    a. distributed equally throughout the retina.
    b. disproportionately located outside the retina.
    c. in the back of the retina, pointing away from the cornea.
    d. in the front of the retinal layer, positioned to receive light as it comes though the lens.

12. Color afterimages, such as seeing blue dots for awhile after someone takes your picture with a camera and a flash, are (were) explained well by:
    a. the fovea.
    b. the trichromatic theory.
    c. the opponent-process theory.
    d. Gestalt psychologists in the 1920s.

13. Which of the following was *not* mentioned in the text as a variety of color deficiency?
    a. dichromat
    b. achromatosis
    c. monochromat
    d. anomalous trichromat

14. In vision, the wave characteristic, *complexity,* corresponds to the saturation level of the hue. What does complexity correspond to in audition?
    a. hertz (Hz)
    b. decibels (db)
    c. timbre
    d. none of the above

15. In order to hear frequencies at the extremes of our range of sensitivity (20-20,000 Hz), the amplitude of the wave needs to be:
    a. higher.
    b. significantly lower.
    c. proportional to the wave's length.
    d. executed in the following sequence: elbow, elbow, wrist, wrist

16. In audition, changes in air pressure (sound waves) are translated into fluid waves when the *stirrup* causes movement of the:
    a. ossicles.
    b. basilar membrane.
    c. tectorial membrane.
    d. oval window of the cochlea.

17. Rock concert is to ear wax as ___ is to ___.
    a. gross; great
    b. soft; loud
    c. central deafness; sensorineural deafness
    d. sensorineural deafness; conduction deafness

18. Microvilli are:
    a. hairs that project from taste receptors.
    b. small clusters of houses in rural areas.
    c. the name for the hair cells on the basilar membrane.
    d. the small gaps between myelin cells on the auditory nerve.

19. When we smell, airborne particles come in contact with our ___, which, in turn, send signals into the CNS.
    a. nasal mucus
    b. olfactory bulbs
    c. thalamic nuclei
    d. olfactory epithelium

20. Inner ear is to muscles and joints as ___ is to ___.
    a. audition; kinesthesia
    b. aching; hearing
    c. kinesthetic sense; vestibular sense
    d. vestibular sense; kinesthetic sense

21. The ability to process more than one source of stimulation at the same time is called:
    a. synesthesia.
    b. schizophrenia.
    c. divided attention.
    d. paranormal perception.

22. ___ is the phenomenon that permits you to recognize a door as a door, even when you see it from its edge.
    a. Feature detection
    b. Shape constancy
    c. Binocular disparity
    d. Good continuation and direction

23. Depth perception, or the ability to see our world three-dimensionally, involves all *but* which of the following:
    a. binocular cues
    b. monocular cues
    c. binocular disparity
    d. retino-depth detectors

24. Which of the following grouping principles is responsible for your ability to fill in gaps in your visual world?
    a. closure
    b. proximity
    c. inclusiveness
    d. good continuation and direction

25. What do flashing road construction sign arrows and cartoons have in common?
    a. nothing
    b. reliance on apparent motion
    c. that only a small minority pays attention to them
    d. all of the above

26. Recall the Ebbinghaus illusion—the illusion that the perceived size of a circle in the center of a group of circles is influenced by the size of the circles that surround it. Staple & Koomen (1997) conducted an experiment using a variation on the Ebbinghaus illusion, using instead pictures of faces surrounded by faces of other objects. Which of the following produced the greatest magnitude of size contrast illusion? When the face was surrounded by:
    a. identical faces
    b. faces of people of the same gender
    c. faces of people of the different gender
    d. nonperson objects such as trucks and handbags

27. Clairvoyance, telepathy, precognition, and psychokinesis are all examples of:
    a. ESP.
    b. horse puckey.
    c. experimentally demonstrable phenomena.
    d. anomalistic psychological (or parapsychological) phenomena.

28. Which of the following, according to your textbook, is partially responsible for the fact that people commonly believe in psychic phenomena?
    a. influence by the media
    b. underestimating chance occurrences and coincidences
    c. many have had psychic experiences, or interpret their experiences as having been psychic.
    d. all of the above

Answers To Labeling Exercise

1. Iris
2. Cornea
3. Lens
4. Vitreous Humor
5. Fovea
6. Optic Nerve
7. Ganglion Cell Layer
8. Photoreceptor Layer
9. Eardrum
10. Semicircular Canals
11. Cochlea
12. Hair Cells

Practice Test Answers And Explanations

1. c. Sensation is the act of receiving stimuli from the environment; perception involves organizing and making sense of the information.
2. a. Transduction is the process of receiving stimuli and translating them into forms that can be used by the nervous system.
3. a. Adaptation is a loss of sensitivity to a stimulus by the receptors as a result of continued presentation of that stimulus.
4. c. The absolute threshold is the minimum amount of energy required for conscious detection of a stimulus 50 percent of the time.
5. d. The question in item 5 is the definition of signal detection theory.
6. b. Changes in perceived hue (or color) result from changes in wavelength whereas manipulating wave height results in shifts in intensity (or brightness).
7. d. Objects that do not emit light are sources of reflected light.
8. b. Radiant sources of light include light bulbs and the sun. By placing gels in front of a source of radiant light, one manipulates (selectively filters) the wavelength qualities of the light.
9. b. Mixing pigments is a subtractive process whereas mixing lights is additive. Note that the primaries for these processes are different.
10. a. Ruby is an elephant (see pages 99 and 100). Work with her has revealed that she chooses paint colors based upon colors in the environments in which she paints.
11. c. Interestingly, the photoreceptors point away from the front of the eye, rather than toward it.
12. c. The opponent-process theory explains the phenomenon of color afterimages.
13. b. The three types of color-deficient people are monochromats, dichromats, and anomalous trichromats.
14. c. Timbre is the acoustic property that has to do with purity of a sound wave. It is what is responsible for the difference in sound generated by two different musical instruments playing the same note.
15. a. In order to hear higher frequency waves, we need them to be of greater amplitude (i.e., louder).
16. d. As the ossicles move, the stirrup (the third middle-ear bone) causes movement of the oval window, which, in turn, sets fluid inside the cochlea into motion.
17. d. Rock concerts can cause sensorineural deafness; ear wax can cause conduction deafness.
18. a. Microvilli are the hairs that project from taste receptors.
19. d. The olfactory epithelium receives airborne molecules and transmits information to the olfactory bulbs.
20. d. The vestibular sense results from activity in the inner ear, whereas the kinesthetic sense stems from receptors in the muscles and joints.
21. c. Divided attention is the ability to process two or more sources of sensory stimulation.
22. b. *Shape constancy* permits the perception of an object's shape as constant despite changes in its retinal image.
23. d. Retino-depth detectors do not exist.
24. a. *Closure* helps us perceive incomplete visual stimuli as complete.
25. b. The illusion of movement in a stationary object is called apparent. Both examples rely on this.

26. a. The greatest effect was found when the picture of a face was surrounded by pictures of the same face.
27. d. Clairvoyance, telepathy, precognition, and psychokinesis are all examples of anomalistic psychological (or parapsychological) phenomena.
28. d. The reasons why people believe in psychic phenomena vary across individuals.

Key Vocabulary Terms

Use the following list to write definitions *in your own words* for each of the key terms from the chapter. Translating the terms into language that is comfortable and familiar for you will facilitate your learning. For further study of these terms, go to the companion Website for the textbook where you will find electronic flash cards that you may use to test your vocabulary.

sensation

perception

transduction

adaptation

Weber's law

just noticeable difference (jnd)

absolute threshold

differential threshold

signal detection theory

subliminal stimuli

wavelength

amplitude

saturation

radiant light

reflected light

accommodation

retina

bipolar cells

ganglion cells

blind spot

optic chiasm

rods

cones

fovea

trichromatic theory

opponent-process theory

color afterimage

monochromat

dichromat

audition

hertz (Hz)

decibel (db)

ossicles

oval window

basilar membrane

organ of Corti

tectorial membrane

place theory

frequency theory

conduction deafness

sensorineural deafness

central deafness

gustation

taste buds

papillae

microvilli

olfaction

vestibular sense

semicircular canals

utricle

kinesthetic sense

cutaneous sense

gate control theory

cutaneous receptors

divided attention

pattern perception

feature analysis theory

perceptual constancy

shape constancy

size constancy

depth perception

binocular cues

monocular cues

binocular disparity

figure-ground relation

proximity

similarity

good continuation

closure

apparent motion

perceptual hypothesis

perceptual illusions

visual search

extrasensory perception (ESP)

Tip for Success: Creating an Effective Study Environment

The Right Place at The Right Time

Think of *where* you would expect to go for each of the following services:
1) to get a manicure
2) to invest a large sum of money
3) to get a paint job on a valuable automobile
4) to get advice on native plants for landscaping
5) to have a delicate surgical procedure performed on you

The people who provide these services have very diverse backgrounds, but they all share at least one thing in common. Their work is done in environments that support their occupations. That is, they work in places that have conditions and resources that permit them to do their very best. Could you imagine: getting your nails done in a dark place without tables and chairs; handing your hard-earned money to someone on the street; getting your car painted outside on a windy day; going to a grocery store to determine which plants would be best for your yard; or having surgery performed on you in an old warehouse? While things might work out all right in each of those scenarios, the conditions are clearly not conducive to the services.

The principles that apply to professional services share things in common with those for establishing an effective study environment. You need the appropriate environment, tools, and access to the resources you may need if you are to make the most of your study time. Anyone would agree that beauticians, stockbrokers, autobody painters, horticulturists, and surgeons need to work in the contexts we usually associate with them. For some reason, though, perhaps because books are fairly portable, it is not uncommon to see students 'studying' in the darndest places. It is curious that students will walk right past the library en route to the busiest building on campus to study. If your goal is to socialize, why not leave the books at home?

List the last four places where you studied:

_____
_____

List four places you think would be ideal for studying:

_____
_____

Did you notice any differences? Why or why not?

_____

The Student Union Is a Great Place to Meet People

But it is a poor place to study, for exactly the same reasons. Because of schedule differences, different people pass through there at different times of the day: the environment is ever changing. Think about how goofy it would be if the professionals mentioned above were to do their same work, but to trade working places for a day. It would be more than disconcerting to hear the horticulturist talking about dirt and microorganisms in the surgery wing of a hospital. Or, what if the surgeon were on the floor of a stock exchange building, with her bright lights, instruments, and hair net, carving away on somebody? It is hard to imagine the brokers in the room attending to the changing of decimal points on the electronic tickertape.

The point is simple. Now that you have established goals, and have organized a schedule that will permit you to make the best use of your time, you need to focus on the places where you work at your most attention-demanding activity: studying. Do not be tempted to think that the portability of books means they are equally useful anywhere you might take them. The books may work equally well in a variety of places, but all they have to do is sit there. You will not work equally well in a variety of environments; find one or two places that will help you maximize learning efficiency. If you work when you should be working, and play when you should be playing, you will be much happier about both activities.

How can studying in a dedicated place help meet your academic and your leisure-time goals?
_____
_____

So Where *Should* I Study?

This may come as a shock: the library is probably the best building on your campus for studying. Think about it. It has the best collection of resources, such as books in every academic field, dictionaries, and likely also computers that can be used to find resources both on and off campus. Libraries are outstanding learning environments for other reasons, too. What comes to mind when you think of the library? Unless you have visited some mighty strange libraries, you probably think of a building that is fairly quiet, in which people work diligently and independently. There is little question concerning whether students who study in libraries are there to do homework. What about the student who sets up camp in the student union?

But, you might say, I do not need those things if I am reading novels for my literature class or working math problems. Or for some unexplainable reason, maybe you are not able to focus at the library. There are plenty of other places on your campus or in your community. What is important is that you identify a place or two that you can use to give your undivided attention (recall the passage in Chapter 3 that discussed the need to focus attention at times such as when driving in busy traffic).

List two or three places that might be good for studying that you have not yet tried.

_____

_____

Characteristics of the Designated Space

When you begin looking for a few places you can use for studying, adopt the criteria for evaluating good libraries. When you enter the context it should be immediately clear to you that you are preparing to concentrate. The place you choose should be quiet. You should have at your disposal, or bring with you, any resources necessary to make the most of your dedicated study time. The place you choose should also be well lit, and heated or cooled appropriately for your comfort needs. In short, aside from having the necessary resources, you need a place that anybody could go to and recognize as a good place to study.

The following are examples to help you get started thinking about where to study.

1) **Empty Classrooms.** Perhaps the best ones are those that you have regular class meetings in when they are not in use, but any empty classroom should be fine.

2) **Study Carrels.** These are distributed throughout the library, and perhaps in other designated spaces on campus. Study carrels can be great places to work because they limit your ability to be distracted and often provide shelving to organize your things.

3) **A Local Community Library.** If, with any regularity, your friends take you away from your studies, you no longer have a situation that is conducive to learning. Find a new one. Local libraries have many of the same characteristics as university libraries and can be great places to study. What is more, you are even less likely to be found in the public library than at your school's library.

4) Bookstores, Coffee Shops, and Galleries. These kinds of places are presently very trendy. If it is a business that sells drinks and snacks, but is also good for studying, the cost of a cup of coffee or a bagel is cheap in exchange for the opportunity to work there. Some businesspeople try to attract students and to maintain good study places.

Regardless of where you go, make sure it is away from distractions, including telephones and friends who do not take their homework as seriously as you do. If you have a cellular phone or pager, TURN IT OFF. You cannot possibly give your undivided attention to your academic goals if you are preoccupied with the phone, email, and the like. If someone needs to get in touch with you, they will. If you have a cellular phone or a pager, you probably also have an answering machine that will take messages for you. Let it do what it is supposed to do.

What three things are most likely to distract you during study time?

_____

_____

_____

Psychologists Study Environments

Classical conditioning (see Chapter 5) helps make an environment more or less effective for a given activity. As an environment becomes familiar, your perceptual systems begin to influence your brain in response to the environmental cues. Have you ever become suddenly hungry when you saw a restaurant advertisement or noticed the time (even though you were not hungry until then)? Environmental cues and temporal cues can influence behavior in powerful ways.

Use your knowledge of classical conditioning to your advantage. If a given context is most strongly associated, for you, with a behavior that is incompatible with focused attention on homework, avoid studying there. For example, the lounge may have many of the characteristics that are appropriate for a good study place, but you may feel compelled to turn on the TV or participate in some other distraction whenever you are there. Avoid tempting yourself. Likewise, your bedroom is designated as a place for resting; trying to study in bed will surely make you tired! Do not allow yourself to be lured into the bed with intentions of learning anything from a textbook.

The real value of identifying one or two places where you will do most of your studying has precisely to do with classical conditioning. Recall the attributes that make libraries effective for studying. That list is the result of conditioning; you have learned that libraries have certain characteristics. Your study places should serve to help you recognize immediately when you should be focusing your attention on homework.

What are some effective cues for letting you know you are in a place that is good for studying?

_____

_____

When One Is Not Enough

It is a good idea to identify two or three places where you can study. Imagine that you have scheduled time to work on your academic goals at your peak time for devoting attention, and that you have found your way to 'your' study carrel in the library. What will you do when someone else is there? What if the library is closed or exceptionally busy? Getting frustrated will only drain your energy and divert your attention from your studies. Smile and head for a quieter place.

Another good reason to have two or more designated study places is to provide some variation on long study days. You may find that you like studying in one place early in the day, but at another in the afternoon or evening. If you prefer to study in a business (e.g., coffee shop), you may need to find another location that has hours that permit you to start working earlier, or to continue later.

List Alternative Places Where You Could Study Effectively and Their Hours of Availability

Location: Time Available to You:

_____

_____

Be Mindful of Others

The previous chapter included a comment on good communication. People who are interested in doing things with you need to know when you will be available, and when you are busy. By making it clear that you will not be available until you finish your homework, people will be less inclined to interrupt you. This is especially important if you have a designated space in your room, or are known to be at a certain place when you are studying. An added bonus to communicating when you will be busy studying is that others may help protect your time.

Be aware that the best places for studying are effective because people respect them as places for quiet reflection. If you get restless, or get the urge to make a lot of noise, be courteous and leave before you ruin the environment for others. Also, avoid taking a project group from one of your classes to discuss the material in a place where people are usually quiet. You may be studying, but if your activity affects others, you are not being respectful.

CHAPTER 4

States of Consciousness

Do You Know?

Do you know that hypnosis has been effective for such phenomena as helping reduce or block sensations of pain and to facilitate focus during memory recall? That is, for a portion of the population hypnosis has real, measurable effects on some facets of sensory perception and behavior. However, it is important to note that not everyone can be hypnotized, and that anything accomplished as a function of having been under hypnosis cannot be explained as such until proper control conditions are conducted to explain away alternative accounts of the phenomenon of interest. Although some findings concerning the power of hypnosis need to be subjected to well controlled experimentation, other findings have held up under scientific scrutiny.

It is interesting to note that it has been popular for entertainers to use hypnosis as part of their acts. Comedy clubs and traveling entertainers, such as those that visit many college campuses, sometimes feature hypnotists. If you have a chance to witness people under hypnosis in one of these settings (or in controlled laboratory settings for that matter), keep in mind that although hypnosis creates a heightened state of suggestibility in some, nobody has been demonstrated to have performed an act—whether based on strength, memorial prowess or lack of humility—under hypnotic influence. That is, if you see someone on stage at a nightclub dressed only in boxer shorts and strutting around on stage clucking like a chicken, such a person is not acting in an unusual way!

Notes from Class and the Textbook

Use the space provided in this outline to record notes from the textbook as well as from class lectures and discussion. Questions related to the *Psychological Detective, Hands On, Myth or Science,* and *Study Tip* sections in the text have been presented in the outline; use the associated space to respond to the questions and to record your own comments about the issues.

I. What Is Consciousness?

II. The Rhythms of Life

    A. Circadian Rhythms

        1. The Sleep-Wake Cycle

How is the 25-hour internal clock related to the fatigue one feels after a weekend?

2. Body Temperature

Use the brief survey on pages 137 and 138 of your textbook to determine whether you are an owl or a lark. Irrespective of which fits you best, consider the implications for the variety and nature of things you do in your daily living and when you do them.

B. Problems with Circadian Rhythms

1. Jet Lag

With respect to internal rhythms and long-distance travel, is it easier to travel from east to west, or from west to east? Why?

2. Shift Work

a. Improving Shift Work

III. The Study of Sleep

A. A Night in a Sleep Lab

B. The Stages of Sleep

1. NREM Sleep

Identify your general sleeping and waking times. Use Figure 4.6, from page 143 in your textbook, to determine when you are likely to be in REM and NREM sleep stages.

    1. REM Sleep

Point your Web browser at the textbook's Web page to see Live!Psych module 4.1.

    C. Differences in Individual Sleep Patterns

Assess your level of sleep deprivation by using the True-False survey on page 146 in your textbook.

    D. The Functions of Sleep

What evidence is there concerning the degree to which people can learn while sleeping? How do the data compare with commercial products and claims concerning learning during sleep?

    E. Sleep Problems

        1. Insomnia

2. Hypersomnias

    a. Narcolepsy

How are the characteristics of REM sleep related to the attacks of muscle weakness that are characteristic of narcolepsy and cataplexy?

    a. Sleep Apnea

3. Parasomnias

    a. Sleepwalking

Is sleepwalking merely the acting out of one's dreams?

    b. Enuresis

    c. Sleep Terrors and Nightmares

How do NREM sleep disorders differ from REM sleep disorders with respect to *when* they occur during a night's sleep?

3. SIDS

G. Dreams: Nighttime Theater

   1. Why We Forget Our Dreams

   2. Interpreting Dreams

IV. Hypnosis

   A. The History of Hypnosis

   B. Hypnotic Induction

   C. Hypnotic Phenomena

      1. Pain Reduction and Medical Treatment

How might the components of hypnosis be useful in reducing pain or alleviating some medical problems?

1. Memory Effects

2. Perception

3. Age Regression

Given that hypnosis is a state of heightened susceptibility to suggestions, what concerns should one have when designing an experiment to test whether hypnosis is effective for age regression?

D. Explanations of Hypnosis

How would you behave if you were hypnotized? What role would your expectations of your behavior play in determining what you would do?

Reread the section in your textbook on hypnosis. In addition to the key terms that are defined in the margins, find at least five other words with which you are less familiar. Copy those words and write definitions for each using the context of the reading material to guide your understanding of the meanings of the words.

1.

2.

3.

4.

5.

V. Altering Consciousness with Drugs

Work with four other people, with one major class of drug (depressants, stimulants, opiates, and hallucinogens) assigned to each of you. Each person should study the class of drugs, and report on it to the group. You may wish to use Table 4-2, found on page 166 in your textbook, to help organize the reports.

A. Depressants

    1. Alcohol

        a. Effects of Alcohol

        b. Factors that Influence Alcohol Use

After reading the section on alcohol, write a short summary describing what you perceive to be the most significant patterns for alcohol use and their consequences.

Point your Web browser at the textbook's Web page to see Live!Psych module 4.2.

        1. Barbiturates and Benzodiazepines

B. Stimulants

C. Opiates

D. Hallucinogens

    1. Designer Drugs

Learning Objectives

After you have studied the chapter, you should be able to respond to the following statements and questions to convey your understanding of the material.

1. How do biological rhythms influence one's ability to sense or perceive stimuli?

2. What variations in awareness can be caused by using psychoactive drugs? How do the changes brought about by drug use compare with changes that one experiences when under hypnosis?

3. Discuss evidence that social factors can influence awareness.

4. What is dreaming? Discuss varying theories about the content of dreams.

5. Describe the characteristics and functions of sleep. What do problems with sleep contribute to our understanding of sleep and consciousness?

Key Word Exercise

Fill in the blanks in the following statements with key words and terms from the textbook. Answer as many as you can without referring to your notes or to the book. If you have blanks after thinking about each item, try using your book. The answers are presented after the practice test.

1. _____ _____ are internal biological changes that occur on a daily schedule.

2. A sleep researcher would use a _____ to measure and record physiological changes during sleep.

3. _____ is more a symptom than a disorder, and involves difficulty falling asleep, frequent awakenings, or poor-quality sleep.

4. *Narcolepsy* and *sleep apnea* are examples from a category of sleep disorders called _____.

5. _____ is the name psychologists use for "bedwetting," a problem that affects about 5 million children in the United States.

6. What is known as *hypnosis* today was once called _____, a treatment that was championed by 18th century physician Franz Mesmer.

7. _____ _____ are chemicals that affect consciousness, perception, mood, and behavior.

8. One is said to have developed _____ when increasing dosages of a drug are needed to achieve the same effect as earlier doses.

9. Most states have adopted 0.10% as the _____ _____ _____ that is the legal definition of intoxication.

10. _____ is a colorless, odorless, and tasteless drug that is derived from the ergot fungus that grows on rye.

Practice Test

Circle the letter that corresponds to the *best* alternative for each of the following items. Read each alternative carefully. The answers are presented at the end of this study guide chapter. Be sure to learn *why* each correct alternative is better than the others.

1. Daydreaming may be called an altered form of consciousness because it is:
   a. usually the result of psychoactive drug use.
   b. different from normal waking consciousness.
   c. the same as dreaming that occurs during normal sleep.
   d. rarely recalled accurately by the daydreamer following an episode.

2. ___ rhythms are to ___ rhythms as shorter than 24 hours is to longer than 24 hours.
   a. Ultradian; infradian
   b. Infradian; circadian
   c. Circadian; ultradian
   d. Infradian; ultradian

3. The internal clock for humans is accurate to within a few minutes for most people. However, it tends to run on a 25-hour clock, and therefore must be reset each day. The brain region that is responsible for resetting the internal clock is the:
   a. fornix.
   b. hippocampus.
   c. suprachiasmatic nucleus.
   d. reticular activating system.

4. Which relationship between circadian rhythm and body temperature is accurate for a person who sleeps in the night and is awake during the day?
   a. Body temperature is lowest during the night.
   b. Body temperature is highest during the night.
   c. Body temperature is stable throughout the day for people who are physically well.
   d. There is no relationship between one's body temperature and time of day or presence/absence of daylight.

5. Whether one is a morning person (lark) or evening person (owl) appears to be influenced by:
   a. the company one keeps.
   b. the time of day of one's birth.
   c. body temperature fluctuations.
   d. an interaction between one's gender and age.

6. With respect to internal rhythms and long-distance travel, it is easier to travel:
   a. from west to east.
   b. from east to west.
   c. from north to south.
   d. from south to north.

7. According to sleep researchers interested in problems associated with shift work, the common *phase advance* cycle is like working successive weeks in ___, ___, and ___.
   a. light; dark; light
   b. east; central; west
   c. planes; trains; cars.
   d. Denver; Paris; Tokyo

8. Non-REM (NREM) stages 1 & 2 are to ___ as NREM stages 3 & 4 are to ___.
   a. dreams; nightmares
   b. disorders; datorders
   c. slow-wave sleep; sleepwalking
   d. later in the night; early in the night

9. Sleep spindles and K complexes are to ___ as eye movements are to ___.
   a. stage 1; stage 2
   b. stage 2; REM sleep
   c. REM sleep; stages 3 & 4
   d. all NREM stages; all REM stages

10. During the course of a night's sleep, the amount of time spent in REM for each successive 90 minute cycle:
    a. gets slightly shorter.
    b. stays about the same.
    c. gets progressively longer.
    d. is impossible to know given today's technology.

11. To sleep like a baby literally is to:
    a. in other words, sleep like a rock.
    b. sleep in a highly efficient fashion.
    c. have several short episodes of sleep.
    d. sleep for a prolonged period of consolidated sleep.

12. REM rebound is:
    a. a term used to describe the bouncing back and forth of the eyes during REM sleep.
    b. a term used to describe the bouncing back down through NREM stages after REM.
    c. a phenomenon that occurs more frequently among those who live nearer to the equator.
    d. an increase in the amount of REM one experiences following reduction in REM sleep due to sleep deprivation or drug use.

13. The best way to deal with *insomnia* is to:
    a. practice good "sleep hygiene."
    b. take prescription sleep medicine.
    c. take over-the-counter sleeping pills.
    d. have a glass of nonalcoholic beer just before bedtime.

14. It is common for victims of *sleep apnea* to:
    a. wake up dead.
    b. awaken hundreds of times each night.
    c. speak aloud during sleepwalking episodes.
    d. be drowsy even though they oversleep regularly.

15. CPAP is a:
    a. treatment for sleep apnea.
    b. treatment for symptoms of insomnia.
    c. sleep disorder that is most common among adults.
    d. sleep disorder that is most common among children.

16. REM sleep behavior disorder (RBD) affects mainly:
    a. adolescent girls.
    b. swing shift workers.
    c. men over 50 years of age.
    d. infants up to 6 months of age.

17. Sleep terrors (a.k.a. night terrors):
    a. are thought to cause SIDS.
    b. is a special class of nightmares.
    c. last up to 45 minutes in adolescents.
    d. are NREM experiences that effect about 5 percent of children.

18. Cross-cultural research on dreaming and dream content has revealed:
    a. little of any substance.
    b. that dreams are universally similar.
    c. that cultural views can influence the probability of dream recall.
    d. multilingual subjects are equally likely to dream in second and subsequent languages as the first.

19. The activation-synthesis hypothesis:
    a. accurately predicted the behaviors of hypnotized subjects.
    b. incorporates both manifest and latent dream content as key influences.
    c. suggests that dreams are the result of cortical activation during normal REM sleep.
    d. suggests that the dream content reported by most people represents 3+ combined dream reports.

20. One's ability to be hypnotized:
    a. is stable over time.
    b. becomes greater with age.
    c. becomes weaker with age.
    d. varies as a function of factors other than one's age.

21. Dissociation is:
    a. a psychological disorder in which one loses one's identity.
    b. a sleep disorder whereby people cannot remember their dreams.
    c. the splitting of conscious awareness that is believed to facilitate pain reduction.
    d. most common among women who have been hypnotized on the witness stand in court.

22. In the United States, the most widely used recreational drugs are:
    a. opiates.
    b. stimulants.
    c. depressants.
    d. hallucinogens.

23. ___ has detrimental effects on a person's health and safety and on social and occupational roles.
    a. Tolerance
    b. Withdrawal
    c. Substance abuse
    d. Substance dependence

24. One's liver can metabolize:
    a. up to one drink each day.
    b. approximately 1 drink per hour.
    c. alcohol during withdrawal only if sufficient tolerance has developed.
    d. only one psychoactive drug at a time, which is why using 2+ drugs at once is dangerous.

25. Barbiturates, like most psychoactive drugs, can:
    a. suppress REM and Stage 4 sleep.
    b. cost less on the street than over the counter.
    c. last for up to three days following administration.
    d. be used with little to no risk for health-related circumstances.

26. Opioids:
    a. is a family of drugs that is also called narcotic analgesics.
    b. are extracted from the coca plant that grows in South America.
    c. are chemicals that the body produces to resemble drugs from outside the body.
    d. are far and away the most commonly abused drugs among high school seniors.

27. Relative to tobacco cigarettes, marijuana cigarettes:
    a. contain more tar.
    b. cost about the same.
    c. contain less carbon monoxide.
    d. are easy for teenagers to get at convenience stores.

Answers to Key Word Exercise

1. Circadian rhythms
2. polysomnograph
3. Insomnia
4. hypersomnias
5. Enuresis
6. mesmerism
7. Psychoactive substances
8. tolerance
9. blood alcohol concentration
10. LSD (lysergic acid diethylamide)

Practice Test Answers and Explanations

1. b. Daydreaming is different from normal waking consciousness and is therefore considered an altered state.
2. a. Ultradian rhythms are shorter than 24 hours (e.g., heartbeat). Infradian rhythms are longer than 24 hours (e.g., menstrual cycle).
3. c. The suprachiasmatic nucleus (SCN) resets the body's clock each day.
4. a. Body temperature drops at night. This is why you often have to pull covers on in the night even if you were warm when you went to bed. It is also why you become chilled when you stay up late.
5. c. The timing with which one's body temperature fluctuates is highly correlated with one's sleeping and waking patterns. Genetic factors appear to influence thermal fluctuations.
6. b. Phase delays that occur during east to west travel extend the sleep-wake cycle to approximate the body's natural 25-hour cycle.
7. d. Phase advances occur when traveling from west to east. Schedules on typical shift rotations are akin to traveling in phase advance. It would be easier for workers to shift in phase delay.
8. d. Stages 3 & 4 predominate NREM early in the night, while 1 & 2 predominate later on.
9. b. Sleep spindles and K complexes are characteristic of stage 2; REM stands for rapid *eye movement*.
10. c. The amount of time spent in REM gets increasingly longer during the course of a night's sleep.
11. c. For up to about 6 months babies sleep in several short episodes each night.
12. d. REM rebound occurs when one has been deprived of the normal amount of REM sleep.

13. a. Good sleep hygiene includes such practices as maintaining a regular sleep-wake cycle, avoiding drug use, exercising, and so on (see Table 5-1 in your text).

14. b. Apnea victims awaken hundreds of times each night. Surprisingly, they get used to awakening, and sometimes go many years without getting an adequate night's rest.

15. a. CPAP (continuous positive airway pressure) is a common treatment that helps prevent airway collapse in apnea victims.

16. c. RBD is a syndrome of injurious or disruptive behavior that occurs most frequently in men over 50.

17. d. These NREM experiences are very frightening for both parents and the children who have them.

18. c. Cultural views can influence the probability of dream recall. Also, dream content may reflect cultural differences.

19. c. The activation-synthesis hypothesis suggests that dreams are the result of haphazard cortical activity.

20. a. The ability of one to be hypnotized remains fairly stable over time.

21. c. According to Ernest Hilgard, dissociation is the splitting of conscious awareness that is believed to facilitate pain reduction.

22. c. The drug classification, depressants, contains alcohol, which by itself is one of the most widely used drugs in the US. Recreational use of depressants in general exceeds use of the drugs in the other categories.

23. c. Substance abuse results in detrimental effects on one's health, and on other factors.

24. b. If one drinks slowly enough, the liver can break down alcohol before it affects you.

25. a. Most psychoactive drugs suppress the most important components of the sleep cycle.

26. a. Opioids are derived from the opium poppy. The drug may be processed to produce morphine and codeine.

27. a. Marijuana contains more tar than tobacco. However, most marijuana smokers use less of the drug than cigarette smokers use tobacco.

Key Vocabulary Terms

Use the following list to write definitions *in your own words* for each of the key terms from the chapter. Translating the terms into language that is comfortable and familiar for you will facilitate your learning. For further study of these terms, go to the companion Website for the textbook where you will find electronic flash cards that you may use to test your vocabulary.

consciousness

daydreaming

jet lag

polysomnograph

non-REM (NREM) sleep

slow-wave sleep

REM rebound

insomnia

hypersomnias

narcolepsy

sleep apnea

parasomnias

sleepwalking

enuresis

sleep terror

nightmare

sudden infant death syndrome (SIDS)

dream

manifest content

latent content

activation-synthesis hypothesis

hypnosis

dissociation

psychoactive substance

substance abuse

substance dependence

tolerance

withdrawal

depressants

alcohol

barbiturates

stimulants

amphetamines

opioids

hallucinogens

lysergic acid diethylamide (LSD)

phencyclidine piperidine (PCP)

marijuana

Tip for Success: Dealing with Distractions

Thus far in the *Tips for Success* sections we have examined essential issues concerning habits and practices that will help you make the most of your college years and beyond. By learning to set goals and monitor progress, to use your time wisely, and to locate environments that are conducive to effective studying, you will make significant strides toward reaching your potential for each of your endeavors. In addition to these skills, you will want to minimize distractions from your attention.

You Are Already Much of the Way There

If you have identified study environments that are effective for you, you have already done much of what you need to do to avoid distractions. However, you will find that in spite of your having designated good places for studying, you can still be distracted from your efforts. In turn, this will marginalize the time you have allocated for working on your goals. Thus, the balance of your schedule will be impacted, as may be your ability to attain your goals. This section was prepared to help you learn to concentrate and communicate, and to avoid the negative impact brought on by distractions.

On Concentration

Things that can serve to distract your concentration fall into two broad categories: those that you can control, and those that you cannot control. The following list identifies a few common issues related to distractions you can control to some extent:

1) **Knowing What to Do.** One of the biggest distractions people face is wondering where to begin, or how to proceed on a given task or set of tasks. This concern with what to do usually results from not having set clearly defined goals, or from having goals that are too broad. In such cases, it may be useful to determine specific objectives on which to work, each of which will support your efforts on a broader goal. For example, when preparing for an exam, you may find it useful to set one objective as mastering new vocabulary, another concerning conceptual issues, and so on; each of these will play an important part in helping meet the goal of understanding material to be presented on an exam. Breaking your goals down into discrete steps will make it easier to know where to begin.

2) **Reducing Stress.** The anxiety that comes from an approaching deadline, having a full schedule, or from any number of personal issues can be very distracting. Whenever possible, begin working early on items, such as writing term papers and preparing for exams, activities that you know will be increasingly stressful as deadlines approach. Exerting control over stressors that you *can* control makes it easier to deal with those that you cannot control.

3) **Be Healthy.** If you feel well, get adequate sleep, exercise regularly, and have a balanced diet, you will find it much easier to concentrate. Alternatively, if you are not generally healthy, concerns about modifying your lifestyle will sometimes preoccupy your mind and distract you from doing your best work. Being healthy benefits you several-fold; you will have more energy to work more efficiently, and will not be preoccupied with your health.

4) **Know When to Say "When."** Your capacity to concentrate is directly related to your productivity. Active studying is time-intensive, fatiguing work. You will benefit the most if you work under peak concentration conditions, and take breaks when you notice you are not processing information as efficiently. Depending on the material you study and issues such as those mentioned above, you should probably plan to work in 20-30 minute blocks. A five to ten minute break should serve to help you regain good concentration. If you cannot remember something you just read, it is time for a break.

Identify four distractors that recently made it difficult for you to concentrate. How will you guard against each of these in the future?

<u>Distractor</u>   <u>Your Plan to Guard Against the Distraction in the Future</u>

1) _____

2) _____

3) _____

4) _____

On Communication

Sometimes you will do everything right—identifying a goal or set of goals to work on, scheduling your time, finding a good place to work—but circumstances beyond your control will divert you as you do your work. Many distractions stem from other people who want your time and attention. Good communication about how you use your time will reduce the likelihood of losing time because of having been distracted by others. Because people will contact you for several different reasons, you will need several different plans for responding to protect your time. The following list addresses some common reasons people may contact you and suggestions about how you might respond.

1) **Roommates and Living Mates.** Those with whom you live are perhaps the most likely to distract you, even though they may want you to do your very best. If you study in a place that others use for other activities, it is a good idea to have another study place that can serve as a back-up. Establishing a plan or schedule for how the space will be used, and when, will help. Consider taking advantage of times when those you live with are asleep or away to do your homework. The first few hours of each day are usually the quietest. Those who live in residence halls or apartments have slightly different issues than those who live at home.

    a) **Residence Hall and Apartment Roommates.** Whether you picked your roommate or had one assigned to you, it will be important to develop ground rules for when the environment needs to be quiet for studying, and when it is ok to have friends over, or to listen to the radio, or to watch TV. Try posting one or more copies of a "quiet hours" schedule where others can see it.

    b) **Family Members.** If you live at home, you will probably find your parent(s) or sibling(s) to be receptive of your requests for quiet time to study. Younger siblings and children, however, have more difficulty understanding the need for uninterrupted time. In addition to setting "quiet hours" for your living quarters, consider signaling others that you are studying by hanging a sign on your door that you can take down when you are not studying.

2) **People Who Stop by Unexpectedly.** You may have friends or family members who periodically stop by unannounced. While sometimes the timing may be perfect and you will welcome a visitor, other times it will disrupt you from your work to have to stop to visit. Occasionally the lure of a friend who wants to do something with you may even cause you to leave your studies behind before you meet your goal. It is in your long-term best interest for you to establish a policy whereby people call ahead rather than just stop by. It is much easier to say "no" when you are on the phone than when you are talking face to face. Also, it is easier to keep a phone conversation short than it is to make a personal visit brief.

3) **The Telephone.** When used properly, the telephone can be a great timesaving tool. Use it to call ahead for appointments, to check on where something you are looking for may be found, or to make arrangements with others. Unfortunately, the telephone can distract your concentration and lead to wasted time as well. When you study, try doing so in an environment that has no phone, or turn the

ringer off on your phone. If the phone disrupts you, consider these suggestions for each of the following kinds of calls:

a) **Telemarketers.** You can usually identify that someone is trying to sell you something within a few seconds after picking up the phone. Whoever called interrupted you. It is ok to interrupt the caller to state firmly that you do not do business over the phone. Repeat as necessary. Or, try telling her or him to give you *their personal phone number* so *you can call them* back at a time that is more convenient for you. That usually gets the point across!

b) **Friends.** If appropriate, state that you are busy but will return the call when you get to a stopping point in your work. This may feel awkward, but bear in mind that you were distracted. If you call back as promised, your friends will not get too upset. To reinforce the need to respect one another's time, and to acknowledge that the phone can be distracting, begin conversations that you initiate by asking whether you called at an acceptable time. If your friends adopt that habit by following your example, it will be easy to avoid having long conversations at inappropriate times.

c) **Sometimes It Is Better to Take the Call.** You may decide to talk on the phone in spite of the timing of a call. When possible, try to keep a list of tasks on hand or in your mind that you can work on while you talk. It will probably be important to have them be tasks that do not demand too much attention. Try putting away dishes or laundry, watering plants, etc., while you talk. Doing this will make help you make the most of the distraction.

4) **Televisions, Stereos, and Other Noisy Things.** Most people concentrate best when the environment is completely quiet. Others, however, find that having something to mask the sounds of neighbors, traffic, and other irregular noises is helpful. It is important not to be distracted, however, by anything that you turn on (e.g., the radio) while you are studying. If you prefer to have music playing while you study, play music that has no lyrics so you are not tempted to sing along. Some people actually turn the radio or TV to a frequency that is in between stations. This produces *white noise*, or a sound that is comprised of all frequencies. Provided that it is not too loud, white noise can be an effective way of masking other noise.

Identify five things you can do to help reduce the distractions given the environment in which you live:

1) _____

2) _____

3) _____

4) _____

5) _____

If you can learn to communicate effectively concerning when you are available and when you are busy, you will become much more productive. Pay attention to the things that divert your attention from your homework and determine some steps for preventing the problem in the future.

CHAPTER 5

Learning

Do You Know?

Do you know that the principles of learning may be used to explain virtually all of the behaviors of you and others? Your text focuses on three important varieties of learning: classical conditioning, operant conditioning, and conditioning in the context of social cognition. For this Do You Know feature, special attention will be given to classical conditioning. However, examples of all forms of conditioning and learning are impossible to miss if you look for them in your everyday life—watch for them and begin thinking like a psychologist by identifying the key parameters that influence your and others' behaviors.

Classical conditioning principles are widely employed in the entertainment industries. One clear example concerns the use of music or other audio-visual cues to predict significant events in television and film. In the film, *Jaws*, a particular musical phrase was repeated each time a character in the movie was about to fall prey to the shark. After only a few pairings, viewers cannot help but become anxious when the music is played in scenes throughout the rest of the movie. In this case, the music is the conditioned stimulus (CS), the unconditioned stimulus is the attack, the unconditioned response is the feeling experienced after seeing a shark attack, and the conditioned response is the anxiety that is produced in anticipation of an attack when the music (CS) is played.

We have been hearing a lot about the roles that fast food restaurant restaurants may have played in creating an obesity problem in the United States. While many dismiss this notion as ridiculous, there may be value in considering the claim, especially from the perspective of conditioning and learning. Critics of fast food complain about the high amounts of fat in most of fast food menu items. Note that many of these items also use sauces and ingredients within high fat dishes, and that these sauces and ingredients have biologically significant taste properties—namely sweet and salty. One could easily argue that the paired tasting of fat and either sweet or salty (or both) flavors might well influence ones preference for the taste of fat because of its association with sweet and/or salt. If classical conditioning can be used to explain acquired anxiety to previously neutral music or other stimuli in films, is it not reasonable to think in terms of people having been conditioned to like the taste of fat because of its consistent association with biologically significant sweet and salty tastes?

Notes from Class and the Textbook

Use the space provided in this outline to record notes from the textbook as well as from class lectures and discussion. Questions related to the *Psychological Detective, Hands On, Myth or Science,* and *Study Tip* sections in the text have been presented in the outline; use the associated space to respond to the questions and to record your own comments about the issues.

I. What is Learning?

II. Classical Conditioning

        A. Basic Elements of Classical Conditioning

On page 186 in your text, the authors describe a demonstration of classical conditioning that involves popping balloons and watching people's responses. All you need for the demonstration will be several balloons and a sewing needle. If you don't have a sewing needle, a stick pin from your bulletin board will do; it is just not as dramatic. You may want to practice the demonstration before showing it to your friends. (Hint: if your balloon is under high tension, you could stick a piece of invisible tape on the balloon and run the needle through the tape.)

Think of your own examples of classical conditioning. To ensure that you understand each of the elements, be certain to identify the CS, UCS, UCR and CR. What do you notice about the qualities of the stimuli? Are the UCR and the CR similar in nature and strength? Think of examples in which the UCR and the CR are similar and others in which they are dissimilar.

B. Classical Conditioning Processes

    1. Acquisition

        a. Sequence of CS-UCS Presentation

        b. Strength of the UCS

        c. Number of CS-UCS Pairings

Point your Web browser at the textbook's Web page to see Live!Psych module 5.1.

    2. Extinction

    3. Spontaneous Recovery

4. Generalization and Discrimination

How do you anticipate Pavlov's dogs responded when an ellipse, that was associated with the absence of food, was gradually altered to look like a circle that had been presented as a signal for food?

C. Applications of Classical Conditioning: Phobias and Beyond

Consider Watson and Rayner's classical conditioning experiment with Little Albert. Consider the costs and benefits of that project. Would a proposal to conduct that experiment today be passed by the review board? Why or why not?

1. Classical Conditioning and Our Motives

D. Trends in Classical Conditioning: After Pavlov

1. Contingency Theory

2. Blocking

E. Evolution and Classical Conditioning: Taste-Aversion Learning and Preparedness

1. Taste Aversion

2. Preparedness

Diagram an experiment to test whether colors or tastes can more easily be conditioned to illness in birds.

3. Learning by Various Species

With a small group of friends, brainstorm and come up with at least five examples of classical conditioning in humans that were not presented in your textbook.

III. Operant Conditioning

    A. Reinforcers: The Basic Concept of Operant Conditioning

        1. Positive and Negative Reinforcers

Consider cheating in school as operant behavior. Can a positive reinforcer be used to encourage unethical behavior such as cheating? Describe the circumstances that would create an outcome such as positively reinforced unethical behavior.

        2. Primary and Secondary (Conditioned) Reinforcers

B. Contingencies and Behavior

Point your Web browser at the textbook's Web page to see Live!Psych module 5.2.

Discuss the process of learning to drive an automobile (especially one with a manual transmission) in terms of *shaping*.

       1. The Premack Principle

   C. Schedules of Reinforcement

A rat is being trained in a Skinner box. The responses by the rat are recorded on a graph called a cumulative record. What does a horizontal line on a cumulative record reveal about the rat's responding?

       1. Continuous Reinforcement

       2. Intermittent (Partial) Reinforcement

          a. Ratio Schedules

          b. Interval Schedules

D. The Partial Reinforcement Effect

E. Operant Conditioning and Stimulus Control

F. Punishment: The Opposite of Reinforcement

Drawing on what you know to be effective for training an organism to perform a response for positive reinforcement, consider what it would take to reduce the performance of a response using punishment. How can punishment be administered in order to maximize its effects?

Create an outline summarizing the basic points of the material on the Skinner box, shaping, and schedules of reinforcement.

IV. Cognitive and Social Perspectives on Learning

    A. The Role of Cognition

        1. Insight Learning

        2. Latent Learning

Create a visual organizer that shows behaviors with cognitive requirements (insight learning , latent learning, and so on) and their most important elements.

    B. Observational Learning

Learning Objectives

After you have studied the chapter, you should be able to respond to the following statements and questions to convey your understanding of the material.

1. Describe *learning* as an adaptive behavior that supports natural selection.

2. What role do sensory and perceptual processes play in learning?

3. What relationships exist between conscious awareness and learning?

4. Differentiate among classical, operant, and observational learning.

Key Word Exercise

Fill in the blanks in the following statements with key words and terms from the textbook. Answer as many as you can without referring to your notes or to the book. If you have blanks after thinking about each item, try using your book. The answers are presented after the practice test.

1. Reactions or reflexes that are elicited automatically when certain stimuli are presented are called _____ _____.

2. _____ is the training stage during which a particular response is learned.

3. When a sprinter has a false start because of hearing a loud noise other than the start gun, _____ is said to have occurred.

4. _____ occurs when a compound stimulus is paired with a US and the more intense (salient) CS elicits a stronger CR.

5. If you have ever become nauseated after eating an unfamiliar food, you probably developed a(n) _____ _____ as a result.

6. A(n) _____ _____ is a stimulus that has innate reinforcing properties.

7. A(n) _____ ___ _____ is a preset pattern of delivering reinforcement.

8. Reinforcement that follows every target response is called _____ _____.

9. Imagine that a child learns the laws regarding when to stop, and when to drive through intersections with traffic lights without ever driving. This would be an example of _____ _____.

10. Experiments have demonstrated that rats can remember a series of events. Thus, rats are capable _____ _____.

Practice Test

Circle the letter that corresponds to the *best* alternative for each of the following items. Read each alternative carefully. The answers are presented at the end of this study guide chapter. Be sure to learn *why* each correct alternative is better than the others.

1. A critical distinction between learned behaviors and those that become possible through maturation, is that learned responses:
    a. are innate, or preprogrammed.
    b. occur as a function of experience(s).
    c. outlast those that are gained through maturation.
    d. are acquired in strictly controlled laboratory conditions.

2. ___ ___ is to ___ ___ as stimulus-stimulus learning is to response-outcome learning.
    a. Classical conditioning; operant conditioning
    b. Operant conditioning; observational learning
    c. Observational learning; classical conditioning
    d. Operant conditioning; instrumental conditioning

3. A conditioned stimulus (CS):
    a. is an automatically produced reaction.
    b. is a stimulus that does not elicit a particular response.
    c. is an event that automatically produces a response without prior training.
    d. starts out neutral, but acquires the ability to elicit a response through training.

4. Unconditioned response (UR) is to conditioned response as ___ is to ___.
    a. sight; sound
    b. pleasure; pain
    c. automatic; learned
    d. None of the above; these terms mean the same thing.

5. The flinching people do when they see a long needle being stuck through a balloon results from learning, and is called:
    a. magic.
    b. extinction.
    c. conditioned excitation.
    d. a conditioned response.

6. Many phobias can be understood in terms of:
   a. operant conditioning.
   b. classical conditioning.
   c. observational learning.
   d. a psychological deficiency.

7. Watson's research with "Little Albert" demonstrated:
   a. what Holmes knew all along.
   b. that white rats can be conditioned to fear children.
   c. that emotional responses may be conditioned in humans.
   d. that children will act violently toward a Bobo doll after watching an adult do the same.

8. Which of the following is not a variable for determining the rate or quality of acquired responding?
   a. the strength of the US
   b. the strength of the CR
   c. the number of CS-US pairings
   d. the sequence of stimulus (CS & US) presentation

9. Spontaneous recovery is:
   a. more common in children than in adults.
   b. a phenomenon that is associated only with lab-based research.
   c. the reappearance of an extinguished CR after the passage of time.
   d. most often associated with patients suffering from mild psychological illnesses.

10. When a musician can recognize a note as "Middle C," rather than another note near "Middle C," this is an example of:
    a. generalization.
    b. discrimination.
    c. dishabituation.
    d. a learned goal (or learned incentive).

11. Contingency theory predicts that the better the CS is able to predict the occurrence of the US, the ___ conditioning will be.
    a. weaker
    b. stronger
    c. longer-lasting
    d. more resistant to extinction

12. ___ is a situation in which the conditionability of a CS is weakened when it is paired with a US that has previously been paired with another CS.
    a. Blocking
    b. Foreshadowing
    c. Overshadowing
    d. Latent Learning

13. An interesting feature of taste-aversion learning is that it:
    a. requires two CSs.
    b. is strong, but often short-lived.
    c. works well with novel and familiar CSs.
    d. occurs when the CS-US interval is lengthy.

14. The fact that some events go together naturally, and are therefore easily learned, is fundamental to the theory of:
    a. preparedness.
    b. easy learning.
    c. relative conditioning.
    d. conditioned associations.

15. A secondary reinforcer:
    a. always follows the CS in classical conditioning.
    b. concerns items of interest after basic needs have been met.
    c. can sometimes go unnoticed by the participant, but is nevertheless powerful.
    d. acquires reinforcing properties by virtue of an association with a primary reinforcer.

16. Hitting the snooze button on your alarm in the morning is:
    a. positively reinforced.
    b. negatively reinforced.
    c. not reinforced if you fall asleep again.
    d. only reinforced if you fall asleep again.

17. Shaping involves:
    a. reinforcement of the target response.
    b. reinforcement of activity other than the target response.
    c. reinforcement that does not follow every target response.
    d. reinforcement of successive approximations of the target response.

18. A cumulative record:
    a. is the peak response rate in a Skinner box.
    b. is a way of displaying results of conditioning trials.
    c. is another name for the acquisition strength of a trial.
    d. is usually released by a band after they have had several hits.

19. The two main types of intermittent schedules of reinforcement are ___ and ___.
    a. interval; ratio
    b. partial; complete
    c. positive; negative
    d. terminal; continuing

20. Conditioning in which we structure perceptual stimuli differently is called ___.
    a. latent learning
    b. insight learning
    c. serial enumeration
    d. perceptual learning

21. Negative punishers are:
    a. painful in nature.
    b. to be avoided at all costs.
    c. the same as positive punishers.
    d. pleasant stimuli that are removed.

22. The partial reinforcement effect:
    a. results from administering only a portion of a reward each time.
    b. is robust with respect to the quality of the reinforcer that is employed.
    c. describes the pattern of responding when one is on a FI schedule and only reacts part of the time.
    d. is reflected when extinction takes longer following intermittent reinforcement than after continuous reinforcement.

23. A stimulus that signals the participant that responding will be reinforced:
    a. is called a discriminative stimulus.
    b. is called a Boojum—as was used in the Snark experiment.
    c. would be Bob Barker yelling, "Come on down," for example.
    d. cannot last fewer than 15 seconds, or longer than 1 hour 25 minutes.

24. When older siblings help their younger siblings learn which behaviors will be punished, and which will be reinforced, the younger siblings experience:
   a. behavior modification.
   b. observational learning.
   c. synthesis of vicarious activation.
   d. prolonged extinction trials for acquired responses.

25. Behavior modification:
   a. is more easily done than said.
   b. was once a common treatment for the mentally ill, but is now considered unethical.
   c. has been defined as the application of the results of learning theory and the application of experimental psychology to the problem of altering maladaptive behavior.
   d. involves placing group housed clients in mental institutions in giant Skinner boxes and rewarding them on schedules as has been done previously with pigeons and laboratory rats.

Answers to Key Word Exercise

1. unconditioned responses	2. Acquisition	3. generalization
4. Overshadowing	5. taste aversion	6. primary reinforcer
7. schedule of reinforcement	8. continuous reinforcement	9. latent learning
10. serial enumeration		

Practice Test Answers and Explanations

1. b. Learning results from experience, whereas changes associated with maturation do not require environmental influence.
2. a. Classical conditioning involves learning about the relationships among stimuli. Operant conditioning involves learning response-outcome contingencies.
3. d. CSs start out as neutral stimuli, but take on meaning after being presented in conjunction with USs.
4. c. URs are automatic reactions that occur without training. CRs are expressed as a function of classical conditioning, or learning.
5. d. Flinching in anticipation of a "bang" when a needle passes through a balloon is an example of conditioned responding.
6. b. Phobias often result from classically conditioned cues associated with an unpleasant experience.
7. c. Watson's research, which would not pass today's APA guidelines, showed the ease with which emotional responses can by conditioned.
8. b. The strength of the CR might be used as an index of the degree of conditioning, but does not influence acquisition as it is the product of acquisition.
9. c. Spontaneous recovery takes place after a CR has been extinguished and there has been a break in conditioning and testing trials.
10. b. Discrimination is the occurrence of a response to a specific stimulus.
11. b. Contingency theory predicts stronger conditioning as a function of the CS's value in predicting the US.
12. a. Blocking refers to one CS impairing another's ability to acquire associative strength and value.
13. d. Taste-aversion learning can occur with CS-US intervals that were surprisingly long when the phenomenon was first discovered.
14. a. Preparedness refers to a theory of biological readiness to learn certain associations.
15. d. Secondary reinforcers are stimuli that take on meaning because they are associated with primary reinforcers.
16. b. An example of negative reinforcement is the termination of an alarm by pushing a button.
17. d. Shaping is also known as the method of (reinforcing) successive approximations.
18. b. A cumulative record is used to show the rate of responding in a conditioning trial.
19. a. Interval and ratio schedules are the two main categories of intermittent reinforcement schedules.
20. b. Insight learning involves the sudden grasp of a concept (the ah-ha experience) as a result of perceptual restructuring.
21. d. Negative punishment involves the termination of a satisfier (e.g., losing privileges).
22. d. The partial reinforcement effect describes the phenomenon of extended responding during extinction of a behavior that was reinforced only some of the time during acquisition.

23. a. A discriminative stimulus signals the participant that reward contingencies are in place for target behaviors.
24. b. Observational, or vicarious learning occurs when one models learning for another (either purposely or otherwise).
25. c. Behavior modification uses learning principles to decrease undesirable behaviors and increase desired ones. See discussion at the end of Chapter 6 in your textbook for more on behavior modification.

Key Vocabulary Terms

Use the following list to write definitions *in your own words* for each of the key terms from the chapter. Translating the terms into language that is comfortable and familiar for you will facilitate your learning. For further study of these terms, go to the companion website for the textbook where you will find electronic flash cards that you may use to test your vocabulary.

learning

classical conditioning

neutral stimulus (NS)

unconditioned stimulus (UCS)

conditioned stimulus (CS)

unconditioned response (UCR)

conditioned response (CR)

extinction

spontaneous recovery

generalization

discrimination

phobia

learned motives

learned goals (learned incentives)

blocking

taste-aversion learning

preparedness

operant conditioning

reinforcer

positive reinforcer

negative reinforcers

primary reinforcer

secondary reinforcer

shaping

cumulative record

schedule of reinforcement

continuous reinforcement

intermittent (or partial) reinforcement

ratio schedule

interval schedule

partial reinforcement effect

discrimination stimulus

punisher

law of effect

punishment

partial reinforcement effect

insight learning

latent learning

observational learning (modeling)

Tip for Success: Getting the Most from the Classroom

The time you spend in class can be very valuable. The classrooms, laboratories, and studios where your classes meet were designed for student learning. The lectures, demonstrations, and discussions you listen to, watch, and participate in were organized by your professors in order to facilitate your understanding of the course material. Your tuition provides you with access to professionals whose interests are the very courses you take, and to facilities that are meant to support your educational experience. What you make of the opportunities you have, however, will depend on how well you are able to extract ideas and information from your classroom experiences. This section offers several suggestions for helping you make the most of your classroom learning opportunities.

Why Notes Are Important

Your notes should represent your perspective on everything that happens in each class you take. Your notes for a given class will represent those elements from the subject that your professor thinks are of importance for students to know. Attend class regularly, pay close attention to the lectures, demonstrations, and discussions, and take thorough notes. The notes you develop as an active, attentive student will be invaluable to you in the future. As you receive assignments, quizzes, and exams back, 3-hole punch them and add them to your notes. Keeping course material organized and together is useful not only as you prepare for exams, but as reference material in subsequent semesters as well. Students are often surprised at how their notes from one class help them in other classes.

No matter how good your memory is, you will not recall everything from class. If your professor is really good at presenting difficult concepts, you may find it tempting to not write notes. Avoid that temptation. Too often, students find themselves frustrated when they do not recall how a given concept was explained in class. The very act of writing something down will help you remember it later. One thing is sure: if you write it down, you can always refer to your notes if you need to; if you do not write it down, you may realize too late that you do not understand a concept completely.

Be Prepared

When you go to a given class meeting, you should have a mindset that enables you to benefit as much as possible from the relatively brief opportunity. You can make an important investment in your career by simply preparing your mind for each class meeting. Learning how to do this, and making a habit of it, are the most effective ways for you to pursue your academic goals. Commit the following list to memory, and discipline yourself to do each step.

1. Know the Topic. Review your syllabus to learn what the topic of each day will be as you progress through the semester. If you have reading or homework assignments, do them. Completing assignments as you go, rather than 'whenever you get around to it,' even if your professor does not check to see if you are caught up, will keep you in touch with the class. At bare minimum you should flip through the pages from your text to review the variety of things you might expect to learn about.

2. Know the Environment. By merely showing up several minutes early, you can usually have your pick of chairs in a classroom. Choose a place in the room that will allow you to see and hear the instructor without having to strain. Any energy you have to spend focusing your attention will detract from your ability to think about the topic at hand. Sitting in the front, center portion of the classroom will allow your professor to see that you are committed to getting the most from your experience. Sitting farther away, or near people who chatter a lot, communicates that you do not think the professor has much of value to offer.

3. Have the Right Tools. Bring the book or books you may be discussing in class. It is rude to read these instead of paying attention, but it is good to be able to refer to your book if it becomes important to do so. Dedicate a 3-ring notebook, or section of a larger binder, to each class, and bring it with you to every meeting. Your notes from each class meeting will be your only reminders of what you did on a given day. By recording them in a well-designated place you will always know where to look when you need information for the class. The 3-ring format will permit you to add handouts from class, exams, and quizzes, etc. Always have *at least* one extra pen or pencil with you. If you are enrolled in a class that may involve performing statistical or mathematical calculations, bring a calculator with you each time as well.

4. Develop Your Own Shorthand. Having a system of abbreviations will help you keep up with comments from class. It is a good idea to keep a reference page in each notebook for the shorthand abbreviation system you develop. If a word is used regularly in your notes, use a standard abbreviation or devise a symbol that takes less time to write. Truncate words when possible. But, be sure to keep a glossary of abbreviations so you do not lose track of your system. If you consider that the time it takes to learn an abbreviation is far less than the time it will take to write the word(s) many times in longhand, you will quickly realize the value of using symbols and abbreviations.

You will want to translate these into your glossary. Look at the following examples, then record several other abbreviations that will save you time in class. Add to your glossary as you develop new shortcuts.

~ = approximately	b/c = because	e.g., = for example
i.e., = in other words	Q: = question	A: = answer
2 = to, too, two	4 = for, fore, four	+ or & = and
B4 = before	etc. = and so forth	→ = leading to
← = resulting from	Ψ = psychology	w/ = with
w/o = without	Δ = change	< = less than
> = more than	@ =at	√ = check
% = percent(age)	Σ = sum	

What are other ways you can simplify your note taking by using abbreviations and symbols?

Be Early, Be Interested, Be Courteous

Being early to and attentive during class shows your commitment. This will give you a few minutes to prepare (e.g., review notes, look through your text) or to discuss the class with your professor or other students. Being late is disruptive and gives the impression that the class is not a priority for you.

Having selected a seat that is front and center in the room, you are well positioned to give your utmost attention. Maintain eye contact with your professor whenever possible. If you are interested in your professor, your professor will be interested in you. Building on this relationship will help you develop and maintain a commitment to studying and doing good work.

To be eligible to teach the class, your professor studied the topic extensively in graduate school. The class you are taking is on a topic that is very important to your professor. If you discover your mind to be wandering, think about what it is that draws people to the discipline. Ask a question that will help your professor convey her or his passion for the subject. Another good way to keep on task is to take notes continuously. It is hard for your mind to wander if you are busy taking notes. Finally, do not close your notebook or put anything away until your professor has closed the class. Often some important points are made in the last few minutes; you cannot record them if you have already put your things away. What's more, closing your books is distracting to others in the classroom.

Approaches to Note Taking

Your notes have to be meaningful to you to be of any use. The most appropriate method for taking notes will depend on your style as a student, your professor's teaching style, the nature of the class, and other variables. Regardless of these things, your notes need to be organized. In addition to dedicating a whole notebook, or section of a larger binder, to each class, you will want to assign a piece of paper to each day. Put each day's date in the same place so that later it will be easy to track what happened by date. If you write on two or more pages, simply rewrite the date and number the page (2, 3, etc.), as appropriate.

Two common methods for taking notes are offered below. Experiment until you find a system that works for you. Take the opportunity to inquire with your professors about the methods that will work best for their particular courses.

1. The Outline Method. Some of your teachers will give highly structured notes that fit well into an outline. If the notes fit an outline format well, use that format. Some notes on using an outline, and a sample of the common outline format are provided near the end of this section.

2. The Cornell System. Another system for recording notes, that works well whether or not the notes follow an outline format, was developed by Walter Pauk at Cornell University. This system involves dividing each page of notes into three parts. See the end of this section for an example of a page. In short, the system uses a large box for notes on the right- hand section of the page, a narrower strip beside the main box for adding detail later on when you study your notes, and a section at the bottom of each page that spans the page's width where summarizing comments about the page can be made.

Things to be Sure to Include in Your Notes

Learning to take good notes takes time and practice. It is better to write too much than to write too little, but sometimes students work so hard to transcribe the class discussions exactly that they miss out on the main point(s). By developing a personally meaningful shorthand system, you will be able to spend less time scribbling in you notebook, and more time paying attention in class.

If you notice that something is reiterated, if your professor draws a picture or diagram on the board, or if you hear something in your professor's intonation that emphasizes a given point, make sure your notes reflect it. If a word is written on the board, write it in your notes.

If you are not sure what your professor is trying to communicate, ask. The chances are that if you are not following something in the class, others are also confused. Most professors appreciate it when their students ask questions; use questions to indicate your interest in class and to communicate that you are paying attention. Many times a question that you may ask will help your professor understand more about you and your commitment, and will also win favor with your fellow students.

Sometimes you understand perfectly well what is being said, but do not have time to record it before your professor moves on to the next topic. Raise your hand and ask that he or she repeat the comment. Again, this will underscore your commitment to getting the most from each class period.

Within a day of taking each set of notes, you should review them, filling in missing information, adding references to figures or text passages from your book, etc. You may even find rewriting your notes to be helpful. The sooner after taking a set of notes that you are able to review them, the better able you will be to fill in gaps, make references to the text, etc.

Notes on Using a Formal Outline

1. Typically there will be at least two points for each level of organization (if there is a I, there should be a II, if there is an A, there should be a B, and so on).

2. Note the numbering and lettering system; it is common to most outlines.

3. Use only key words and sentence fragments. The point of the outline it to record the main points; details are added when the outline is used as a basis for writing a paper or delivering a speech.

Sample Outline Format

I. Major topic (sentence fragment that reflects the main point of the topic or section)

    A. 1st important supporting point

    B. 2nd supporting point

        1. 1st detail to clarify I.B.

        2. 2nd detail relating to I.B.

            a. 1st small point relating to 2nd detail

            b. 2nd small point for 2nd detail under I.B.

                i. Minute piece of information about 3rd detail

                ii. 2nd minute piece of information

II. Second Topic

    A. 1st point

    B. 2nd point

    C. 3rd point

III. Third Topic

    A. 1st point

    B. 2nd point

Example of Layout for the Cornell Method

The table below represents a piece of 8.5" x 11" notebook paper:

	date (xx/xx/xx) - p.#
← ~2.5" → **Cue Column** Leave blank while in class. Add detail to this area when you review your notes. Draw diagrams, highlight terms and concepts, or refer to pages in the text book.	**Class Notes Section** Use formal or informal outline format to record notes from class in this section. Include the following: Drawings & diagrams Key concepts & ideas Q:s & A:s from class Q:s to ask your professor Other item, as appropriate

↑
2"
↓   **Summary Area**
Fill in this section after you review your notes. It should
contain summarizing comments about the rest of the page.

CHAPTER 6

Motivation and Emotion

Do You Know?

Do you know that the same theoretical process—Richard Solomon's Opponent Process theory of emotion—handles explanation of behaviors that occur in emotional contexts and the acquisition of drug tolerance equally well? Solomon's theory is a two-process theory that presumes that each emotional process is associated with another process of opposite emotional sign. Particularly, the theory holds that after experiencing one emotion, such as fear in the context of skydiving as presented in your textbook, one experiences the opposite emotion. In the case of the skydiving example, fear gives way to thrill and excitement, both of which are desirable emotional states. The theory allows for the primary, or A Process emotion to be of any sign; thus, if you have ever experienced letdown or even mild depression following an exciting event such as a vacation, you understand firsthand how a positive emotional experience may come to yield to a negative one.

Solomon's theory is based upon homeostatic mechanisms and learning theory, and suggests that, as in the case of skydiving, when the B Process emotion is desirable, it may lead to increased behavior that leads to the A Process emotion in order that one may experience the B Process. This mechanism offers a means for understanding why people who experiment with high-risk behavior tend to repeat performance of the behavior.

Interestingly, another application of the theory also helps understand the acquisition of drug tolerance. Consider the A and B Processes as physiological events. If the A Process is attributable to the physiological influence of a given drug on the body, the B Process represents the compensatory responding of the body as it strives to achieve homeostasis with respect to the biological effects that are thrown out of balance by use of the drug. However, the B Process, according to an expanded version of Solomon's theory, lags behind the A Process in time, both with respect to its development of amplitude (how strong the compensatory response is) and with respect to the time course of the process. Initial use of the drug is unanticipated by the body, so has an A Process that is comparatively larger than the resulting B Process. With repeated use of the drug, the body learns to respond to the classical conditioning cues associated with the drug, and therefore counteracts the drug insult more effectively. Thus, in order for the user to have the same experience as with initial use of the drug, larger quantities of the drug need to be administered. Finally, because the B Process trails behind the A Process in time, just as the user may experience a "high" upon administration of the drug, the high gives way to a relative low—or crash—when the A Process ends and the B Process is still active.

Notes from Class and the Textbook

Use the space provided in this outline to record notes from the textbook as well as from class lectures and discussion. Questions related to the *Psychological Detective, Hands On, Myth or Science,* and *Study Tip* sections in the text have been presented in the outline; use the associated space to respond to the questions and to record your own comments about the issues.

I. What is Motivation?

II. Theories of Motivation

    A. Biological Theories

        1. Ethology

        2. Internal States, Drives, and Drive Reduction

3. Optimum-Level Theories

Why might changes in thermal stimulation be desirable? How does this implicate motivation?

B. Cognitive Theories

1. Cognitive-Consistency Theories

2. Incentive Theories

3. Maslow's Hierarchy of Needs

From memory, list the five levels in Maslow's hierarchy of needs. For each level, list as many examples of that need as possible.

III. Specific Motives

    A. Hunger

Diagram the chain of events that the hypothalamus sets in motion in response to external signals and/or internal stimuli.

        1. Nutrition and Eating

        2. How Does My Weight Compare?

How could you collect information to make comparisons between your weight and others?

        3. The Body Mass Index (BMI)

        4. The Biology of Obesity

Consider set-point theory as it relates to the maintenance of body weight during fluctuations in amount and quality of diet. What are the implications of dieting on metabolism according to this theory?

5. Social Factors and Weight

6. Dieting

7. Eating Disorders

B. Sex

1. External Factors

How are humans and nonhuman animals different with respect to sexual arousal? What are the consequences of these differences?

2. Hormones

3. Brain Mechanisms

4. The Sexual Response

C. Achievement

IV. The What and the Why of Emotion

    A. Relating Emotions and Behavior: The Evolutionary Perspective

V. The Physiological Components of Emotions

    A. Early Theories of Emotions

        1. The James-Lange Theory

        2. The Cannon-Bard Theory

Compare and contrast the James-Lange and Cannon-Bard theories of emotions. Which do you find more compelling? Why?

    B. Physiological Differences among Emotions

    C. The Role of the Brain in Emotion

If each time you hear a tone you receive a mild electric shock, how would this contingency change your behavior?

    1.   The Brain's Hemispheres and Emotions

    2.   Lack of Emotion

    3.   The Opponent-Process Theory

  D. Evaluating the Lie Detector

How might the anxiety associated with taking a lie detector test increase or decrease the likelihood of the machine detecting a lie when you tell the truth?

VI. The Expressive Components of Emotions

  A. Universal Elements in the Facial Expression of Emotion

Point your Web browser at the textbook's Web page to see Live!Psych module 6.1.

    1.   How Many Emotions Are There?

Examine Robert Plutchik's list of eight basic human emotions (Figure 6-13, page 257 in your textbook). Act out the expressions and have a friend guess which expression matches which label. Trade roles with your friend.

    2.   The Facial Feedback Hypothesis

How does your ability to smile or frown influence your emotionality?

    3.   Display Rules: The Effects of Culture

    4. Smiling

Is a sincere smile different from an insincere one? If so, how?

B. Nonverbal Communication

    1. Body Language

    2. Paralanguage

C. Gender Effects

VII. The Cognitive Components of Emotion

A. The Language of Emotion

    1. The Schacter and Singer Appraisal Model

    2. Other Appraisal Theories of Emotion

B. The Development of Emotion

    1. Emotional Intelligence

Learning Objectives

After you have studied the chapter, you should be able to respond to the following statements and questions to convey your understanding of the material.

1. Differentiate between biological and cognitive theories of emotion.

2. Identify the four basic categories of motives that were outlined in your book. How are they similar and how are they different?

3. How is the brain involved in the regulation of emotions?

4. What elements of emotions are universal?

5. How is cognition related to emotion?

Key Word Exercise

Fill in the blanks in the following statements with key words and terms from the textbook. Answer as many as you can without referring to your notes or to the book. If you have blanks after thinking about each item, try using your book. The answers are presented after the practice test.

1. _____ _____ are triggered or released by specific environmental events called *releasing stimuli*.

2. _____ _____ of motivation suggest behavior is motivated by the goal the organism seeks to attain.

3. Deciding whether to study for a quiz instead of going out with friends <u>or</u> to go out with friends and risk failing an exam is an example of an _____-_____ _____.

4. When considering making a purchase, you may find yourself attracted to and repulsed by a variety of goals. The term for this circumstance is: _____ _____ _____ _____.

5. The menstrual synchrony found among lesbian couples has supported speculation about the role of _____ in controlling some aspects of human behavior.

6. During the resolution phase of the sexual response cycle, physiological changes associated with sexual arousal gradually _____.

7. The _____ _____ theory of emotion can be used to explain why people participate in anxiety-provoking activities such as skydiving.

8. Research on the universality of emotions has demonstrated that there are at least _____ emotions that are recognized everywhere.

9. _____ _____ are cultural norms that tell us to laugh when someone (particularly one's boss) tells a joke.

10. _____ _____ includes such abilities as motivating oneself, persisting in the face of frustrations, and controlling impulses, as well as being aware of the emotions one is experiencing.

Practice Test

Circle the letter that corresponds to the **best** alternative for each of the following items. Be sure to read each alternative carefully and to learn why each correct alternative is better than the others. The answers are presented at the end of this study guide chapter.

1. The study of motivation has three aspects. Which of the following is not one of these?
   a. the goal(s) toward which the behavior was directed
   b. the factor or motivational state prompting the behavior
   c. the reasons for differences in the intensity of the behavior
   d. All of the above are aspects associated with the study of emotions.

2. Instincts are:
   a. essentially reflexes.
   b. smells that come from within.
   c. the building blocks for motivation.
   d. unlearned behaviors that are more complex than reflexes.

3. The red spots on the bellies of male stickleback fish:
   a. are releasing stimuli for other males.
   b. occur because the fish swim too close to the ground.
   c. develop as the fish mature and become large enough to mate.
   d. fade to gray when the fish are no longer interested in mating.

4. A compelling feature of the sociobiology theory is that it:
   a. is interdisciplinary in nature.
   b. can explain altruistic behavior.
   c. successfully predicted homelessness would be a problem.
   d. explains human and animal behavior without presuming motives.

5. Homeostasis is the tendency of the body to maintain balance. Drive reduction theory suggests physiological needs known as ___ motivate activity that will restore balance.
   a. drives
   b. homeostats
   c. psychophysical wants
   d. the 'basics' (for humans these include the need to shop, for example)

6. Which theories of motivation stress the processing and understanding of information?
   a. ethology
   b. sociobiology
   c. optimum-level theory
   d. cognitive theories of emotion

7. When a person has inconsistent or incompatible thoughts or cognitions, this is called:
   a. hysteria.
   b. mass confusion.
   c. cognitive dissonance.
   d. feeling wishy-washy.

8. Drive-reduction theories are to incentive theories as ___ is to ___.
   a. go; stop
   b. push; pull
   c. accelerate; brake
   d. slow down; speed up

9. Maslow's hierarchy of needs has five categories of motivated behavior that can be ordered in hierarchical fashion along which dimension(s)?
   a. the *type* of motivation
   b. the *strength* of motivation
   c. both a. and b.
   d. neither a. nor b.

10. Self-actualization:
    a. is met concurrently with basic needs.
    b. is reached by most people by the time they are 30.
    c. comes from developing one's unique potential to develop fully.
    d. takes a lifetime to accomplish; since most people do not live that long it is rare.

11. Money, diamonds, gold, and concert tickets are examples of:
    a. rare commodities.
    b. intrinsic motivators.
    c. valued natural resources.
    d. learned goals or incentives.

12. Which category of conflict is characterized as having only one goal?
    a. approach-approach
    b. approach-avoidance
    c. avoidance-avoidance
    d. multiple approach-avoidance

13. Which category of specific motives is hardest to define precisely?
    a. sex
    b. hunger
    c. affiliation
    d. achievement

14. The concept of *set point* has to do with which category of motive?
    a. sex
    b. hunger
    c. affiliation
    d. achievement

15. Human sexual behavior is a function of an interplay between all but which of the following?
    a. genetic factors
    b. prenatal factors
    c. environmental factors
    d. All the above factors are involved.

16. The James-Lange theory of emotions, and the commonsense view of emotions:
    a. are opposite.
    b. are very similar.
    c. were developed simultaneously.
    d. both implicate physiological arousal as the cause of emotion.

17. In some respects, the Cannon-Bard theory is:
    a. a reaction to the James-Lange theory.
    b. a variation of the commonsense view.
    c. a compromise between the commonsense view and the James-Lange theory.
    d. the most significant theory in psychology's short history as it is right on the mark.

18. Experiments that measured autonomic nervous system arousal as the dependent variable demonstrated which of the following with respect to emotional expressions?
    a. Categorically different emotions produce different levels of autonomic arousal.
    b. Autonomic arousal changes as a function of emotional intensity, irrespective of the category.
    c. Though they may 'feel' different, all the emotions are very similar in terms of autonomic arousal.
    d. None of the above are true.

19. The ___ is a component of the limbic system and is essential in evaluating the emotional meaning of stimuli.
    a. amygdala
    b. hippocampus
    c. hypothalamus
    d. cerebral cortex

20. The opponent-process theory of emotion is:
    a. based on homeostatic mechanisms.
    b. supported by research using the polygraph.
    c. an interesting model, but holds little scientific value.
    d. based on the need for cognitive appraisal of an emotion's hedonic value.

21. Eckman's research that involved showing pictures (of people expressing a variety of emotions) to people from the world over revealed:
    a. that there are four basic emotions.
    b. while emotions may be common, their expression varies widely.
    c. that the number of emotions one may experience varies with cultural exposure.
    d. that there is a high degree of agreement across cultures in recognizing basic emotions.

22. According to the facial feedback hypothesis, holding your face in a frown:
    a. is metabolically expensive.
    b. will cause it to get stuck that way.
    c. provides feedback that will influence your emotionality.
    d. None of the above; the text mentions no such hypothesis.

23. Display rules are:
    a. more for children.
    b. examples of cultural norms.
    c. really more like guidelines than rules.
    d. directions for confederates in emotion research experiments.

24. The meanings of gestures (also called emblems):
    a. are fairly universal.
    b. are difficult to discern unless you are part of the in-group.
    c. are determined by the emotional experience of the communicator.
    d. vary from culture to culture, though sometimes the meanings are shared.

25. The German term *schadenfreude*, and the Japanese term *ijirashii* refer to:
    a. the same things.
    b. the opposite things.
    c. emotions for which the English language has no labels.
    d. emotions that are basically positive, but are unlike anything experienced by an American.

Answers to Key Word Exercise

1. Instinctive (or innate) behaviors
2. Incentive theories
3. avoidance-avoidance conflict
4. multiple approach-avoidance conflict
5. pheromones
6. decline
7. opponent-process
8. six: anger, disgust, fear, happiness, sadness, and surprise
9. Display rules
10. Emotional intelligence

Practice Test Answers and Explanations

1. d. Answers a. – c. represent the range of aspects addressed in the study of emotion.
2. d. Instincts are unlearned behaviors that play roles in determining motivation. That is, they are native (innate) to the species of interest.
3. a. The red spots serve to identify that the territory an intruder is entering is already occupied.
4. b. Sociobiological theory posits that individuals act in unselfish ways to perpetuate their genes. According to the theory, sometimes this means giving one's life so that (genetic) relatives live.
5. a. Drive reduction theory, as the name implies, suggests that drives motivate behavior.
6. d. Cognitive theories stress the active processing of information.

7. c. Cognitive dissonance is an aversive state that occurs when thoughts are incompatible.
8. b. Drive-reduction theories say drives push us toward goals (thirst causes us to engage in seeking something to drink); incentive theories suggest that we are pulled by the goal (money might encourage your behavior).
9. c. Maslow's hierarchy uses both dimensions: type and strength of motivation.
10. c. Self-actualization, according to Maslow's theory, is the need to develop one's fullest potential.
11. d. These are examples of learned goals or learned incentives. Each can act as a powerful motivator.
12. b. An approach-avoidance conflict has one goal that has good and bad aspects associated with it.
13. d. Achievement is difficult to define, but usually involves behaviors directed toward attainment of a goal or avoiding an aversive event. The abstract nature of what goals or events influence achievement motivation makes it hard to define.
14. b. One's *set point* is a range of weight that the body usually maintains.
15. d. Factors a. – c. all interact to influence human sexual behavior.
16. a. The two are opposite with respect to perspective on when bodily changes occur.
17. c. Although it has its shortcomings, the Cannon-Bard theory, which is a bit of a compromise between the commonsense view and the James-Lange theory, was a good idea for its time.
18. a. Different categories of emotion are associated with different patterns of autonomic activity.
19. a. The amygdala is important for processing emotional information.
20. a. The opponent-process theory of emotions assumes a need for emotional homeostasis and posits opposing processes to account for the range of experiences we have.
21. d. There is a high degree of agreement among people of widely varying cultures about what expressions convey.
22. c. The facial feedback hypothesis suggests that making a certain expression will produce the corresponding emotion.
23. b. Display rules are examples of cultural norms, and concern which emotions to display, to whom, and under which circumstances.
24. d. Gestures' meanings vary from culture to culture. The meaning of a given gesture may be in stark contrast to what people think they are communicating when using gestures.
25. c. These terms refer to experiences that English-speaking people understand, but for which they have not developed specific words.

Key Vocabulary Terms

Use the following list to write definitions *in your own words* for each of the key terms from the chapter. Translating the terms into language that is comfortable and familiar for you will facilitate your learning. For further study of these terms, go to the companion website for the textbook where you will find electronic flash cards that you may use to test your vocabulary.

motivation

instincts

drive

drive-reduction model

optimum-level theory

cognitive dissonance

hierarchy of needs

self-actualization

set point

obesity

body mass index (BMI)

anorexia nervosa

bulimia nervosa

sexual orientation

pheromones

achievement

emotion

James-Lange theory

commonsense view of emotions

Cannon-Bard theory

opponent-process theory

polygraph

facial feedback hypothesis

display rules

nonverbal communication

paralanguage

Tip for Success: Getting the Most from Your Textbook

Textbooks are packed densely with information and can be exhausting to read. Studying your textbook must be an *active* process in order for you to gain the most from it. It is better to study chapters over several study sessions, rather than in a single sitting. Consider the *serial position effect* (see Chapter 7, Memory). According to the serial position effect, you will remember the most from the first and last portions of your study sessions. With this in mind, there are two things to consider when organizing your study sessions: 1) *minimize the middle* portion of your study sessions, and 2) *study actively*.

By minimizing the middle portion, or extending the "ends" of your study session, you will take advantage of the primacy (early part of study session) and recency (last part of study session) components of the serial position effect. By making the process of studying active, you will capitalize on what you will learn about levels of processing in the chapter on memory. In brief, the deeper you process information, the greater your chances are of remembering the information.

In addition to taking full advantage of this study guide, there are two well-known approaches you may wish to consider for studying your textbook. As with discovering which method of *note taking* will work best for you, try different approaches until you find a good fit for your learning style (there is more about understanding your learning style in the *Tip* section at the end of Chapter 8 in this study guide).

What Does Not Work

It is unfortunate that perhaps the most widely used method for studying a textbook is probably the least effective. Look around at your classmates' books and notice how many people highlight or underline passages of text with fluorescent markers. *Indiscriminate* highlighting is a common practice among students who are at the early stages of learning to study. If you prefer to highlight, that may be just fine; the important thing is to consider carefully what text you will identify, and why.

Material should be highlighted because the reader plans to reread the passage again later. If each page looks as if it were dipped into a bucket of ink, the notion of rereading highlighted material can be daunting. As a result, many never reread that which they took so much time identifying.

What Does Work

A few methods of studying textbook material have been developed through the years. A combination of these may provide you with the best approach. In addition to considering the merits of the following methods, know that this study guide you are reading was organized expressly for facilitating the process of extracting information from your textbook. First, the two main methods for studying text:

> **1. SQ3R.** This is an acronym that stands for steps in the process of studying text: Survey, Question, Read, Recall, and Review.

>> **a. Survey.** Spend several minutes orienting yourself to the material you are about to study. Knowing where you are headed will make it far easier to recognize the key landmarks along the way. The following sub-steps should be part of the survey step: examine chapter overviews, read summaries at the end of chapters, and read the headings from throughout the chapter. Take time to look at the figures and tables and note how they fit with the sections of the text with which they are associated.

>> **b. Question.** As you begin studying either a single paragraph or a larger portion of a chapter, stop first and ask yourself what you are about to learn. Write things down. This can be as simple as rephrasing a paragraph heading into a question. Do not rely on your memory. Write it down.

c. Read. Having surveyed the material and prepared yourself by asking what you expect to learn, you will be prepared to read. Read with the questions you posed in mind. Do not bog down and spend your time just staring at words. If you cannot remember what you just read, you are not reading effectively. One way to keep from bogging down is to keep track of how much time you spend reading each page. If you push yourself slightly, you will retain more than if you slow down and relax too much while you read. Summarize the main points from what you read in your notebook. Make sure to do this in your own words. By translating the messages from the text into *your own language,* you are processing it, and thereby improving your chances of remembering it.

d. Recall. Look away from your book and notes, even close your eyes if it helps, and use mental imagery to recall what you just read. What words stand out? What was communicated in the tables and figures? If you were to draw a diagram or picture to represent the information, what would it look like?

e. Review. Refer to your questions, notes from reading, and textbook to see how well you recalled the information. Take note of any omissions. What needs more attention? Do not go on until you master each page. Generally speaking, it is difficult to benefit from subsequent paragraphs and pages until you understand the ones you have already studied.

This may sound like a time-consuming way to read. In the long run, it is more efficient. Take time to learn the material during your first exposure and you will save yourself from having to reread later. If you sit down with the idea of finishing a portion of a chapter, rather than trying to study the whole thing, you will find that you can make better use of discrete chunks of time.

What does SQ3R stand for and why does it work so well?

_____

_____

The next technique for studying text, the *Notes in the Margin Method,* is used effectively by itself by many students. Consider, however, using it in conjunction with the SQ3R method to improve your potential for learning the material.

2. Notes in the Margin Method. Quite literally, this technique involves using the blank space in your textbook to record notes as you read. However, you may wish to record your notes in a notebook. By writing in the notebook, you will preserve the quality of your book and be better able to read your notes without missing some of your comments.

a. Do Not Mark in Your Text as You Read. Having identified a reason to read a paragraph (see B, above, for comments on asking questions), you are ready to read. Read with an eye for information that will come up in class lectures and discussions, or on quizzes and exams.

b. Adopt Your Professor's Perspective. *After* reading a section of text, adopt your professor's perspective and write a question or two-record them in your notebook. If you develop your skills at *asking questions,* including multiple choice items with all the alternatives, you will also develop your skills for *answering questions.*

c. Refer to the Text. Next, find the passage in the text that provides the answer to your question. This is the material you could underline or highlight. Better yet, translate the passage into your own words and write it in your notes.

d. Study Your Notes. If your goal is to learn course content, study your notes from the textbook and quiz yourself with your own questions. Active notetaking will help you learn; studying your notes compounds the effect.

Summarize the steps of the "Notes in the Margins Method":

_____

_____

3. Use of this Study Guide. The chapters in this study guide were organized to help you benefit the most from your textbook. Attend to the structure of the outline. Which sections are related to which larger topics from the text? How are the vocabulary words related to the material you are studying? The following suggestions may help you combine the methods that were described above and make the best use of this study guide as a learning tool.

    a. Examine the Outline in this Study Guide. The outline in this study guide, which always follows the chapter overview, was extracted exactly from the textbook. When surveying the material you are about to study, you may find it helpful to study the outline from the study guide first.

    b. Learn the Language. Many students struggle with the language of psychology. Each chapter of the study guide includes a list of each key word from the chapter; the key words are listed near the end of the study guide chapters and are presented in the order in which they are presented in the textbook. Take time to record a definition for each word. Do this *in your own words,* rather than copying verbatim from the text.
    c. Use the Space. In addition to providing space for rewriting key word definitions, you will find space to jot down a few summarizing comments for each section of each chapter. Use this space.

    d. Destroy this Study Guide! As you work through the outlines, key word exercises, and practice tests, tear the pages out and insert them in the proper places in your 3-ring notebook.

How can using this study guide help you get the most from the textbook?

_____

_____

_____

You noticed, no doubt, that each of the suggestions for using your textbook involved *active* processing of the text material. If you do not study the material actively, chances are you will not gain as much from it. Also, make sure to study only for reasonable units of time. If you can *minimize the middle* portions of your study sessions, you will retain the most from them.

CHAPTER 7

Memory

Do You Know?

Do you know that the basis of all memories is physiological? Through the years psychologists have developed several models of human (and nonhuman) memory systems. While these models have not always reflected the underlying physiological processes that are necessary for memory formation, they are not mutually exclusive with such processes either. Indeed, the function of memory modeling has largely been to organize phenomena that have been discovered and measured in well controlled laboratory studies. The models that have been developed by cognitive psychologists have not only contributed to understandings of different memory systems, but have also provided contexts for developing ever clearer perspectives on how memory works, including at physiological levels.

Cognitive neuroscience is an exciting, new interdisciplinary area of inquiry. As the name implies, people working in this area are interested in the biological underpinnings of cognitive processes. Models such as those presented in the memory chapter in your textbook have been very important in the quest to understand the conditions under which memories are formed. Aspects of research in this area have focused on mechanisms involved in encoding, storage, and retrieval of memorial information. While cognitive psychologists have been busy refining their models of memory to account for all of the phenomena that have been discovered through research, computer scientists have been busy developing artificial models that mimic the organic ones. Not surprisingly, information and ideas have flowed both ways during these related inquiries into memory. What is more, researchers trained in physiological methodologies have contributed information about neuronal activity to both groups while also borrowing ideas from the models in order to inform new approaches to their research.

Several interesting findings have developed as a result of inter- and cross-disciplinary interest in memory. For example, researchers in psychology and medicine documented very closely the outcome of H.M.'s bilateral hippocampal surgery. As a result, we have a clearer understanding of the anatomy of declarative memory and we have better models of human memory that account for the profound results of that experimental surgery. Studies of H.M.'s memorial deficiencies that resulted from the surgery have also helped distinguish declarative from procedural memory. Armed with the understanding that the brain regions involved in these distinct memory systems are likely to be different, neuroscientists have performed numerous experiments on both types of memory. Although our understandings are still developing, it seems clear that procedural memories are stored and maintained in more primitive brain regions, while declarative memories appear to depend upon more recently developed tissue.

Notes from Class and the Textbook

Use the space provided in this outline to record notes from the textbook as well as from class lectures and discussion. Questions related to the *Psychological Detective, Hands On, Myth or Science,* and *Study Tip* sections in the text have been presented in the outline; use the associated space to respond to the questions and to record your own comments about the issues.

I. Initial Studies

How many ways could an experimenter measure a participant's memory for nonsense syllables?

A. The Curve of Forgetting

Point your Web browser at the textbook's Web page to see Live!Psych module 7.1.

B. Recognition and Relearning

II. Traditional Models of Memory

A. Human Memory as an Information Processing System

Point your Web browser at the textbook's Web page to see Live!Psych module 7.2.

1. Encoding

2. Storage

3. Retrieval

Who was your fourth grade teacher? What process(es) did you use to retrieve the name?

Is there such a thing as photographic memory, or is it more likely that some people just have very good memories? Reread the section at the top of page 276 on Leonardo da Vinci and Napoleon Bonaparte.

Create a diagram of the human memory system. Include short definitions of each component of the system.

B. The Stages-of-Memory Model

    1.   Sensory Memory

What causes the sensation that one feels *after* having rubbed a hand against the edge of a desk, tapping fingers, or other form of sensory stimulation?

    2.   Short-Term Memory

Write down the three phone numbers from the *Psychological Detective* section. Why would it be easier to handle two versus three numbers?

Write down as many of the 15 words as you can. Did you perform better than 7+/-2? If so, why?

3. Long-Term Memory

   a. Forgetting

Point your Web browser at the textbook's Web page to see Live!Psych module 7.3.

III. Other Approaches to Learning and Memory

   A. The Levels-of-Processing Model

Compare the stages-of-memory and Craik and Lockhart models of memory. Which makes more sense to you, and why? Should a good model of memory include elements from each model?

   B. Alternate Approaches

   1. Transfer-Appropriate Processing

2. Parallel Distributed Processing

C. Different Types of Long-Term Memory

   1. Procedural Memory

   2. Semantic Memory

Write the answers to the *Psychological Detective* section questions. How many answers were just "on the tip of your tongue"?

Conduct the self-test of states' capitals that is presented on page 288 in your textbook.

   3. Episodic Memory

   4. Priming or Implicit Memory

Work with three other people—each person should provide a brief report on one of the four types of long-term memory. Brainstorm together to identify several examples of each type.

D. Retrieval

1.   Retrieval from Short-Term Memory

Why is it necessary to *retrieve* information that is in our consciousness?

2. Retrieval from Long-Term Memory

3. Encoding Specificity

Consider the importance of context in encoding. How can you guard against having to depend upon contextual cues to aid your retrieval of information?

4. Eyewitness Testimony

5. State-Dependent Memory

E. The Repressed-Memory Controversy

F. Memory Illusions

IV. Techniques for Improving Memory

A. Influential Factors

B. Processing Strategies

Point your Web browser at the textbook's Web page to see Live!Psych module 7.4.

1. Imagery

2. Method of Loci

How can familiar songs, places on an often-traveled path, or rooms in your childhood home be used to help remember lists of information?

3.   Pegword Technique

4.   Grouping (Chunking)

5.   Coding

6. Acronyms and Acrostics

V. The Physiological Basis of Learning and Memory

    A. Amnesias

        1.   Anterograde Amnesia and the Hippocampus

Why do H.M.'s daily experiences consist exclusively of things he can maintain in STM, except for things he learned prior to 1953?

        2.   Retrograde Amnesia and the Consolidation Hypothesis

Learning Objectives

After you have studied the chapter, you should be able to respond to the following statements and questions to convey your understanding of the material.

1. What are some uniquely human aspects of learning and memory?

2. What contributions did Ebbinghaus make to the study of memory?

3. Compare and contrast the Atkinson-Shiffrin Model with the Levels-of-Processing Model.

4. What are some strategies and devices for improving memory?

5. What are amnesias? What have symptoms of amnesias contributed to our understanding of memory?

Key Word Exercise

Fill in the blanks in the following statements with key words and terms from the textbook. Answer as many as you can without referring to your notes or to the book. If you have blanks after thinking about each item, try using your book. The answers are presented after the practice test.

1. _____-_____ _____ is a technique that is often used to learn the vocabulary for a foreign language.

2. Identifying a suspect from a police line-up is an example of a _____ _____.

3. Information cannot be retrieved for a test unless it is first _____ and then stored.

4. Sperling elegantly gathered data on the capacity of _____ _____ by assigning tones, to act as signals, to each of three rows in a 12-letter stimulus matrix.

5. _____-_____ _____ is a relatively permanent store that depends on rehearsal or practice.

6. That people do better recalling information from a word list if they are instructed to rate the pleasantness of each word, versus counting the number of letters in each word, is evidence for the _____-_____-_____ _____.

7. Remembering how to rollerblade is an example of _____ _____.

8. Psychologists refer to memory of one's personal experiences as _____ _____.

9. People do not always know whether to tip waitstaff when eating out at a pizza place because the context does not exactly match the _____ for either a fast-food joint or for a restaurant.

10. Retrograde amnesia may exist for items that occur just prior to a traumatic event because _____ of the information concerning the items has not taken place yet.

Practice Test

Circle the letter that corresponds to the *best* alternative for each of the following items. Read each alternative carefully. The answers are presented at the end of this study guide chapter. Be sure to learn *why* each correct alternative is better than the others

1. Ebbinghaus used nonsense syllables in his studies of how associations between stimuli are formed:
   a. because they were short.
   b. because they were supposed to have no meaning.
   c. in order to encourage people from countries that spoke other languages to replicate his work.
   d. because generating the consonant-vowel-consonant sequence was easy to do with a computer.

2. A learning procedure in which material that has been learned may be repeated in any order is called:
   a. the recognition test.
   b. the free recall procedure.
   c. the serial learning procedure.
   d. the randomized recall procedure.

3. One of Ebbinghaus' most important findings was:
   a. the method of loci.
   b. anterograde amnesia.
   c. the curve of forgetting.
   d. the Atkinson-Shiffrin model of memory.

4. The difference between the time it takes to learn material once and the time necessary to learn it a second time is:
   a. called a savings score.
   b. commonly referred to as the difference score.
   c. usually shorter among children than with adults.
   d. is long unless the information is particularly salient.

5. The human information processing system has been characterized as having all *but* which of the following stages?
   a. storage
   b. retrieval
   c. encoding
   d. transferring

6. Leonardo da Vinci and Napoleon Bonaparte had in common which of the following?
   a. the capacity for eidetic imagery
   b. the capacity to form flashbulb memories
   c. anterograde amnesia due to a closed head injury (e.g., stroke)
   d. retrograde amnesia stemming from an open head injury (e.g., foreign object entering the head)

7. Which component of the Atkinson-Shiffrin model had the smallest capacity?
   a. sensory memory
   b. long-term memory
   c. short-term memory
   d. the environmental input channel

8. Information in short-term memory is usually lost after:
   a. 20 seconds or so.
   b. about 15 minutes.
   c. a good night's rest.
   d. new information is admitted.

9. The magic number that was proposed by George Miller was:
   a. three: many aspects of memory seem to involve the number three.
   b. not a single number, but span of numbers from about five to about nine.
   c. 8675309: a number that was later treated as a woman's phone number in a pop song.
   d. one. Three Dog Night described *one* as the loneliest number, but Miller thought it was magic.

10. Working memory was proposed:
    a. as a second phase of STM.
    b. as a treatment for broken memory.
    c. as a hypothetical construct to explain processing in LTM.
    d. by Ebbinghaus to explain improved recall for certain items.

11. Saving information for a specified period of time is to ___ as adding to the material to be remembered is to ___.
    a. storage; retrieval
    b. retrieval; encoding
    c. temporal encoding; summation encoding
    d. maintenance rehearsal; elaborative rehearsal

12. With respect to what is recalled (as opposed to what is sought in a memory task), old memories are to new memories as ___ is to ___.
    a. anterograde amnesia; retrograde amnesia
    b. retrograde amnesia; anterograde amnesia
    c. retroactive interference; proactive interference
    d. proactive interference; retroactive interference

13. The levels-of-processing theory states that which of the following relationships exists between processing depth and likelihood of recall?
    a. positive—as processing depth increases, probability of recall increases
    b. negative—as processing depth increases, probability of recall decreases
    c. no relationship—the probability of recall is independent of processing depth
    d. inverse—the probability of recall occurs as a mathematical expression equal to one over the depth of processing

14. The transfer-appropriate processing (TAP) model suggests:
    a. we process information in several subsystems simultaneously.
    b. that content is learned best when it is processed at deep versus shallow levels.
    c. we only transfer to memory that which is appropriate, as the model's name implies.
    d. the best learning and memory occur when the encoding and retrieval processes are the same.

15. Which of the following was *not* discussed in your text as a type of long-term memory?
    a. episodic memory
    b. personal memory
    c. semantic memory
    d. procedural memory

16. The tip-of-the-tongue (TOT) phenomenon is sometimes used to investigate the nature of:
    a. semantic memory.
    b. procedural memory.
    c. flashbulb memories.
    d. none of the above; TOT is strictly a phenomenon and hinders rather than helps investigators.

17. The topic of interest when discussing the role of prior exposure to stimulus items in aiding subsequent learning is:
    a. flashbulb memory.
    b. retrograde amnesia.
    c. anterograde amnesia.
    d. priming or implicit memory.

18. Multiple choice is to essay test as ___ is to ___.
    a. hard; easy
    b. recall; recognition
    c. recognition; recall
    d. semantic memory; episodic memory

19. A network of related concepts that are linked together is called a(n):
    a. schema.
    b. semantic network.
    c. flashbulb memory.
    d. eidetic memorial network.

20. State-dependent learning is closely related to the ___ hypothesis.
    a. flashbulb memory
    b. encoding specificity
    c. eyewitness memory
    d. repression of content

21. A distinction between "memory illusions" and true memories is:
    a. in their relative durations.
    b. in the time it takes to form them.
    c. that memory illusions are usually less detailed.
    d. that memory illusions are usually more detailed.

22. The serial position effect:
    a. is used extensively in determining how to stock shelves in the breakfast aisle in grocery stores.
    b. is most easily demonstrated in experiments that employ tasks including learning word pairs.
    c. refers to the tendency for people to show improved recall for items at the beginning and end of a list in comparison to items in the middle.
    d. refers to the phenomenon whereby participants perform better on recall tests of word lists when the words are from the middle rather than the end of the list.

23. John plays the game *Monopoly* frequently. He recently inferred from studying for his psychology class that he could use his memory for the game's board to his advantage. To his surprise, he finds it easy to recall terms when he associates them with places on the board. He is using a variation on:
    a. imagery.
    b. method of loci.
    c. pegword technique.
    d. flashbulb technique.

24. Acronym is to acrostic as ___ is to ___.
    a. word; saying
    b. saying; word
    c. opposite; same
    d. same; opposite

25. With respect to lost memories, anterograde amnesia is to retrograde amnesia as ___ is to ___.
    a. new; old
    b. old; new
    c. declarative; procedural
    d. procedural; declarative

Answers to Key Word Exercise

1. Paired-associate learning   2. recognition task   3. encoded
4. sensory memory   5. Long-term memory   6. levels-of-processing theory
7. procedural memory   8. episodic memory   9. schema
10. consolidation

Practice Test Answers and Explanations

1. b. Ebbinghaus chose to use nonsense syllables because he thought they would have no meaning. It turns out that these syllables sometimes do have meaning, and therefore may confound experiments.
2. b. The *free recall* procedure permits subjects to recollect information in any order they wish.
3. c. Ebbinghaus discovered the curve of forgetting when testing his own memory.
4. a. The savings score is the time saved by having learned the material previously.
5. d. The system involves three steps—encoding, storage, and retrieval—in that sequence.
6. a. Both men were reported to have had the capacities for eidetic imagery (photographic memory).
7. c. The short-term memory component of the model has the smallest capacity.
8. a. Information in STM lasts only 10-20 seconds before being lost from consciousness.
9. b. Miller proposed 7+/-2 (5 to 9) as the limit for normal STM capacity.
10. a. Working memory is considered to be a second component of STM in which attention and conscious effort are used to process material.
11. d. Maintenance rehearsal is used to keep information (e.g., a phone number) for a specified time. Elaborative rehearsal is used when expanding (elaborating) memory.
12. d. Retroactive interference involves new memories being recalled in place of old ones; vice versa for proactive interference.
13. a. The levels-of-processing approach states that greater processing depth results in improved recall.

14. d.   The TAP model suggests that the best learning and memory occur when the encoding and retrieval processes are the same. This model, however, has been criticized.

15. b.   The other three were discussed as types of LTM, as was *priming or implicit memory*.

16. a.   Investigators sometimes use items the evoke TOT to study semantic memory as both TOT and semantic memory involve general knowledge.

17. d.   *Priming, or implicit memory*, is unconscious memory processing in which prior exposure to stimulus items may aid in subsequent learning.

18. c.   Multiple choice tests are examples of recognition tasks, whereas essay tests examine recall.

19. b.   Semantic networks are clusters of related concepts.

20. b.   State-dependent learning is an example of learning that supports the encoding specificity hypothesis.

21. c.   True memories generally have more detail than memory illusions.

22. c.   The serial position effect is the tendency for people to do better when recalling items from the beginning and end of a word list.

23. b.   John uses a variation on the method of loci technique, in which familiar places on the game board become associated with items on a word list.

24. a.   Acronyms are words in which each letter stands for something. Acrostics are verses or sayings in which the first letter of each word is important.

25. a.   Anterograde amnesia is an inability to store new memories, while retrograde amnesia is an inability to recall information that was stored prior to a traumatic event.

Key Vocabulary Terms

Use the following list to write definitions *in your own words* for each of the key terms from the chapter. Translating the terms into language that is comfortable and familiar for you will facilitate your learning. For further study of these terms, go to the companion website for the textbook where you will find electronic flash cards that you may use to test your vocabulary.

memory

nonsense syllables

serial learning

paired-associate learning

free recall

recognition test

relearning test

savings score

encoding

storage

retrieval

sensory memory

short-term memory (STM)

working memory

long-term memory

maintenance rehearsal

elaborative rehearsal

proactive interference

retroactive interference

levels-of-processing

procedural memory

semantic memory

tip-of-the-tongue (TOT) phenomenon

episodic memory

flashbulb memory

priming or implicit memory

semantic network

schema

encoding specificity

state-dependent learning

serial position effect

mnemonic devices

imagery

method of loci

pegword technique

acronym

acrostic

amnesia

anterograde amnesia

retrograde amnesia

consolidation hypothesis

Tip for Success: Preparing for and Taking Exams

Under the best circumstances, tests are instruments that serve both teachers and students. Teachers rely on them for measuring student progress, and students use them for feedback on the depth and breadth of their understanding. Additionally, students can use tests to demonstrate their enthusiasm for a course. For many students, taking tests is the only way they communicate with their instructors.

Because tests are often closely linked to course grades, it is common for students to become anxious about them. Unfortunately, anxiety sometimes distracts students from focusing entirely on content when preparing for tests, and from performing their very best when taking tests. This section was developed as guide to preparing for and taking exams.

Things to Do Before the Test

1. Be Prepared. Preparation for a test can be overwhelming and should be broken into manageable units. Identify test days on your calendar, and set specific preparation goals that maximize your use of available time. By starting early, and proceeding only after mastering each unit along the way, you will save yourself a great deal of anxiety and frustration as the test day draws closer.

2. Be Early. Be early to every class meeting, but be especially early on test days. When you are running late, you will be more anxious. By being early you will be able to make full use of the time available for taking the test. It is unreasonable to ask for additional time on a test if you do not show up on time.

3. Stake Your Claim. You learned about state-dependent learning in Chapter 7 of your textbook. State-, mood-, and context-dependent learning can facilitate recall of information at test time. While the effects of any of these may not be whopping, anything that helps, counts. If your goal is to perform well, you will want to take advantage of anything that might facilitate your performance. In general, you want to maintain the same conditions at retrieval time as were in place when information was encoded. Consider the following suggestions:

   a. Keep Your Physiological State Constant. Do not drink 19 cups of coffee prior to an exam unless you drink that much coffee before regular class meetings. By changing your physiological state, you disrupt normal functioning, and may not be sensitive to feedback that would normally help cue recall. What is more, you will be distracted by the changes in your bodily activity.

   b. The Same Goes for Mood. There are data that indicate that some learning is mood-dependent. Thus, do not show up on test day angry, anxious, or otherwise discombobulated, unless you are that way on regular class days. Maintaining an even temper and stable mood will serve you well in many facets of life.

   c. Keep Your Seat. By keeping your normal classroom seat you are holding constant the contextual cues from the environment. Since those cues are part of a context where you think and learn about the course material, they may help improve your performance on test day.

4. Know Your Professor's Style. Whenever possible, review samples of the questions and other test items your professor has used in the past. Getting these may be as simple as asking her or him if there is a test file you may review, or if he or she would share some samples so you can become better acquainted with their style. Other students who have taken a course from your professor previously may also be of some assistance.

Get as much information as possible that will help you know how to prepare for the test. If there will be multiple choice items, will they focus on definitions, or should you know how to *apply* what you have learned? Will you have to solve analogy problems? In general, your preparations should match the type of text you will take. Learn to anticipate test items, and practice responding to them. Specific ideas for different categories of exam items will be given below.

5. Recognition Is Easier than Comprehension. Do not convince yourself that you understand material just because you recognize it. This goes for material from textbooks as well as for that which is presented in class. Good books make the most difficult material accessible to a student who is new to the field; good teachers can make challenging concepts seem easy to understand. Beware that even though you may take in material as you read or hear it, additional effort may be required to comprehend it fully. Challenge yourself to recall as much as possible about a given topic without cues from your textbook or notes.

At the Test: Objective Items

There is no substitute for understanding the material. The best thing you can do to improve your score is to study and thoroughly understand the material. Sometimes, though, you will be faced with challenging alternatives, or with an essay question that requires you to think differently than you had anticipated. Learn the following suggestions and use them as appropriate to help you during an exam.

1. Multiple –Choice Questions. This is a common variety of test item because it allows your instructor to probe your understanding at a variety of depths. The following tips may help:

a. Break Each Question into the Stem and the Alternatives. Study each alternative. Sometimes the wording of alternatives reveals that they are poor fits for the stem. Sometimes there are alternatives that simply do not make sense. *After* reading each alternative, cross out those that you know are incorrect. If you do not identify a clear best answer, move on to the next item.

b. Avoid Absolute Statements and Extremes. More often than not, answers that are absolutes or extreme statements are decoys, and should be avoided.

c. Beware of Jargon. If an alternative is filled with complicated language, it may not be the right answer.

d. Use Your Familiarity with Prefixes, Suffixes, and Root Words. When you are presented with an unfamiliar word, break it down and try to discover its meaning *in context*. Also, do not be afraid to ask your professor to define a word for you.

e. Study the Grammar. Sometimes the grammar used in a multiple–choice alternative will help give it away as either the correct answer or as a decoy. Pay attention to grammar as it may provide helpful clues.

f. If You Must Guess. Sometimes you simply cannot determine which answer is the best one. If you must guess, do so after eliminating one or two alternatives. Your chances of guessing correctly get significantly better with each alternative you are able to eliminate. If you are not penalized for guessing incorrectly, you should respond to each item.

2. True-False Items. Some professors use true-false items to test their students' mastery of detailed information. Consider the following tips for responding to these items.

a. Only Two Options. A statement can be either true or false. If you do not know the answer, guess. With true-false items, you have a 50-50 chance of guessing correctly.

b. True Means Always True, False Means Always False. If a given answer is *true,* it must be true under every circumstance. Test the accuracy of statements by trying to think of examples of when the statement is false.

c. Qualifiers. If a statement is qualified (e.g., some, many, usually, frequently), this may be a cue that it is true.

d. Check Names and Dates. Details such as names and dates can easily be mixed up to test your knowledge of who did what, when.

3. Matching Sets. It is important to read directions carefully for matching sets, as the rules sometimes permit re-using alternatives, and sometimes there will be extra items. If you determine that every item will be used once, you have the advantage of being able to use the process of elimination to simplify guessing from among any remaining alternatives.

a. Look for Relationships. Often one column is devoted to terms, and the other to definitions for the terms. Determine whether this or another relationship is present in the set before proceeding as it may help in eliminating alternatives.

b. Save Time. It takes less time to read a long definition and scan a list of short terms for a match, than vice versa. If a matching set has lengthy definitions that are to be paired with short terms, read the longer items first.

c. Start with What You Know. If you are not confident of which alternative should go with a given item, skip it and come back to it later. The process of eliminating alternatives for matches you are confident about may make it easier to decide from among remaining alternatives later.

Comment on Returned Objective Tests

You will need to review your answers to determine which alternatives are correct. While taking an exam, jot notes beside each item to reflect your decision for an alternative. Make a list of the stems and alternatives that go together. This may require some digging in your notes or in the textbook. If your instructor will not let you take the exam home, ask if you can take notes from it; if so, you will be glad you have developed a shorthand system.

What can you do to improve your preparation for objective exams? How can you use your exams as learning tools after you get them back?

_____

_____

_____

Before the Test: Essay Items

Some professors give out a pool of essay questions from which they will choose the one(s) you will write on during an exam; if this is the case in your class, you have no excuse for not preparing thoroughly. Other times you may get some hints about particular content to focus on when preparing for the essay portion of an exam. Take note of these hints. If you have no direction from your professor, there are still some important things you can do to prepare.

As you study your text, you will note that some material seems to lend itself well to objective (i.e., multiple–choice, matching) items, while other material does not. If a portion of a chapter contains information that is more easily described in narrative text than in discrete definitions, or if there are important concepts or relationships between and among concepts, these items may be good essay item candidates.

Frequently students are able to anticipate the broad topic that will be addressed in essay questions. Practice reviewing the text and writing essay items of the same format and style that your professor uses. You will get better at this with practice.

Once you have generated a list of potential questions, write outlines for responses to each item. Include in your outline any key words or examples that would be useful for communicating your understanding of the topic or relationship. It is not necessary to write out your whole answer in longhand if you can include all the topics and elements in your outline. Study the outline to review for the exam.

At the Test: Essay Items

1. Know the Directions. Read the directions for the essay section carefully. Sometimes professors will expect grammatically correct answers; sometimes they are merely looking for lists. If you are unsure, ask. Attend to whether you are directed to answer each item, or a subset of the items. How many points is each item worth? It is a good idea to start working on the more valuable items first.

2. Jot Down Notes. Take a few minutes to make comments on scratch paper, or in the margins about things to include in each essay. If you observe that there will be overlap in your answers, you may wish to simplify them, and to refer to the content of one while writing the other. This will save you time and energy during the test.

3. Budget Your Time, and Stick to Your Schedule. Unless you have been granted unlimited time to work on your exam, you will need to attend to the time that you have available for writing on the essay item(s). If each item you are to answer is of equal length and complexity, distribute your time evenly. You may want to allocate more time to an item if it is weighted more heavily, or if your response to it will have more detailed information. Be sure to allow ample time to reread your essay. A careful review of your efforts should help minimize grammatical errors and word omissions.

4. Make an Outline. Borrowing from the list of things you wish to include, organize a brief outline or diagram that prescribes the flow of your response. Doing this will help keep you from having to erase, cross out, or reorganize major portions of your essay. Your professor will be more favorably impressed by a well-organized, succinctly written essay than one that is wordy and hard to follow.

5. Write Carefully. Write legibly and do not rush yourself. The organizational steps you have taken should help the essay flow smoothly onto your paper. Attend to your expression of ideas, keeping your reader in mind. Is your task to write for a well-informed or a naive audience?

6. Reread Your Essay. When you have finished writing your exam, re-read the essay questions as if you were a journal editor. If you write more than one essay, finish writing each one before moving on to editing your work. As you read, ask yourself the following questions: Are your ideas presented clearly? Did you make good use of transitional sentences? Are there any sentence fragments? Are there subject-verb agreement errors? Is the language gender- or culture-biased? Have you used effective examples to illustrate your points?

How can you improve the quality of your essays through preparation and planning before you begin writing?

_____

_____

_____

CHAPTER 8

Thinking, Language, and Intelligence

Do You Know?

Do you know that it would be impossible to develop a culture-fair intelligence test? That is to say, an intelligence test void of bias cannot exist. When developing a test, the individual or group undertaking the task cannot help but build in language and examples from their own experiences. Even if a large committee of well-rounded people were to design a test, they could not possibly represent the diversity of life experiences that would characterize an apparently compatible group of people to be tested, and to hope the instrument could be used across cultures that use different languages, have different schooling systems, and so on would be futile at best. Intelligence is so intimately tied to experience that it is certainly impractical, and probably impossible to assess consistently across groups.

In spite of the inherent difficulties in assessing intelligence across cultures, and even though the concept of intelligence itself is difficult to define, testing can be quite useful in diagnosing and understanding individuals' intellectual capacities. Reliability and validity tests help guard against problematic test items, and the standardization process helps eliminate some sources of bias. As a result of these measures to eliminate unexplainable variation among scores, the tests produce reasonably consistent performance when they are administered repeatedly to the same people. Differences between cultures may also be consistent, and it is clear that the impossibility of culture-fair tests will make this difference impossible to eliminate. It is important to note, though, that while differences between cultures may result as artifacts of biased test construction, such differences represent probabilistic trends and not absolute differences in groups.

By analogy, consider the common claim that men are taller than women. While this is true based on the average heights of men and women, it does not hold that all men are taller than all women. There is significant overlap in the heights of men and women. As a result, some women are taller than most men, and most women are taller than some men. Similarly, culture-based differences in intelligence test performance do not define absolute differences for all members of the groups in question. Tests designed, however unintentionally, such that they benefit members of a given culture will be more difficult for those from outside the culture, and the reverse is also true.

Notes from Class and the Textbook

Use the space provided in this outline to record notes from the textbook as well as from class lectures and discussion. Questions related to the *Psychological Detective, Hands On, Myth or Science,* and *Study Tip* sections in the text have been presented in the outline; use the associated space to respond to the questions and to record your own comments about the issues.

I. Thinking

    A. Cognitive Psychology

        1. Images

How can researchers draw inferences about the mental processes involved in answering questions concerning the relatedness of stimuli, such as the pairs of three-dimensional objects shown in Figure 8-1 on page 308 in the textbook?

        2. Concepts

Study the geometric figures in Figure 8-2 on page 310 in your textbook. What rule groups items one and four together while excluding items two and three? After you have thought about the problem, check your response on page 356 in your textbook.

B. Problem Solving

1. Problem-Solving Methods

a. Algorithms

Solve the anagram on page 312 in your textbook. As you solve the problem, pay particular attention to the approaches you use in arriving at a solution.

Point your Web browser at the textbook's Web page to see Live!Psych module 8.1.

b. Heuristics

2. Obstacles and Aids to Problem Solving

3. Setting Subgoals

Solve the river crossing problem from page 313 in your textbook. How does your response compare with the answer presented in the textbook? How did you arrive at your response?

4. Approach to Representing Problems

Examine Figure 8-4 from page 314 in your textbook. How would you solve the problem? The answer is presented on page 356 in your textbook.

5. Rigidity

Point your Web browser at the textbook's Web page to see Live!Psych module 8.2.

Describe a solution to the problem presented in Figure 8-7, page 315, in your textbook. You may compare your solution against the one that is presented on page 356 in your textbook.

6. Set Effect

Work with two other people to create an outline of the basic problem-solving process. In your outline, label the steps according to the material that is presented in the text.

C. Making Decisions

    1. Seeking Information to Confirm a Solution

    2. Representativeness

You are to guess the outcome of the toss of a coin that has just landed heads-up five times in a row. What is your guess? Why?

    3. Availability

    4. Comparison

    5. Framing

Design icons or graphic images to help you remember each of the decision-making heuristics.

D. Creativity

    1. Defining Creativity

    2. Measuring Creativity

    3. Personal Factors in Creativity

4. Situational Factors in Creativity

5. Enhancing Creativity in Work

II. Language

    A. Language and Development

        1. The Acquisition of Language

        2. American Sign Language

    B. Thinking and Language

        1. Using Language to Limit Thought

        2. Language and Gender

Rewrite the sentences from page 333 in your textbook such that they are gender-neutral.

III. Intelligence

Write down several characteristics and behaviors that are shared by intelligent people.

A. Cultural Views of Intelligence

B. The History of Intelligence Testing

    1. The Stanford-Binet Intelligence Scale

    2. The Wechsler Scales

Create a timeline illustrating the history of intelligence testing.

C. Principles of Psychological Tests

    1. Reliability

    2. Validity

    3. Standardization

D. Extremes of Intelligence

    1. Exceptional Children

    2. Savant Syndrome

E. Kinds of Intelligence

    1. Spearman's Model

2. Sternberg's Model

3. Gardner's Multiple Intelligences

Describe the major theories of intelligence, illustrating with examples, as appropriate.

F. Misuse of Intelligence Tests

G. Heredity and Environmental Determinants of Intelligence

1. Hereditary Determinants

How could researchers interested in intelligence determine the contributions of genetic factors (heritability)?

2. Environmental Determinants of Intelligence

What is the relationship between birth order and intelligence? Read the passage on page 352 and consider the varieties of support that have been marshaled for and against notions that intelligence is negatively correlated with birth order.

Examine Figure 8-18. What components demonstrate the contributions of environmental factors to intelligence?

3. Explaining Differences in Intelligence Scores

Learning Objectives

After you have studied the chapter, you should be able to respond to the following statements and questions to convey your understanding of the material.

1. What are some problem solving and decision making abilities that differentiate humans from nonhuman animals?

2. How can we be mislead in problem solving and decision making?

3. What is creativity and how might its use be fostered in the workplace?

4. Describe the sequence in which language is typically acquired.

5. How are thinking and language related?

6. What are the implications of the fact that only humans devise ways of measuring their intellectual achievements?

7. What three principles apply to all psychological tests?

8. Discuss variations in intellectual ability in terms of extremes of intelligence.

9. Describe the models of intelligence (Spearman, Sternberg, Gardner).

10. What roles do heredity and environment play in determining one's intelligence?

Key Word Exercise

Fill in the blanks in the following statements with key words and terms from the textbook. Answer as many as you can without referring to your notes or to the book. If you have blanks after thinking about each item, try using your book. The answers are presented after the practice test.

1. _____ involves the manipulation of information in the form of mental images and concepts.

2. If you listed on your resume that you raised grain-consuming animal units, rather than saying you raised farm animals, you would be employing a kind of _____.

3. Chess players do not use _____ because it would take centuries to examine all the possible arrangements of the chess pieces.

4. Sometimes it is helpful when trying to solve a problem to break it into manageable intermediate _____.

5. Functional fixedness is a specific example of _____.

6. The fact that inducing positive feelings can enhance creativity is an example of _____ _____ in creativity.

7. _____ is an understanding of word order necessary to convey ideas.

8. The _____ _____ is calculated by dividing an estimate of one's mental age by one's chronological age and multiplying by 100.

9. The procedures for administering the SAT test are the same no matter where the test is given. This is because the test has undergone _____.

10. Describing a hypothetical experiment in which seeds are planted in different kinds of soil would be analogous to comparing _____ influences on intelligence.

11. _____ _____ was Charles Darwin's cousin, but is best known for his early work in the area of intelligence testing.

Practice Test

Circle the letter that corresponds to the *best* alternative for each of the following items. Read each alternative carefully. The answers are presented at the end of this study guide chapter. Be sure to learn *why* each correct alternative is better than the others.

1. When Scott Smith injected himself with curare, a poison that causes paralysis, he did so:
   a. because he had done poorly on an intelligence test.
   b. because people had criticized his cognitive abilities.
   c. to test whether he could think in spite of not being able to move.
   d. to test whether his paralysis would be passed on to his offspring.

2. Cognitive psychologists infer mental processes:
   a. from the observable behaviors of the people they study.
   b. based on little or no empirical data to support their inferences.
   c. in spite of the fact that by studying carefully, one can actually observe these processes.
   d. based largely on the reports offered by subjects regarding their notions about problem solving.

3. Interestingly, mental images are not exclusively visual in nature. Which other sensory modalities were presented in the text as being capable of evoking images?
   a. audition
   b. olfaction
   c. both a. and b.
   d. neither a. nor b.

4. High-imagery words are to ___ as low-imagery words are to ___.
   a. smell; hear
   b. nouns; verbs
   c. two pegs; meaning alone
   d. one syllable; multi-syllabic

5. A prototype is a specific example of a particular:
   a. model .
   b. concept.
   c. construct.
   d. classification.

6. "Doublespeak" or euphemisms may be cited as:
   a. evidence that our words determine our thoughts.
   b. examples of universal insults to the intelligence of others.
   c. often as necessary when one is describing problem–solving abilities.
   d. indices that careful selection of words can be designed to steer our thoughts.

7. Well-defined problems have all but which of the following characteristics?
   a. a clearly specified solution state
   b. a clearly specified beginning state
   c. a clearly specified set of steps for solving the problem
   d. a set of clearly specified tools or techniques for finding the solution

8. Samantha is trying to solve a problem by systematically evaluating all possible solutions until the correct one is found. That is, she is using:
   a. an algorithm.
   b. the availability heuristic.
   c. the trial-and-error procedure.
   d. the representativeness heuristic.

9. The familiar spelling rule, 'i before e except after c,' is:
   a. highly overrated.
   b. an example of a heuristic.
   c. effective only with five–letter words.
   d. more complicated than the algorithm that many use in the same circumstances.

10. Jim just used a dime to open the battery bank on his camera. In doing so he overcame:
    a. frigidity.
    b. poor framing.
    c. confirmation bias.
    d. functional fixedness.

11. The gambler's fallacy is the faulty assumption that independent events are linked: for example believing that four consecutive 'heads' tosses *will be* followed by a 'tails' toss. The gambler's fallacy is an example of:

a. the law of averages.

b. the set effect at work.

c. why gambling is evil.

d. a representative heuristic.

12. It is safer, in statistical terms, to fly in an airplane than it is to drive to the airport. People who debate this fact often cite a recently publicized plane crash to support their contention. In so doing, they:

a. use the availability heuristic.

b. violate the representativeness heuristic.

c. increase the likelihood of causing a plane crash.

d. deny the truth about why planes crash in the first place.

13. Terri is trying to talk her dad into taking her fishing tomorrow. After seeing the weather forecast, she realizes she will have to do some fast-talking. When she turned to her father and reported there was a 30% chance of sunshine for tomorrow she:

a. ignored confirmation bias.

b. told her father a boldfaced lie.

c. manipulated the framing of her report.

d. hoped he would use the representativeness heuristic.

14. Defining *creativity* is not easy. However, one characteristic of creativity is an ability to use ___ thinking.

a. random

b. diverging

c. emerging

d. converging

15. Tests of intelligence may not be appropriate for use in cultures other than the US because:

a. only US citizens are intelligent.

b. the tests cannot be translated into other languages.

c. intelligence is so hard to manipulate experimentally.

d. definitions of intelligence appear to vary widely across cultures.

16. Binet and Simon proposed the concept of ___ on the basis of having observed age–related differences in ability levels.

a. eugemcs

b. mental age

c. intelligence

d. chronological age

17. The smallest unit of sound in language is to the smallest unit of meaning in language as ___ is to ___.

a. phoneme; morpheme

b. morpheme; phoneme

c. syntax; grammar

d. grammar; syntax

18. Producing consistent scores is to ___ as measuring what is intended is to ___.
    a. reliability; validity
    b. validity; reliability
    c. standardization; validity
    d. reliability; standardization

19. A normal curve is:
    a. a characteristic of the forehead shape of someone with an average IQ.
    b. thrown with the first two fingers in perpendicular orientation to the seams.
    c. a bell-shaped distribution of scores with the majority clustered around the middle.
    d. produced when there is a strong positive relationship (correlation) between variables.

20. A person with mental retardation who manifests at least one remarkable ability:
    a. is said to have a learning disability.
    b. would have the rare savant syndrome.
    c. would be able to use a calculator extremely quickly.
    d. would probably be placed in a gifted and talented curriculum.

21. Which of the following is *not* part of Sternberg's triarchic theory of intelligence?
    a. social intelligence
    b. creative intelligence
    c. practical intelligence
    d. analytical intelligence

22. The proportion of intelligence that is attributable to genetics is called the ___ of intelligence.
    a. biology
    b. heredity
    c. chemistry
    d. heritability

23. If environmental variables were the key determinants of intelligence, which pair of people would score most similarly?
    a. fraternal twins reared apart
    b. identical twins reared apart
    c. adoptive siblings reared together
    d. adoptive siblings reared apart for six years, then reared together for six more years

24. Identical is to Fraternal as ___ is to ___.
    a. one ovum; two ova
    b. two ova; one ovum
    c. x chromosome; y chromosome
    d. y chromosome; x chromosome

25. In Gardners's model of intelligence, *g* refers to:
    a. genetics
    b. general intelligence
    c. the "thousand contributors to intelligence"
    d. the denominator in an equation that is used to predict native ability

Answers to Key Word Exercise

1. Thinking	2. doublespeak	3. algorithms
4. subgoals	5. rigidity	6. situational factors
7. Syntax	8. intelligence quotient	9. standardization
10. environmental	11. Francis Galton	

Practice Test Answers and Explanations

1. c. Smith demonstrated that thinking does not require sub-vocal mouth movements as had been thought previously.
2. a. Many believe that the data cognitive psychologists use needs to be public and replicable.
3. c. In addition to visual imagery, people are capable of evoking auditory and olfactory images.
4. c. High-imagery words provide two pegs for hanging memories, whereas low-imagery words require memory for meaning alone.
5. b. A prototype is a special case of a concept. For example, a carrot is a prototypical vegetable.
6. d. Doublespeak is an acceptable or inoffensive term that is used in place of an offensive one.
7. c. Specifying the steps to the solution would be to give away the problem.
8. a. An algorithm is a systematic procedure that involves evaluating all solutions until one is found.
9. b. 'I before e, except after c' is a heuristic (or rule of thumb).
10. d. Functional fixedness is the inability to see new uses for familiar objects (e.g., not recognizing that a dime can be a screwdriver).
11. d. The gambler's fallacy is an example of the representativeness heuristic (a failing problem–solving strategy).
12. a. The availability heuristic is a failing problem–solving strategy that involves estimating the probability of an event based on how easily it comes to mind (how available it is in one's memory).
13. c. She manipulated the framing, or presentation of negative and positive outcomes.
14. b. Creative solutions tend to be diverging, or moving in search of multiple answers.
15. d. Definitions of intelligence vary widely across cultures.
16. b. Mental age was proposed as a way of assigning people to categories based on test scores.
17. a. Phonemes are the smallest units of sound that are understood as parts of language, whereas morphemes are the smallest units of sound that convey meaning in language.
18. a. Reliability is the degree to which a test can yield consistent scores over repeated administrations; validity has to do with how well a test measures what it was designed to measure.
19. c. A normal curve is bell-shaped with most scores in the middle of the distribution.
20. b. Persons who have mental retardation, but who possess one or more remarkable abilities have *savant syndrome*.
21. a. Social intelligence is not part of Sternberg's model.
22. d. The heritability of intelligence is the proportion that is attributable to genetic factors.
23. c. If environmental conditions were key in determining intelligence, people who were reared most similarly should score most similarly, regardless of parentage. However, it appears that genetics also plays a significant part in determining intelligence.
24. a. Identical twins come from a single egg, or ovum. Fraternal twins come from separate ova.
25. b. The *g factor* in Gardner's theory is generalized intelligence.

Key Vocabulary Terms

Use the following list to write definitions *in your own words* for each of the key terms from the chapter. Translating the terms into language that is comfortable and familiar for you will facilitate your learning. For further study of these terms, go to the companion website for the textbook where you will find electronic flash cards that you may use to test your vocabulary.

cognitive psychology

thinking

concepts

prototype

algorithm

heuristics

functional fixedness

set effect

confirmation bias

representativeness heuristic

availability heuristic

framing

creativity

phoneme

morpheme

syntax

intelligence

mental age

intelligence quotient (IQ)

reliability

validity

standardization

norms

normal curve

savant syndrome

heritability

identical twins

fraternal twins

Tip for Success: Learning Styles

In Chapter 8, *Thinking and Intelligence,* you learned about theories of intelligence. There are several theories of intelligence, each with different features and emphases. A common theme in them, though, is that intelligence is not a unitary, homogeneous entity. Prevalent theories such as Spearman's, Sternberg's, and Gardner's, propose that there are several types of intelligence.

Briefly describe Spearman's *g*.

_____

_____

What are the components of Sternberg's Triarchic Theory of intelligence?

_____

_____

_____

List the eight kinds of intelligence as proposed by Gardner:

_____

_____

_____

_____

_____

_____

_____

_____

Given the widespread attention models of multiple intelligences have received in recent years, it is becoming clear that intelligence is complicated and involved, and is not a homogeneous, unitary entity as has been thought previously. It does not matter whether research supports each of these theories, one at the exclusion of the other, or other ideas altogether. It is important, however, that education and industry take stock of the fact that different people have different intellectual strengths--different intelligences--and that one's ability to excel in a given area will depend in part on her or his native abilities. By logical extension, people should, to some degree, be channeled into curricula in schools, and also into various career tracks, based on their type(s) of intelligence.

More specifically, different people learn and adapt differently, based on their abilities. In order to improve interest and performance in school, and, later on, productivity and satisfaction in a career, it is important that people discover their learning styles.

What Is Learning Style?

Take a few minutes to reread pages xxii through xxvii in the textbook preface. If you have not already done so, take the Pathways to Learning questionnaire on page xxiv. Note the extent to which each of your eight intelligences, according to Gardner's Model, are developed. If you show particular strength in one or two domains over and above the others, you may want to use this information to inform your approach to studying. Drs. Davis and Palladino have gone to great lengths to develop study suggestions that are tailored to four of the learning styles: verbal/linguistic, logical/mathematical, visual/spatial, and interpersonal. While anyone may certainly take advantage of each of the study tips presented in the book, you may want to pay particular to suggestions that fit your learning style profile most closely. For convenience, the study tips in the chapters are color coded; the legend for these is on the first page inside the cover of your textbook.

Why Are You in School?

Your answer to this question may vary depending on your learning style. Some people approach their classes with a perspective of finding a purpose for anything they learn. If they cannot find an immediate personal application for information, they would just as soon not learn it. Others are not so concerned with how information can be applied to their personal lives, and want to learn for the sake of learning. Some want to challenge the ideas they are exposed to by testing them in various situations; for them learning is solidified in experience-based activities. Still others are interested in how information can be applied to environments, cultures, and the larger world. It is as though these people view content through a filter that allows them to see how their knowledge can be used to benefit other people and places.

It is helpful to realize the variety of perspectives your classmates use. You may get more from a given class by approaching it from a perspective that is different than your normal one. Sharing perspectives with people who view course content in different ways can make a class more enriching for everyone. There is no best way to learn material. Each approach has its merits; the key is to learn to benefit from as many perspectives as possible.

Learning styles vary by individual. However, teaching styles are fairly consistent from one instructor to another, and do not often reflect the diversity of learning style strengths for a given class.

How can you benefit most from the classes you take in light of your unique learning style?

_____

_____

_____

Things to Consider

    1. Get Out of Your Comfort Zone. Some of the most valuable experiences you will have will result from your willingness to try new things. Humans are creatures of habit, and tend to avoid uncomfortable situations. By trying new things and adopting different perspectives, you will discover exciting things about you and the world. You may even learn that a different career path fits your strengths and abilities better than the one you had been considering.

    2. Adjust Your Learning Style. Your courses will be far more meaningful if you accept them for what they are. If you are enrolled in a class that has little application to your personal life, try to enjoy it as an opportunity to expand your knowledge base.

    3. Be in Control. You are ultimately responsible for what you get out of your education. Do not allow yourself to get into a rut of thinking that your professor, the textbook, your classmates, or anything else is stifling your ability to get the most from the class. Nowhere is it stated that you cannot supplement your learning experiences by doing additional reading, or experiments, or by organizing discussion groups or trips to visit people or places that will expand your exposure to material. On the contrary, doing these kinds of things will help you develop your understanding of the topics at hand and give you a record of career-oriented activity to describe when pursuing options such as employment or graduate school; the skills one develops in independent projects are often highly desired.

4. Learn from Others. Often you will have opportunities to work with others in your classes in group projects. More frequently, you will have opportunities to discuss class material with others as you complete assignments and prepare for exams. As often as you can, team up and compare notes with people who take school seriously, but who have a different perspective than you do. You can learn from one another, plus you will develop appreciation for other ways of thinking as a result of collaborative learning.

5. Ask for Guidance. Think of your professors as learning resources. In addition to preparing for your daily class meetings, you may find it helpful to do additional work in order to gain the most from the class. Your instructor can help you identify interesting topics to explore in the library, resources to consult for further study on a topic of particular interest to you, and may even include you in her or his research if you show some interest and initiative.

CHAPTER 9

Development across the Lifespan

BASIC ISSUES IN DEVELOPMENTAL PSYCHOLOGY
Nature and Nurture
Research Methods

DEVELOPMENT FROM CONCEPTION TO BIRTH

Heredity
Prenatal Development
Birth

DEVELOPMENT IN INFANCY
Sensory Abilities
How Newborns Learn
Maturation

PSYCHOSOCIAL DEVELOPMENT IN CHILDHOOD
Temperament
Personality Development
Attachment
The Father's Role
Day Care
The Peer Group
Television

COGNITIVE DEVELOPMENT IN CHILDHOOD
Piaget's Theory
Moral Development

ADOLESCENCE
Physical Changes
Cognitive and Intellectual Changes
Personality and Social Changes

EARLY ADULTHOOD
Physical Changes
Cognitive and Intellectual Changes
Personality and Social Changes

MIDDLE ADULTHOOD
Physical Changes
Cognitive and Intellectual Changes
Personality and Social Changes

LATE ADULTHOOD
Physical Changes
Cognitive and Intellectual Changes
Personality and Social Changes

DEATH, DYING, AND BEREAVEMENT
Attitudes toward Death
Confronting Death
Bereavement, Grief, and Support

Do You Know?

Do you know that the average American child will have watched more than 25,000 hours of television before he or she graduates from high school? For years, researchers have debated what this vast exposure to television means for people's values, comfort with violence, and so on. A recently published longitudinal study by Huesmann, Moise-Titus, Podolski, and Eron (2003)* addressed some of the common topics in that debate.

The paper by Huesmann et al. revealed that childhood exposure to media violence for both boys and girls predicts aggressive behavior among the same population when they are young adults. Based on the study, such aggression is predicted irrespective of individual's initial childhood levels of aggression. The most influential programming was that in which the children can identify with one or more of the characters in the program.

The data from this project and others imply a relationship between the viewing of television violence and one's propensity to commit aggressive acts later in life. Given this probable link, plus the fact that television programming is increasingly explicit in nature, even on network (i.e., not cable) television, one might reasonably predict that we will see increased acts of aggression in the public and private lives of people in our culture in the years to come. Although definitive causal data are practically impossible to gather on this topic (we cannot experimentally control the lives of anyone, let alone many research participants for the length of time necessary to demonstrate the effects with proper control groups, etc.), we may be better off safe than sorry. Parents can exercise precautions by watching programming with their children and/or by imposing viewing restrictions by using ratings, perhaps employing technology to block access to some channels.

*Huesmann, L.R., Moise-Titus, J., Podolski, C.L. & Eron, L.D. (2003). Longitudinal relations between children's exposure to TV violence and their aggressive and violent behavior in young adulthood: 1977-1992. *Developmental Psychology, 39*, 201-221.

Notes from Class and the Textbook

Use the space provided in this outline to record notes from the textbook as well as from class lectures and discussion. Questions related to the *Psychological Detective, Hands On, Myth or Science,* and *Study Tip* sections in the text have been presented in the outline; use the associated space to respond to the questions and to record your own comments about the issues.

I. Basic Issues in Developmental Psychology

    A. Nature and Nurture

To what extent are musical ability, athletic ability, shyness, and activity level genetically determined? To what extent are they environmentally determined?

    B. Research Methods

        1. Longitudinal versus Cross-Sectional Studies

II. Development from Conception to Birth

    A. Heredity

Point your Web browser at the textbook's Web page to see Live!Psych module 9.1.

    1. Polygenic Heredity

    2. Determination of Sex

    3. Sex-Linked Traits

B. Prenatal Development

    1. Barriers to Prenatal Development

        a. Teratogens

        b. Drugs

        c. Smoking

        d. Alcohol

    2. Checking the Health of the Fetus

        a. Ultrasound

        b. Amniocentesis

C. Birth

Create flash cards for all of the terms defined in the margins of the section on development from conception to birth. With a study partner, test one another until each of you clearly understands the vocabulary.

III. Development in Infancy

    A. Sensory Abilities

        1. Voice Recognition

        2. Vision

        3. Taste and Smell

    B. How Newborns Learn

        1. Classical Conditioning

How could you demonstrate classical conditioning in a newborn? Outline a demonstration, naming the components of the conditioning paradigm.

        2. Operant Conditioning

3. Imitating Others

C. Maturation

    1. Development of the Brain

    2. Physical Development

IV. Psychosocial Development in Childhood

  A. Temperament

  B. Personality Development

    1. Sigmund Freud

    2. Erik Erikson

  C. Attachment

    1. Ethological Theory

    2. The Strange Situation Test

  D. The Father's Role

  E. Day Care

F. The Peer Group

G. Television

What steps can parents take to ensure the television programming their children are exposed to is not detrimental?

V. Cognitive Development in Childhood

    A. Piaget's Theory

        1. The Sensorimotor Stage

        2. The Preoperational Stage

        3. The Concrete Operational Stage

        4. Challenges to Piaget's Theory

Summarize Piaget's stages of cognitive development in children. Underline or highlight important terms.

B. Moral Development

VI. Adolescence

A. Physical Changes

B. Cognitive and Intellectual Changes

1. Adolescent Thought Patterns

C. Personality and Social Changes

1. Possible Outcomes of Identity Formation

2. Adolescent Peer Groups

3. Family Influences

4. Making a Commitment

VII. Early Adulthood

A. Physical Changes

B. Cognitive and Intellectual Changes

Outline a research project that would help determine whether intellectual ability declines with age.

        1. Types of Intelligence

    C. Personality and Social Changes

        1. Intimacy versus Isolation

        2. Marriage

        3. Children

        4. Parenting Styles

        5. The Feminization of Poverty

        6. Career Development

VIII. Middle Adulthood

    A. Physical Changes

    B. Cognitive and Intellectual Changes

C. Personality and Social Changes

      1. Midlife Crisis

      2. Other Stresses during Middle Adulthood

What are some possible reasons for couples having greater marital satisfaction after their children leave home?

IX. Late Adulthood

A. Physical Changes

Consider the five true-false statements on page 402 in your textbook. Commit to an answer for each item, then check your answers against the information presented in the subsequent paragraphs.

Page 403 in your textbook contains an exercise to simulate loss of sensory acuity. Get the suggested materials and try the exercise with a few friends, each of you taking turns in the simulation. Finally, discuss the questions presented in your text at the end of the Hands On section.

B. Cognitive and Intellectual Changes

Create a timeline showing Erik Erikson's stage theory of personality development. Use different colors, or draw icons, to represent the different stages.

      C. Personality and Social Changes

          1. Retirement

          2. Aging

X. Death Dying, and Bereavement

      A. Attitudes toward Death

          1. Childhood

          2. Adolescence

          3. Young Adulthood

          4. Middle Adulthood

          5. Late Adulthood

      B. Confronting Death

C. Bereavement, Grief, and Support

Learning Objectives

After you have studied the chapter, you should be able to respond to the following statements and questions to convey your understanding of the material.

1. Discuss two primary research methods for studying psychological development. What are the advantages and disadvantages of each?

2. Give a few examples of how newborns and infants learn.

3. Discuss what happens to the temperaments of children as they mature.

4. Identify the steps of cognitive development that were suggested by Piaget. What does it mean that all humans develop cognitive abilities in roughly the same way?

5. Identify Kohlberg's proposed primary levels of moral development.

6. Differentiate between fluid and crystallized intelligences. What is the relationship between these as one develops across the lifespan?

7. What stages of Erikson's theory of psychosocial crises are typically addressed during adolescence, early, middle and late adulthood?

8. Identify and describe the five stages of dealing with death that were offered by Kübler-Ross.

Key Word Exercise

Fill in the blanks in the following statements with key words and terms from the textbook. Answer as many as you can without referring to your notes or to the book. If you have blanks after thinking about each item, try using your book. The answers are presented after the practice test.

1. _____ is a procedure that involves withdrawing fluid from the womb for analyses regarding genetic abnormalities of the fetus.

2. Emma, an infant girl, has learned to kick her leg in order to be reinforced by the movement of a mobile. She has demonstrated an ability to learn from _____ conditioning.

3. _____ is the developing of motor and cognitive abilities at an early age.

4. The _____ theory of attachment states that attachment evolved because of its adaptive value to the infant.

5. A form of social influence that usually includes classmates and neighborhood children, and can have both positive and negative influences on the development of a child, is called a _____ _____.

6. A _____ is common in some societies and is the key to manhood for boys.

7. Tomorrow, Mr. Johnston will have surgery on his eyes. This is because he has _____, a condition whereby his lenses have become clouded.

8. One form of dementia is _____ _____, a degenerative brain disorder that results in progressive loss of intelligence and awareness.

9. A(n) _____ _____ is developed by some adolescents in response to the expectations their parents have for them.

10. Peter is experiencing grief, the emotional changes that are associated with _____ following his mother's death.

Practice Test

Circle the letter that corresponds to the ***best*** alternative for each of the following items. Read each alternative carefully. The answers are presented at the end of this study guide chapter. Be sure to learn *why* each correct alternative is better than the others.

1. Which of the following statements would best characterize John B. Watson's view on the role of heredity in shaping human behaviors?
   a. There is no such thing as an inheritance of capacity, talent, temperament, or mental constitution.
   b. Key human characteristics develop depending mainly on training that goes on in the crib.
   c. It is a unique combination of heredity and environment that permits humans to develop their idiosyncratic abilities and characteristics.
   d. Given the complexities of the human nervous system, coupled with the rich nature of the rearing environment, it is impossible to know which is the greater of environment and heredity.

2. Nature is to nurture as ___ is to ___.
   a. Watson; Piaget
   b. Kohlberg; Erikson
   c. environment; heredity
   d. heredity; environment

3. It is important to note when studying people from different age groups that while they may share many demographic characteristics, they have not had the same life experiences. That is, they are from different:
   a. cohorts.
   b. cultural strata.
   c. phases and stages.
   d. socioeconomic groups.

4. Which sequence represents the order in which prenatal (before birth) development occurs?
   a. embryo, fetus, zygote
   b. zygote, embryo, fetus
   c. fetus, zygote, embryo
   d. embryo, zygote, fetus

5. The principle whereby complex traits are determined by many genes is called:
   a. genetics.
   b. behavior genetics.
   c. polygenic inheritance.
   d. the principle of deoxyribonucleic acid (DNA).

6. The placenta is important in prenatal development because it does all but which of the following?
   a. produces hormones
   b. transmits nourishment
   c. filters out certain harmful substances
   d. neutralizes the teratogenic effects of alcohol

7. The outline picture that is produced by projecting sound waves onto the fetus, uterus, and placenta is called a(n):
   a. sonogram.
   b. genetic diagram.
   c. amniocentesis scan.
   d. ultrasound procedure.

8. Which of the following is *not* one of the three stages of birth?
   a. labor
   b. anoxia
   c. delivery
   d. afterbirth

9. While it is initially poor, infant visual acuity improves to about 20/20 by:
   a. 3 weeks of age.
   b. 4 to 10 weeks of age.
   c. 6 to 12 months of age.
   d. the time the child reaches her or his second year.

10. Watson and Rayner demonstrated:
    a. that older infants can be classically conditioned to fear.
    b. the processes of meiosis and mitosis under strict laboratory conditions.
    c. the power of genetic influence in determining whether and what a child can learn.
    d. that "Little Albert" could learn to avoid painful stimuli by operating a manipulandum.

11. Erikson's theory of development stresses:
    a. attachment.
    b. psychosocial crises.
    c. psychosexual stages.
    d. the acquisition of morality.

12. Harlow's research with infant monkeys demonstrated:
    a. the role of contact comfort in attachment.
    b. that they all are raised with the same basic parenting style.
    c. the value of attending to the critical window during early development.
    d. little other than that the assumptions about humans generalize well to primates.

13. Which was not identified as one of three common parenting styles?
    a. permissive
    b. dictatorship
    c. authoritarian
    d. authoritative

14. Young Tim and his sister Carrie are having grain burgers for lunch. Each got the same amount, one patty, but when their father cut the patties to make them easier to eat, he cut Carrie's into more pieces than Tim's. Tim whined and complained that he got shorted, thereby demonstrating that:
    a. he had not yet reached the sensorimotor stage of cognitive development.
    b. he had not yet reached the preoperational stage of cognitive development.
    c. he had not yet reached the formal operational stage of cognitive development.
    d. he had not yet reached the concrete operational stage of cognitive development.

15. With respect to the development of full sexual maturity, girls are to boys as ___ is to___.
    a. menarche; nocturnal emissions
    b. growth of axillary hair; changes in skin
    c. primary sex characteristics; secondary sex characteristics
    d. secondary sex characteristics; primary sex characteristics

16. Presbyopia is to presbycusis as ___ is to ___.
    a. male; female
    b. female; male
    c. hearing; vision
    d. vision; hearing

17. Sarah is beginning to show symptoms of dementia. As a result of dementia, she:
    a. ceases to ovulate and menstruate.
    b. will experience memory loss and disorientation.
    c. may have to have corrective surgery to restore normal vision.
    d. will have to use greater caution in activity as her risk for bone damage will increase.

18. Ability to see new relationships is to ___ as ability to retrieve and use information is to ___.
    a. middle adulthood; late adulthood
    b. late adulthood; middle adulthood
    c. fluid intelligence; crystallized intelligence
    d. crystallized intelligence; fluid intelligence

19. An interesting characteristic of adolescents in Erikson's *intimacy versus isolation* crisis is that:
    a. the crisis is more common among boys than among girls.
    b. the crisis is more common among girls than among boys.
    c. boys usually develop strong autonomy before becoming intimate, while girls may never have a strong sense of autonomous identity.
    d. girls usually develop strong autonomy before becoming intimate, while boys may never have a strong sense of autonomous identity.

20. The feminization of poverty in the *U.S.* is ___ it is in other industrialized nations.
    a. less than
    b. greater than
    c. about the same as
    d. a less important issue than

21. The *hospice movement* is:
    a. cruel and inhumane.
    b. essentially an application of humanistic psychology.
    c. an interesting behavior shown by many middle-aged adults.
    d. more a way of using the workforce than providing service to those who need it,

22. The *personal fable:*
    a. includes self-centered ideas and a sense that one is invulnerable.
    b. the term psychologists use to describe the life stories told to them by aging people.
    c. is longer, but not near as loaded with moral messages than the ones recorded by Aesop.
    d. is demonstrated in the young adult woman who thinks she can "solve the world's problems" by becoming a psychologist.

Answers to Key Word Exercise

1. Amniocentesis	2. operant	3. Precocious
4. ethological	5. peer group	6. rite of passage
7. cataracts	8. Alzheimer's disease	9. negative identity
10. bereavement		

Practice Test Answers and Explanations

1. b.   Watson was a strict behaviorist who believed that the only thing that mattered was environment.
2. d.   Heredity is associated with natural, or biological issues, while nurture refers to training or upbringing.
3. a.   A cohort is a group of individuals born in the same period.
4. b.   Zygotes are formed by the union of a sperm and an ova; next, the embryo develops, then the fetus.
5. c.   As its name implies, polygenic inheritance involves many genes influencing traits.
6. d.   The placenta passes alcohol through to the developing baby in the same concentrations that are found in the mother's blood.
7. a.   A sonogram is a picture that is produced using the ultrasound procedure.
8. b.   Anoxia is a reduction in or lack of oxygen that can cause brain damage during the birthing process.
9. c.   Visual acuity usually develops to 20/20 by one year of age.
10. a.   They conditioned fear in "Little Albert," who was an older infant at the time.
11. b.   Erikson's theory of development focused on a series of psychosocial crises.
12. a.   Harlow's work was useful in demonstrating the need for contact comfort during early development. However, other forms of attachment between parent and offspring are important too.
13. b.   Dictatorship was not discussed as a parenting style.
14. d.   During the concrete operational stage children learn the principle of conservation-recognition that a physical change in a substance does not change the amount of that substance. Relax, Tim, most adults get too big a container when putting away leftovers.
15. a.   Menarche (the first menstrual period) marks full sexual maturity for a girl; the ability to ejaculate semen (often in nocturnal emissions) marks sexual maturity for boys.
16. d.   Presbyopia is farsightedness that normally develops in middle adulthood; presbycusis is a middle-dulthood related hearing disorder.
17. b.   Dementia is a general decline in intellectual ability that is associated with old age.
18. c.   Fluid intelligence concerns the use of new relationships, whereas crystallized intelligence involves the ability to use information that has been learned.
19. c.   Girls are less likely to develop autonomous identities prior to establishing intimate relationships.
20. b.   Because of the high divorce rate, coupled with the fact that children of divorced parents usually stay with their mothers, more women are impoverished in the U.S. than in other countries.
21. b.   Hospice, which is characterized by a philosophy of treatment for the terminally ill, is an excellent example of the application of (humanistic) psychology.
22. a.   Personal fable is a term used to describe the thoughts and behaviors of adolescents who act as though they do not have to play by the same rules as other members of society.

Key Vocabulary Terms

Use the following list to write definitions *in your own words* for each of the key terms from the chapter. Translating the terms into language that is comfortable and familiar for you will facilitate your learning. For further study of these terms, go to the companion website for the textbook where you will find electronic flash cards that you may use to test your vocabulary.

developmental psychology

nature

nurture

behavior genetics

longitudinal study

cross-sectional study

cohort

zygote

mitosis

embryo

chromosomes

genes

deoxyribonucleic acid (DNA)

polygenic inheritance

fetus

placenta

teratogen

critical period

fetal alcohol syndrome (FAS)

ultrasound procedure

sonogram

amniocentesis

anoxia

rooting reflex

palmar or grasp reflex

moro reflex

Babinski reflex

cesarean section

maturation

precocious

psychosocial crisis

basic trust versus basic mistrust

autonomy versus shame and doubt

autonomy

initiative versus guilt

industry versus inferiority

attachment

contact comfort

ethological theory of attachment

peer group

cognitive development

assimilation

accommodation

sensorimotor stage

object permanence

mental representation

preoperational stage

symbolic representation

egocentrism

concrete operational stage

conservation

preconventional level

conventional role conformity

autonomous moral principles

adolescence

puberty

pubescence

secular trend

primary sex characteristics

menarche

secondary sex characteristics

formal operational stage

personal fable

imaginary audience

identity versus identity confusion

identity achievement

foreclosure

negative identity

identity diffusion

moratorium

early adulthood

fluid intelligence

crystallized intelligence

intimacy versus isolation

middle adulthood

presbyopia

presbycusis

menopause

osteoporosis

midlife crisis

generativity versus stagnation

empty nest syndrome

late adulthood

cataracts

dementia

Alzheimer's disease

ageism

integrity versus despair

bereavement

grief

mourning

hospice

Tip for Success: Stress Management

Thus far, the *Tips* sections in this study guide have addressed goal-setting, strategies for making the most of your resources (e.g., time, textbook, classroom experiences, study environment), preparing for and taking exams, and identifying your learning style. Managing all these activities can be both challenging and rewarding. In order to strive for and reach your potential, it is important to think and feel your very best. Sometimes, though, the pressures associated with having a multitude of responsibilities may create stress that will keep you from performing optimally. This *Tip* section was written to help you understand stress, and to learn some ways of keeping stress levels at a minimum.

What is Stress?

Stress refers to that which produces pressure, strain, or tension. Often, stress occurs as a function of perceived or real restraints on time to perform some task or function. However, impending time is not always the source of stress. Think, for example, of the last occasion when you had to speak to a crowd, or perform an attention-demanding task.

Identify several sources of occasional stress in your life:

_____

Stress Is in the Eye of the Beholder

It is interesting to note that stressful events are different for different people. Sometimes you may find that the relative amount of stress associated with an item in your life changes. You, circumstances, or an interaction between both can cause you to be more (or less) stressed by a task or behavior. Why are things stressful sometimes and not stressful at other times?

An old saying is that *perception is reality*. If that is the case, then it might provide some insight into the reasons why events change with respect to the amount of stress with which they are associated. If that is the case, it means that you can control the amount of stress you experience at a given moment by learning to alter your perception in order to manage the potentially stressful circumstance.

This idea is probably not new to you, but it is important nonetheless. For example, you may have heard some interesting advice about using imagery to reduce stress while giving a public speech. Some say it is helpful to imagine that your audience is in their underwear. The idea is that they would have more to be embarrassed about than you, and that this should put you at ease. It is important, however, that you imagine that they, and not you, are the ones in underclothes!

The key message here is that your perceptions govern, to a large degree, whether something is associated with stress. Learning to take things in stride, and not to getting too worked up about them, will be helpful.

Not All Stress Is Bad

The Yerkes-Dodson law of motivation says that optimal levels of performance are associated with moderate levels of stress or anxiety about the event. If stress is too low, one is not sufficiently interested in the event. High levels of stress interfere with one's ability to perform well. You may have had this range of experiences when writing a paper or preparing for an exam. Students sometimes find it difficult to get interested in studying too far in advance. At the other end of the spectrum, they find it difficult to concentrate during the last minutes or hours for a large project that they have put off until it is too late. Somewhere in between is a happy medium: the amount of stress that is necessary to focus your attention without being distracting.

Some people say they work best under pressure. What is the role of stress when this is the case?

High Levels of Stress Can Impair Performance

The *Health Psychology* branch of the discipline covers many facets of the stress response. Please refer to that chapter for a thorough explanation of stress and stress-related issues. In brief, however, you should know that when one experiences stressors (anything that causes an organism to display the nonspecific stress response), a series of responses typically follows. That series of responses, known as the general adaptation syndrome, is associated with changes in vital organ functioning and biochemical activity that can be hard on one's body. Stress can increase one's susceptibility to disease and illness.

Therefore, then, not only do high levels of stress impair the level and quality of behavior, but they take a toll on physiology and physical health as well. Sufficiently high levels of stress suppress immune-system functioning and put one at risk of illness.

Maladaptive Responses to Stress

Imagine someone who has a high-pressure job, such as a salesperson whose income is based on commission. The circumstances of such jobs cause the people who have them to experience tremendous levels of stress. Unfortunately, they often turn to maladaptive behaviors to combat the stress, thereby exacerbating the problem. For example, smoking and consuming large amounts of caffeine cause one to become more, not less, restless. After a day of drinking coffee and smoking (both caffeine and nicotine are behavioral stimulants), some will even choose to "relax" with a few alcoholic drinks (alcohol is a central nervous system depressant)

Caffeine, nicotine, and alcohol all impair one's ability to get productive (i.e., REM) sleep. Thus, this pattern of drug use impairs a person's ability to get adequate sleep, which in turn produces feelings of fatigue. Fighting fatigue with caffeine and nicotine is a losing battle. As you can see, using drugs, whether to maintain alertness, or to relax, may produce more stress than it alleviates.

Some respond to stress by overeating or eating unhealthy food. Excessive sugar intake will cause wild fluctuations in energy levels. Consuming fats will lead to weight gain, and perhaps to obesity. Overconsumption of either fats or sugars causes people to feel bad about their bodies and about their health. These feelings lead to increased stress. As with the use of drugs, improper diet can have dramatic negative impact on one's health; this will lead to increased health-related stress.

What Can You Do?

Use your critical thinking skills to identify the *causes* that produce the *effect* of stress. Whenever possible, strive to reduce exposure to stimuli and circumstances that produce stress. By eliminating the cause, you will also rid yourself of the effect. For example, if working up to deadlines is highly stressful for you, learn to complete your work earlier so you are not pressured by time.

To do your best, you need to feel your best. This means taking measures to maintain good health, and to eliminate unwanted stressors from your lifestyle. Take the time to learn about behaviors and their effects that will contribute positively to your personal well-being.

List several things you can do to alleviate stress in your life:

CHAPTER 10

Sex and Gender

Do You Know?

Do you know that there are several notable male-female differences in behavior? Common examples are in areas such as linguistic, spatial and mathematic abilities and the capacity to recognize and interpret nonverbal communication. Although over the range of sex-based difference, the differences reflect probabilistic trends, as discussed earlier with respect to measuring intelligence across cultures, and are not necessarily large. Indeed, evidence suggests that the differences are diminishing over time—a phenomenon that suggests environmental and not biological variables may be largely responsible for at least some of the differences.

Although some sex-based differences may ultimately be attributable to environmental (including cultural) difference, it is likely that there will always be some male-female behavioral differences. The reason for this is that the brains of males and females reveal consistent differences, and, given that behavior originates from the brain, it is reasonable to assume that structural differences will mean differences in functioning as well.

What is critical with respect to the issue of male-female differences, whether we are considering structural or behavioral sex-based distinctions, is that these differences be acknowledged without using them to foist political agendas and discrimination. Each sex appears to be associated with relative strengths. Again, recognize that we are referring to sometimes trivial statistical differences that represent probabilistic trends and not absolute differences. As psychologists develop increasingly better means for studying behavior, it is likely that additional differences will be discovered. Also, as we develop cultural and pedagogical approaches that are equally encouraging of both sexes, any differences will be minimized. All male-female statistical differences notwithstanding, it is important to remember that each individual has her or his own strengths and weaknesses, and that one should not allow sex-based preconceptions to influence one's treatment of another in the context of a particular behavioral domain.

Notes from Class and the Textbook

Use the space provided in this outline to record notes from the textbook as well as from class lectures and discussion. Questions related to the *Psychological Detective, Hands On, Myth or Science,* and *Study Tip* sections in the text have been presented in the outline; use the associated space to respond to the questions and to record your own comments about the issues.

I. Sex and Gender: An Introduction

    A. The Biology of Sex

        1. The Genetics of Sex

        2. Genetic Abnormalities

        3. Male Vulnerability

Create a visual organizer containing and describing the aspects of male vulnerability (in the context of the biology of sex).

B. Sexual Behavior

    1. Sexual Orientation

How is the sexual behavior of humans different than that of nonhumans? What are the consequences of the differences?

    2. Differences in Sexual Attitudes and Practices

    3. Sexual Dysfunctions

        a. Sexual Aversion Disorder

        b. Male Erectile Disorder

        c. Sexual Pain Disorders

C. The Development of Gender Roles

    1. Psychodynamic Theory

What does learning theory contribute to our understanding of gender roles?

    2. Cognitive Developmental Theories

    3. Gender Schema Theory

D. Gender Stereotyping

E. Cultural Differences in Views of Masculinity and Femininity

How could you study the presence of gender stereotyping in young children who have not acquired the language that would permit simple questioning?

Define gender stereotyping and summarize the section in your textbook that goes into detail on this topic.

1. Components of Gender Stereotypes

2. Mass Media and Gender Stereotypes

II. Similarities and Differences Between males and Females

    A. Biological Differences: Fact and Fiction

        1. Brain Differences

    B. Early Analyses of Sex Differences

    C. The Cognitive Realm

        1. Verbal Abilities

        2. Mathematical Abilities

        3. Visual-Spatial Abilities

What explanations, other than biological-based ones, might account for sex–based differences in mathematical and spatial abilities?

Outline male-female differences in the cognitive realm.

        D. The Social Realm

            1. Communication

            2. Helping Behavior

            3. Aggression

III. Social Issues

        A. Education

            1. Elementary School

How would you investigate the existence and extent of gender bias in the classroom? Would you ask teachers if such bias exists? Are there better ways to investigate possible gender bias in the classroom?

2. High School and Higher Education

In a small group, consider gender roles in education. Consider the roles that were implemented during your pre-college years, and the effects they may have had on you and your choices.

B. Work and Careers

    1. Sexual Harassment

    2. Frequency of Sexual Harassment

    3. Perceiving Sexual Harassment

    4. Gender Stereotyping on the Job

    5. Women as Leaders

C. Family Responsibilities

    1. Juggling

Learning Objectives

After you have studied the chapter, you should be able to respond to the following statements and questions to convey your understanding of the material.

1. What factors are instrumental in developing gender roles?

2. How do stereotypes influence various types of behavior?

3. Describe the trends in academic performance differences and similarities among men and women.

4. What is sexual harassment?

Key Word Exercise

Fill in the blanks in the following statements with key words and terms from the textbook. Answer as many as you can without referring to your notes or to the book. If you have blanks after thinking about each item, try using your book. The answers are presented after the practice test.

1. During the seventh week of embryonic development, internal reproductive organs develop. If androgens are not present at this stage, the sex of the child will be _____.

2. An individual's potential to respond sexually to persons of the same sex, the opposite sex, or both is called _____ _____.

3. According to _____ _____ _____, people develop masculine and feminine characteristics as a function of their accumulated experiences.

4. _____ _____ are reflected in behaviors ranging from the courses students enroll in to the occupations they pursue. As a result, boys are less likely to enroll in home economics courses and girls are less likely to work in construction.

5. _____ tend to use communication to establish and maintain relationships. _____ tend to use communication to exert power, to preserve independence, and to enhance status.

6. If one were subjected to _____, one would receive differential treatment on the basis of his or her sex.

7. Consistent with gender stereotypes, _____ are taught to be assertive and independent, while _____ are taught to be dependent and passive.

8. A recent review focused on the effectiveness of men and women in leadership and managerial roles. The results indicated that men and women were _____ _____.

9. Statistically, when both wife and husband work outside the home, the majority of the housework and child-care tasks remain the responsibility of the _____.

10. _____ tend to help more when the situation is dangerous and when the helping takes place in public. _____ are more likely to help when there are no observers and when a nurturing type of help is needed.

Practice Test

Circle the letter that corresponds to the *best* alternative for each of the following items. Read each alternative carefully. The answers are presented at the end of this study guide chapter. Be sure to learn *why* each correct alternative is better than the others.

1. The word sex is to ___ as the word gender is to ___.
   a. female; male
   b. biology; culture
   c. culture; biology
   d. within the U.S.; outside the U.S.

2. Males and females constitute roughly equal proportions of the population that is up to about 30 years old. After 30:
   a. that pattern continues.
   b. males begin to outnumber females.
   c. females begin to outnumber males.
   d. it is hard to tell because people tend to stop wearing appropriately colored clothing.

3. *Adrenogenital syndrome* refers to a condition in which:
   a. females develop adrenal glands in place of genitals.
   b. females develop genitals resembling those of males.
   c. people have the functional reproductive anatomy of both genders.
   d. males develop secondary sex characteristics resembling those of females.

4. Researchers have discovered that a nucleus in the hypothalamus (the sexually dimorphic nucleus) is twice as large in men as it is in women. The nucleus is - in heterosexual men in comparison to homosexual men.
   a. utterly nonexistent
   b. about the same size
   c. two to three times larger
   d. one to two times smaller

5. The *gender-schema theory* for explaining the development of gender distinctions:
   a. combines elements of social learning theory and cognitive developmental theory.
   b. combines elements of the psychodynamic theory and cognitive developmental theory.
   c. says that people exert control over secondary sex characteristics based on external events.
   d. says that primary sex characteristics develop in response to predictable environmental stimuli.

6. Gender stereotyping
   a. is the exclusive determinant of one's future.
   b. has profound influence over how people shape their lives.
   c. was a serious problem in the 1950s, but thankfully is a thing of the past.
   d. helps boys and girls choose the proper paths when making career and familial decisions.

7. Individuals who have high levels of characteristics associated with both males and females are:
   a. referred to as bisexual.
   b. referred to as androgynous.
   c. most likely to suffer from identity confusion.
   d. usually females with an extra y chromosome.

8. Guidelines for gender-inclusive language include:
   a. using gender-neutral job titles.
   b. avoiding gender-exclusive comments whenever possible.
   c. using plural forms of pronouns whenever possible.
   d. All of the above are guidelines for promoting unbiased language.

9. A woman who experiences a stroke in the left hemisphere is more likely to retain language abilities than a man with the same damage probably because:
   a. the left hemisphere is significantly larger in women.
   b. men have better spatial abilities instead of improved language capacity.
   c. women have proportionately more fibers bridging the two hemispheres (corpus callosum).
   d. None of the above have been offered as explanations for this phenomenon.

10. A *meta-analysis* is:
    a. a procedure for combining the results from several studies.
    b. a means of carefully studying the brain to examine gender differences.
    c. a way of examining metas, or social units that are formed to promote androgyny.
    d. an approach used by developmental psychologists to study gender stereotyping directly.

11. The most consistent finding concerning spatial ability is that:
    a. males and females score alike.
    b. males outperform females on mental rotation tasks.
    c. females outperform males at identifying the direction North.
    d. None of the above are supported in the research on spatial ability.

12. The disappearing of sex differences in cognitive ability may have to do with:
    a. the diversification of sexual preferences.
    b. when the tests are administered rather than the tests themselves.
    c. concerted efforts by classroom teachers to treat everyone the same.
    d. changes that influence gender stereotyping and its effects on education.

13. Imagine that you have just been asked whether males are more aggressive than females. Given what has been presented in your textbook, a good answer would be:
    a. yes, without question.
    b. no, the two genders are strikingly similar.
    c. it depends, the type of aggression under consideration is significant.
    d. how should I know, my psychology book did not mention gender- or sex-based differences in aggression.

14. Pat has just earned a bachelor's degree. With no additional information about Pat, you would predict that Pat is a ___, because since academic year 1984-85 ___ have earned more bachelor's degrees than ___ in American undergraduate colleges and universities.
    a. male; men; women
    b. woman; women; men
    c. athlete; athletes; non-athletes
    d. hermaphrodite; hermaphrodites; pseudohermaphrodites

15. Judy has hit a glass ceiling. That is, she:
    a. displayed her strength in an act of aggression directed toward the air.
    b. is facing barriers to getting a job with greater responsibilities and better pay.
    c. is a painter and just whapped her head on the ceiling because she had not noticed how close she was to the ceiling.
    d. none of the above.

16. Incidences of sexual harassment can take which form?
    a. Quid pro quo (Latin for "this for that")
    b. Hostile work environment (degrading, intimidating, or offensive)
    c. Both a. and b.
    d. Neither a. nor b.

17. Which of the following statements is true about sexual harassment?
    a. Every state, and many cities and towns have civil rights laws that deal with sexual harassment.
    b. Sexual harassment is relatively new and laws regarding it are just being developed.
    c. Presently there are no laws (federal, state, or civil in nature) that deal with incidences of sexual harassment.
    d. The federal government has issued sexual harassment legislation that supercedes any laws set forth by states and cities.

18. With respect to perceptions of sexual harassment, men and women ___ when the instances are explicitly coercive, and ___ when the instances are less explicit.
    a. agree; agree
    b. disagree; agree
    c. agree; disagree
    d. disagree; disagree

19. Self-reported data on child-care involvement has indicated that:
    a. men and women share child-care involvement roughly equally.
    b. men tend to have far greater levels of involvement in child-care in every category.
    c. women tend to have far greater levels of involvement in child-care in every category.
    d. women tend to more of the child-care related tasks that were rated as unpleasant, while men and women had more comparable involvement in enjoyable tasks.

20. Many women who have careers also do a majority of the house-related work in their homes. Which of the following seems to reflect the impact of juggling multiple (job- and home-related) tasks?
    a. Men seem better equipped to take on a variety of tasks than women.
    b. Women seem better equipped to take on a variety of tasks than men.
    c. Juggling multiple roles seems to insulate women (and men) against depression.
    d. Juggling multiple tasks is the single leading cause of depression in American women.

Answers to Key Word Exercises

1. female
4. Gender stereotypes
7. boys; girls
10. Men; Women

2. sexual orientation
5. Females; Males
8. equally effective

3. gender-schema theory
6. sexism
9. wife

Practice Test Answers and Explanations

1. b.   *Sex* refers to one's biological make-up (e.g., anatomy, genetics). *Gender* refers to social and psychological phenomena as defined by a given culture.
2. c.   Females make up an increasing percent of the population as age increases.
3. b.   Adrenogenital syndrome, which results from excessive exposure to androgens during fetal development, causes females to have genitals resembling those of males.
4. c.   The reduced size of the sexually dimorphic nucleus in homosexual men provides some support for theories that sexual preference is determined biologically.
5. a.   The gender schema theory combines elements of social learning theory and cognitive developmental theory.
6. b.   Gender stereotyping constantly impacts decisions people make, thereby shaping their lives.
7. b.   Androgyny is the possession of both male and female behavioral characteristics.
8. d.   The American Psychological Association, among other entities, recommends a. - c.
9. c: The corpus callosum seems to be larger in women than in men.
10. a.   A meta-analysis is a technique that facilitates the combination of data from several research projects for comparison in a single project.
11. b.   Males outperform females on mental rotation tasks (spatial ability). However, the similarities of cognitive abilities, including mathematical and language abilities, are far more striking than any small differences between the sexes.
12. d.   Societal changes in gender stereotyping and its effects on education seem to be at play.
13. c.   Whether a male will react more or less aggressively than a female depends on the type of aggression, and on the context.
14. b.   Women have outperformed men at earning bachelor's degrees for the last several years.
15. b.   *Glass ceiling* is a term that refers to the differential treatment received by men and women as they pursue the same jobs. It is harder for women to get promoted.
16. c.   Incidences of sexual harassment can take two forms: quid pro quo, or hostile work environment.
17. a.   Every state, and many cities and towns have civil rights laws that deal with sexual harassment.
18. c.   Men and women agree that an incidence constitutes sexual harassment when it is explicit, but disagree when the instance is less explicit.
19. d.   Women tend to more of the child-care related tasks that were rated as unpleasant, while men and women had more comparable involvement in enjoyable tasks.
20. c.   Juggling multiple roles seems to insulate women (and men) against depression.

Key Vocabulary Terms

Use the following list to write definitions *in your own words* for each of the key terms from the chapter. Translating the terms into language that is comfortable and familiar for you will facilitate your learning. For further study of these terms, go to the companion website for the textbook where you will find electronic flash cards that you may use to test your vocabulary.

sex

gender

hermaphrodite

pseudohermaphrodite

adrenogenital syndrome

androgen insensitivity syndrome

gender roles

cognitive developmental theory

gender-schema theory

stereotype

sexism

sexual harassment

Tip for Success: Critical Thinking

People in and out of academe value *critical thinking*. The scientific method depends on researchers' abilities to think critically about their own work, as well as when they are reviewing others' work. The subject matter of psychology sometimes requires well-honed thinking skills to ensure that causal inferences and conclusions are made only after carefully considering alternative explanations.

What Is Critical Thinking?

The term *critical thinking* is so commonplace that it has become a cliché. It is frequently used because it describes so well a process that is important in innumerable ways. Consider definitions of the two words that comprise the term. Critical means *requiring careful judgment*. Thinking means *to form or have in the mind*. Combined, *critical thinking* means *having careful judgment in the mind*.

Rewrite the definition of critical thinking in your own words:

_____

_____

Critical Thinking Is Everywhere

Critical thinking is represented in good communication of all forms: reading, listening, speaking, and writing. Part of the active reading process is to consider carefully that which you read. Likewise, a good listener does not merely soak up information like a sponge, but takes it in attending to all the subtleties of meaning in the message. When you communicate with others, whether verbally or in writing, it is important that *your* message reflects logical reasoning and appropriate expression of *your* conclusions. Be cautious about making or conveying assumptions.

Comment on why assumptions not welcome in critical thinking?

_____

_____

Seek the Truth

Critical thinking involves concern for that which is accurate. Science in general depends on patterns of research findings that corroborate, or are consistent with one another. Science is based on very carefully calculated inferences; virtually nothing is really known to be true in any scientific discipline, and psychology is not an exception.

If *your* mission is to understand the truth, it will be necessary for you to let go of some theories and hypotheses that once seemed plausible. As new theories incorporate the valid aspects of old ones, they simultaneously discard explanations that are rendered invalid in light of new data. As a critical thinker, it is vital that you admit mistakes and recognize flaws in you own and others' thinking. If you strive to improve your understanding of a given phenomenon, you will, at times, be stumped. Do not be afraid to say: "*I do not know.*" If you carry this practice into your everyday reasoning and communication, you will feel liberated from having to infer or guess at explanations of things you do not understand fully. That is a mark of a critical thinker.

Critical Thinking in Problem Solving

Problem solving can be both challenging and fun. When you search for solutions to problems, you often find yourself trying approaches until you find one that works. How do you determine that a solution does not work? The answer is simple: you think critically about the problem at hand, the proposed solution, and readily identify the shortcomings of the solution. As you get closer and closer to a solution, you will note that it gets increasingly difficult to find its faults. This circumstance requires that you fine-tune your thinking skills and consider carefully any oversights or shortcomings of the solution.

Qualities of a Critical Thinker

All critical thinkers share many of the same characteristics. Critical thinkers are systematic, open minded, analytical, patient, curious, informed, and aware. Consider these characteristics:

1. Systematic. Adopt a methodical, organized approach to asking and seeking answers to questions. Organization and focus are important components of this quality. As you work through problems, keep track of information and keep sight of your objective.

2. Open-Minded. Celebrate differences in opinion and different ways of thinking. By welcoming different approaches to thinking about problems, one often gains valuable insight.

3. Analytical. Recognize statements and conclusions that need support. If a claim cannot be substantiated, it is not of value. Similarly, beware of exaggerated claims. A perennial favorite is the famous estimated frequency of occurrence: 99.99 percent of the time.

4. Patient. There are many ways of approaching a problem, and many problems have more than one solution. Listen carefully to others and take your time. Wisdom comes from experience, and experience comes from awareness. It takes patience to be aware.

5. Curious. Curiosity may have "killed the cat," but it makes critical thinkers. Critical thinkers need to know *why* things occur, and do not accept "Just because" as an answer. One can spend a lifetime asking and answering questions and looking for ways of using the information gained.

6. Informed. Seek clear answers and definitions. Gather all the facts. Informed judgments are the best ones. Reserve criticism until you have all the relevant information. If you think you have all the information, but do not understand someone's idea or comment, ask good questions. Sometimes it is necessary to adopt a different perspective.

7. Aware. Does the person sharing an idea stand to gain from it? Knowing why someone would make a comment can be helpful in understanding the idea. If an idea gets your support, then what? By being aware of the implications of a given idea or solution, people are sometimes better able to evaluate the idea.

Whether you are purchasing products or buying into others' theories and ideas, learning to be a critical consumer will serve you well. How can you use the thinking skills and characteristics that are presented in this section to be a critical consumer?

CHAPTER 11

Personality

Do You Know?

Do you know that the concept of personality has been of interest to people for thousands of years, yet it still vexes psychologists as much as any other topic in the discipline? Your textbook defines personality as a relatively stable pattern of behaving, feeling, and thinking that distinguishes one person from another. On its surface, that definition is quite compelling, and to be sure, it is rather akin to definitions you might find in any other textbook. While there seems to be widespread agreement on the definition, it is important to note that these definitions do not lend to straightforward research questions that can be addressed such that they provide unambiguous data to clarify understanding of the concept of personality.

Whether considering the early approach of Hippocrates, the widely known one of Freud, or any of a large number of contemporary ideas, it is clear that tackling the task of understanding personality is difficult, and it is therefore likely that it will continue to puzzle researchers and theorists for generations to come. The difficulty, no doubt, stems from the very concept being hypothetical in nature, and not something that lends itself to measurement. Try the following thought experiment. Imagine two people whom you know reasonably well, and whom you consider to have very different personalities. Next, describe different tests that you might conduct on these two in order to probe their differences and underscore their personalities. If you had limitless resources and perfect compliance from your subjects, you would likely still fall short of definitive descriptions of their personalities. This is precisely because hypothetical constructs are not objective enough that they can be defined to the satisfaction of everyone. Not until personality is defined in objective, measurable terms will we be able to address the features that make us unique in ways that will be meaningful over time. Given the complexity of humans and human nature, it is difficult to imagine objective ways of defining personality that will work equally well in characterizing all people.

Notes from Class and the Textbook

Use the space provided in this outline to record notes from the textbook as well as from class lectures and discussion. Questions related to the *Psychological Detective, Hands On, Myth or Science,* and *Study Tip* sections in the text have been presented in the outline; use the associated space to respond to the questions and to record your own comments about the issues.

I. Analyzing Personality

    A. Defining Personality

    B. Assessing Personality

        1. Self-Report Inventories

        2. The Minnesota Multiphasic Personality Inventory

        3. The California Psychological Inventory

4. Limitations of Self-Report Inventories

5. Projective Tests

6. Limitations of Projective Tests

7. The Barnum Effect

Why do people accept feedback on their personalities from sources such as horoscopes, computer- and Internet-based programs, etc.?

8. Other Measures

C. Is Behavior Consistent?

1. Challenges to the Idea of Consistency

2. In Defense of Consistency

Does volunteering to work for charity provide evidence of the consistency of altruism over time? Why or why not?

3. Evidence of Consistency Based on Multiple Measures

II. Trait Approaches

Complete the "Big Five" Test on pages 467 and 468 of your textbook. The scoring key for the test appears at the end of the chapter in the textbook on page 499.

    A. Factors in Personality: Raymond B. Cattell

    B. Categorization of Traits: Hans Eysenck

What do people described as extroverts and introverts prefer doing? Write down a few answers before moving on to the next section.

    C. The "Big Five" Traits

        1. The Big Five and Job Performance

    D. Alternatives to the Big Five

III. Biological Factors in Personality

    A. Early Biological Approaches

Trepanation, operating on the skull in order to facilitate blood flow in the capillaries of the brain, received mixed support as a medical practice. While it is illegal in the United States and Europe, it has its advocates. What are your thoughts on this controversial practice?

        1. Humors and Bumps

        2. Body Types

        3. Sensation Seeking

Complete the Sensation Seeking Scale that appears on pages 476 and 477 in your textbook. The scoring key for the scale appears at the end of the chapter in the textbook on page 499.

Write a paragraph describing what you have learned about yourself according to your scores on the Big Five Test and the Sensation Seeking Scale.

B. Twin Studies

How do you differentiate between a coincidence and an explainable event? Does the distinction change if the event is explained in terms of genetic versus environmental factors? Consider these questions in light of the similarities and differences in the behaviors of twins.

Point your Web browser at the textbook's Web page to see Live!Psych module 11.1.

C. Personality and the Evolutionary Perspective

IV. The Psychodynamic Perspective

A. Basic Concepts

1. Psychic Determinism

What, if anything, does it really mean when someone makes a *Freudian slip*?

2. Instincts

3. The Unconscious

B. The Structure of the Mind

   1. The Id

   2. The Ego

   3. The Superego

   4. Interaction of Id, Ego, and Superego

C. Defense Mechanisms

How could you test the idea that someone's id, ego, and superego are in conflict?

D. Stages of Psychosexual Development

   1. The Oral Stage

   2. The Anal Stage

Pair up with a study partner and act as Rotter and Bandura. In your role–playing exercise, reflect the theorists' perspectives on personality through a question and answer dialogue.

VI. The Humanistic Perspective

      1. Abraham Maslow

         a. Basic Needs

         b. Self-Actualization

      2. Carl Rogers

How can information from the Q-sort be used to study the relationship between one's real and ideal selves?

Learning Objectives

After you have studied the chapter, you should be able to respond to the following statements and questions to convey your understanding of the material.

1. What methods and tools have been developed to measure personality?

2. How are environmental and genetic variables involved in determining personality?

3. Describe the psychodynamic perspective on personality. Why has it been so appealing to people over the years? What are its shortcomings?

4. What has been contributed by the learning and cognitive perspectives on personality?

5. Identify the strengths and weaknesses of the humanistic approach to personality.

Key Word Exercise

Fill in the blanks in the following statements with key words and terms from the textbook. Answer as many as you can without referring to your notes or to the book. If you have blanks after thinking about each item, try using your book. The answers are presented after the practice test.

1. Psychological tests in which individuals answer questions about themselves, usually by responding *yes or no* or *true* or *false* are called _____-_____ _____.

2. The *Thematic Apperception Test* is an example of a(n) _____ _____.

3. _____ is a summary term that describes the tendency to behave, feel, and think in ways that are consistent across situations.

4. Sheldon's terms, *endomorph, mesomorph,* and *ectomorph,* came from an early approach to investigating personality based on _____.

5. _____ estimates suggest that genetics are responsible for between 20 and 50 percent of personality characteristics.

6. Freud's model for explaining personality development was based on his idea that people seek to experience pleasure in several parts of the body called _____.

7. _____ complex is to girl as _____ complex is to boy.

8. *Denial, projection, rationalization,* and *repression* are examples of _____ _____.

9. Freud's theory has been highly criticized by psychologists because it is not _____.

10. Bandura labeled one's expectancy about her or his ability to engage in effective behaviors _____ _____.

Practice Test

Circle the letter that corresponds to the *best* alternative for each of the following items. Read each alternative carefully. The answers are presented at the end of this study guide chapter. Be sure to learn *why* each correct alternative is better than the others.

1. Your friend just took a test with over 500 true-false items on it. Which of the following was it?
   a. the Self-Report Inventory
   b. the Thematic Apperception Test
   c. the Minnesota Multiphasic Personality Inventory
   d. the Generalized Personality Analysis (GPA) Questionnaire

2. A back translation is:
   a. a normal translation that is performed after the fact.
   b. a procedure used to ensure that adaptations of a test in another language are translated appropriately.
   c. a maneuver used by many Olympic platform divers that requires a combination of athletic agility and personality.
   d. done when someone is unsure what a person from another culture has done behaviorally, and describes it to someone back home who can make sense of it.

3. Projective tests involve:
   a. looking into the future.
   b. presentation of unstructured or ambiguous stimuli.
   c. assigning clients to projects and testing their abilities to do the work.
   d. overhead projectors that display images on huge screens for interpretation by subjects.

4. To say that someone has fallen subject to the Barnum effect is to say:
   a. they are depressed.
   b. they just had a good time at the circus.
   c. they actually believe in the work of Sigmund Freud.
   d. they just accepted a generalized description as an accurate statement.

5. Eysenck's theory posits that:
   a. personality consists of three basic traits.
   b. airplane pilots, musicians, and artists are basically the same.
   c. the id, ego, and superego are in constant battle with one another.
   d. that there are 16 personality factors (which may be measured using the 16PF scale)

6. The "big five" traits:
   a. were proposed by Cattell.
   b. were offered by Eysenck.
   c. are really just extensions of the three that Freud originally suggested.
   d. are gaining widespread support, and can be remembered using the acronym OCEAN.

7. Although there is a fair amount of debate about determinants of behavior, it seems clear that:
   a. genetics have insignificant influences on behavior.
   b. situational variables influence behavior in significant ways.
   c. it will always be impossible to know why people do the things they do.
   d. none of the above.

8. Which of the following did Hippocrates *not* consider as one of the four bodily humors?
   a. blood
   b. phlegm
   c. black bile
   d. vitreous humor

9. You and a friend were strolling through an antiques and curios store when you noticed a porcelain model of a human head with various labels that would have corresponded to parts of the brain that were theorized to control various behaviors. You realized that it was derived from the 1800's idea of ___ that was championed by Franz Joseph Gall.
   a. Oedipus
   b. phrenology
   c. mystic tea vessels
   d. the stream of consciousness

10. Skydivers, race car drivers, divers, and others who regularly seek stimulation from a variety of sources are known as:
    a. nuts.
    b. riskers.
    c. death wishers.
    d. sensation seekers.

11. The study of identical twins who were separated early in life:
    a. allows researchers to isolate the effects of nature from those of nurture.
    b. has been restricted to the U.S. states of Ohio and Minnesota because it is cruel.
    e. takes relatively little time and effort compared to studying fraternal twins the same way.
    d. is a common practice among developmental psychologists as such separation is commonplace.

12. Research comparing differences between identical twins reared apart, and those reared together,:
    a. has yet to be done in a systematic way.
    b. yielded similar results on many of the MMPI sub-scales.
    c. is by its very nature *longitudinal,* and therefore has not been completed.
    d. helped psychologists realize the greater similarity of fraternal versus identical twins.

13. The size of the genetic effect—estimated by what is called *heritability*—indicates that:
    a. Ohio twins outscore Minnesota twins.
    b. fraternal twins outscore identical twins.
    c. differences among most people are due at least as much to environmental influences.
    d. the parents of fraternal twins are often strikingly similar in comparison to other sets of spouses.

14. Freud's notion of psychic determinism:
    a. assumes that all behaviors result from early childhood experiences.
    b. developed out of the research that was first begun by phrenologist Franz Gall.
    c. is that one's sex determines the varieties of defense mechanisms on which he or she will rely.
    d. assumes that all behaviors result from resonating psychic energy that is in one's home, but cannot be measured.

15. Freud's model for understanding personality can be likened to a(n):
    a. iceberg.
    b. river barge.
    c. enormous cigar.
    d. canyon created by a river.

16. *Id* is to ___ as *ego* is to___.
    a. Maslow; Freud
    b. identical twin; fraternal twin
    c. steam locomotive; houseboat
    d. pleasure principle; reality principle

17. According to Freud, the *superego:*
    a. is an exceptionally good ego.
    b. is far above the surface of awareness.
    c. incorporates societal and parental standards.
    d. develops out of the ego as one resolves one's innate desire for the opposite sex parent.

18. By and large, the Neo-Freudians:
    a. were Freud's offspring.
    b. found Freud's idea of *ego* to be ridiculous.
    c. disagreed with Freud's focus on the *id* and sexual motives.
    d. All of the above are true about the Neo-Freudians.

19. A widespread criticism of Freudian theory:
    a. has not existed to date.
    b. is that it is largely untestable.
    c. was offered by the man himself at the close of his life.
    d. stemmed from Freud's having an unresolved Oedipal conflict.

20. A significant contribution to personality theory was offered by Julian Rotter, who:
    a. developed a scale to measure the *locus of control.*
    b. invented the idea of *sensation seeking* as a way of explaining his own behavior.
    c. was the first name relative of Julian Lennon, son of John Lennon (one of the Beatles).
    d. basically followed in the tradition of the behaviorists in emphasizing noncognitive factors.

21. *Reciprocal determinism* is an idea that was proposed by Albert Bandura:
    a. to compete with Freud's notion of *psychic determinism.*
    b. to explain the interaction of person variables, situation variables, and behavior.
    c. a psychologist who began his career in the automotive industry–the source of the term.
    d. when he observed that after children hit Bobo dolls the dolls retaliated by kicking the children.

22. Abraham Maslow, who is well known for having developed the *hierarchy of needs,* thought which of the following?
   a. Humanistic psychology was the "third force" in psychology.
   b. Cognitive psychology was the creation science of psychology.
   c. Humanistic psychology would bring the downfall of the discipline.
   d. His idea fit better with traditional Freudian ideology than with Humanistic psychology.

23. Carl Rogers is probably best known for his term:
   a. ego-ideal.
   b. self-actualization.
   c. unconditional positive regard.
   d. conditional reward contingency.

24. Research on the *self* in social contexts has revealed:
   a. that John Watson was right.
   b. that most people are antisocial in nature.
   c. little to nothing of lasting value to psychology.
   d. that there are significant cultural differences with respect to conceptions of the *self.*

Answers to Key Word Exercise

1. self-report inventories	2. projective test	3. Trait
4. body type	5. Heritability	6. erogenous zones
7. Electra; Oedipal	8. defense mechanisms	9. testable
10. self-efficacy		

Practice Test Answers and Explanations

1. c.   The MMPI is a test that scores people according to 10 different dimensions. It has been adapted for use in at least 22 languages.

2. b.   A back translation is performed when testing how well a term or concept from a test translated into another language. The term is translated back into the original language.

3. b.   Projective tests involve the presentation of unstructured or ambiguous stimuli and recording people's responses to the stimuli.

4. d.   The Barnum effect is based on P. T. Barnum's statement about the circus, there is a "little something in it for everybody." Here, it means that a generalized statement is accepted as an accurate description of one's personality.

5. a.   Eysenck's model suggests that personality is comprised of three basic traits: extraversion, neuroticism, and psychoticism.

6. d.   There is growing agreement about the five basic traits, although there is some disagreement about their labels. They are: openness, conscientiousness, extraversion, agreeableness, and neuroticism.

7. b.   Among other influences, it is clear that situational variables influence behavior in significant ways.

8. d.   The four bodily humors Hippocrates championed were black bile, blood, phlegm, and yellow bile.

9. b.   The model was based on Gall's idea, *phrenology,* which presumed that a lot could be learned about one's cognitive abilities and behavioral propensities by feeling the bumps on the head.

10. d.   *Sensation seeking* is the characteristic of engaging regularly in risky behavior, seeking thrills, and participating in novel experiences through the mind and senses.

11. a.   Though it is not easy to find such twins, researchers like to study identical twins that were separated early as it helps separate the environmental influences on development.

12. b.   University of Minnesota researchers compared 44 pairs of twins that were separated early in life, and found striking similarities between them in light of their comparability to twins reared together.

13. c.   Heritability research, including that done with identical twins reared together and apart, indicates that differences among most people are due at least as much to environmental influences.

14. a. Freud's *psychic determinism* assumes behaviors stem from early experiences, especially conflicts related to sexual instincts.

15. a. Freud's model of personality is often compared to an iceberg. See "The Structure of the Mind" section in your textbook.

16. d. Freud's hypothetical construct (hypothetical construct is a fancy name for idea) *id was claimed to* operate according to what he called the pleasure principle. The *ego,* he said, was guided by reality.

17. c. The *superego,* according to Freud, is the element that incorporates societal and parental standards in what is commonly referred to as the *conscience* as well as the idealistic *ego ideal.*

18. c. The Neo-Freudians disagreed with Freud's focus on the *id* and sexual motives.

19. b. Freud's theory has received much criticism since it does not lend itself to testing. Even when his ideas do lend themselves to testing, the results are mixed and do not support it well.

20. a. Rotter developed a scale to measure *locus of control.* His research and ideas may be considered extensions of Skinner's, but Rotter's interests include cognitive components such as *expectancies.*

21. b. Reciprocal determinism is Bandura's idea for explaining the interaction of person variables, situation variables, and behavior.

22. a. Maslow thought that Humanistic psychology was the "third force" in psychology because it offered an alternative to psychodynamic theory and behaviorism.

23. c. Rogers, a Humanist and a contemporary of Maslow, coined the term unconditional positive regard. He believed that growing up believing affection is conditional causes one to distort experiences.

24. d. There are significant cultural differences with respect to conceptions of the *self.*

Key Vocabulary Terms

Use the following list to write definitions *in your own words* for each of the key terms from the chapter. Translating the terms into language that is comfortable and familiar for you will facilitate your learning. For further study of these terms, go to the companion website for the textbook where you will find electronic flash cards that you may use to test your vocabulary.

personality

self-report inventory

projective test

Barnum effect

trait

psychic determinism

unconscious

id

ego

superego

defense mechanism

oral stage

fixation

anal stage

phallic stage

Oedipal complex

Electra complex

latency stage

genital stage

social learning theory

locus of control

reciprocal determinism

self-efficacy

humanistic psychology

self-actualization

Tip for Success: Leadership Skills

At some level, everyone is a leader. By asking or answering a question, or otherwise redirecting the attention of your classmates and teacher, you are a leader in your class. Similarly, when you provide input to project group members, you are assuming a leadership position. When you are a leader, you shape your experience and help determine what your future opportunities will include. Sharing your insights is a sure way to ensure that your needs are understood. Alternatively, if you shy away from sharing your perspective, you may have to live with the consequences of others' interests and motives.

This *Tip* section will focus on ways you can shape your educational and career-related experiences by being a leader. There is no time like the present for you to begin shaping your life by assuming more leadership in your endeavors. The list that follows provides several suggestions for developing and maintaining leadership roles. Your ideas need to be heard. With a little effort, you will set in motion your future as a leader with a range of opportunities.

1. Be Willing to Make Mistakes. An old say goes, "nothing ventured, nothing gained." This saying fits a number of topics that involve taking risks. As a leader, you will be constantly making decisions that could result in failure. That is OK. Everyone falls short of her or his expectations from time to time. The hope is that, on balance, your advances will outweigh your setbacks.

Name three things that you avoided doing because you were afraid of making a mistake.

_____

_____

What was the worst thing that could have happened if you had made a mistake? What did you stand to gain?

_____

_____

2. Challenge Yourself. Take a few moments and think of several prominent leaders from history. What set them apart from everyone else? Most likely it was that they made significant contributions or accomplishments in their fields. The only way to make significant accomplishments is to take on challenging tasks. Identify a challenging goal, make a promise to yourself and others about the goal, and go for it! You will keep your interest in your endeavors peaked if you continue to take on meaningful challenges.

What challenging opportunities await you in your near future?

_____

_____

3. Leaders Are Role Models. By assuming leadership positions, you will have unique opportunities to help others and to share your insight into problems and issues. By maintaining your focus, you will encourage others to do the same. When things do not go as planned, keep your focus. Without having to divert energy, everyone will benefit.

4. Communicate Objective Truths, Make "I" Statements, and Be in Control. Leaders take ownership in their feelings and ideas. A very important leadership skill is to make statements that reflect either objective truths or personalized opinions. If you state something that is *not* an objective truth, preface it with *I think, I feel,* or *I believe.* Always resist passing judgment on others. Pointing fingers and placing blame only makes you feel bad and causes others to harbor resentment.

Only you have the power to decide how you will respond to what others do or say. When you place blame on someone else, you are indicating that you are out of control. If you begin to feel you are losing control, indicate that such is the case by making an *I statement* (e.g., I feel as though I am not in control of what is happening).

Think of three occasions when you have made statements that involved placing blame or pointing your finger at others. Write an *I Statement* that you could have made on each occasion instead.

_____

_____

_____

5. Focus on the Issue. By and large, your friends and colleagues are interested in succeeding at the endeavors they take on. If you are working together on something, and meet with frustration, do not blame others. Chances are they want to succeed too. Focus your attention on aspects of the problem that merit your attention rather than on other people who are also frustrated.

6. Give Credit to Others. The most satisfactory feeling that one can experience when something goes well is just that, a feeling. Have you ever noticed that many people like to brag, but that nobody likes hearing someone brag? This has a significant implication for those occasions when you meet with success in your endeavors. Rather than accepting responsibility for your successes, redirect attention to those whose efforts made your success possible. That will make them feel better and have more positive feelings about you.

Identify an accomplishment that you took credit for, even though someone else helped (even if he or she played a minor role that nobody was aware of):

_____

7. Have *Silent Pride*. Sometimes your successes are well deserved, and are due entirely to your own efforts. When things go your way and you are not able to redirect attention to others who played a role in the success, try being quietly humble. Being quietly humble, or having *silent pride*, will help others to see you more favorably and to wonder why you are not bragging. Since nobody likes to hear someone brag, this behavior will be intriguing. It is better to be intriguing than obnoxious.

Identify an example of someone bragging about her or his success at something. How would that occasion have been different had they adopted the silent pride response?

_____

8. Be Assertive. To *assert* is to state something positively. Being assertive means making clear statements about your ideas and feelings. Assertive comments and behavior typically come from those who are confident and respectful of others. Aggressive comments and behavior, on the other hand, are divisive and tend to break down relationships. Learn to control your aggression and to assert your position when appropriate.

9. Listen. When you adopt a position of leadership, it is important that you listen carefully to what others say. Failure to listen to, and respond to, others' comments reflects poor leadership. If you lead others, it is critical that you understand and represent their interests.

Identify the leadership skills you already practice. Which ones should you attend to?

_____

_____

CHAPTER 12

Psychological Disorders

Do You Know?

Do you know that diagnosis of psychological disorders is sometimes very difficult? Unlike many medical diseases that are diagnosable based upon a few defining symptoms, psychological disorders have less precise diagnostic criteria and therefore are more difficult to pinpoint definitively. What is more, some psychological disorders involve cyclical or periodic expression of symptoms, and unless the diagnostic criteria for all of the symptoms are viewed by the clinician or team that makes the diagnosis, persons with psychological disorders may not be properly diagnosed. A couple of familiar diagnoses will serve to illustrate examples of the importance of observing all of the features of someone's behavior in advance of performing diagnostic evaluation.

Dissociative identity disorder, which was previously called multiple personality disorder, typically takes several years to diagnose. This is not so much because the disorder's diagnostic criteria are so difficult to define, rather it typically takes several attempts to determine a proper diagnosis and course of treatment before it becomes clear that someone has the disorder. At one time the disorder was considered to be extremely rare, so clinicians did not necessarily consider it as a candidate when performing diagnoses. Instead, people were diagnosed with such disorders as depression, schizophrenia, and substance abuse disorder. Only after having gathered information on people for several years do patterns emerge that make it clear that the person in question may have dissociative identity disorder.

Another example of complicated diagnosis is with bipolar disorder, or manic depression as it was once called. Bipolar disorder is a mood disorder that involves the person's experiencing periods of depression and mania (the opposite of depression) in alternating fashion. Because people do not typically find manic phases to be maladaptive and undesired, it is not common for them to seek treatment when in that phase. Instead, only when people experience depression do they consider that they may need clinical help. If the clinician only witnesses the person in depressive phases, and is otherwise unaware that the person also experiences manic phases, he or she cannot offer the proper diagnosis. Because the treatments for (unipolar) depression and bipolar disorder are different, bipolar disorder may persist without effective treatment indefinitely until a more comprehensive diagnosis is made.

These are but a couple of examples of the complications clinicians experience when performing diagnoses. Inasmuch as the key criteria are typically behavioral in nature, it is not surprising that diagnosis is so difficult. As brain imaging techniques, cerebrospinal fluid assays, and other more objective tests of structural and functional abnormalities become part of the diagnostic evaluation, it is likely that the criteria for determining whether someone has a disorder, and if so which one, will become more precise.

Notes from Class and the Textbook

Use the space provided in this outline to record notes from the textbook as well as from class lectures and discussion. Questions related to the *Psychological Detective, Hands On, Myth or Science,* and *Study Tip* sections in the text have been presented in the outline; use the associated space to respond to the questions and to record your own comments about the issues.

I. Abnormal Behavior

    A. Criteria of Abnormality

        1. Statistical Rarity

        2. Interference with Normal Functioning

3. Distress

4. Deviance from Social Norms

B. A Working Definition

C. The Concept of Insanity

How often is the insanity plea used? What sources guide people's thinking about the frequency of use of the insanity plea? How often does it result in acquittal?

D. Models of Abnormal Behavior

1. The Medical Model

2. The Psychological Models

3. Culture and Disorders

II. Classifying and Counting Psychological Disorders

A. DSM-IV

Create flash cards with the names of the major categories of disorders listed in the DSM-IV. Put the disorder type on one side, and an example on the other side. Work with two other students. Have one call out either the disorder type or an example, and the other student give the other piece of information. Trade the cards around until each student can name an example of a disorder type when given an example, and vice versa.

   B. The Labeling Issue

   C. The Prevalence of Psychological Disorders

III. Anxiety, Somatoform, and Dissociative Disorders

   A. Anxiety Disorders

      1. Phobias

      2. Panic Disorder

Why do only some of the 15 to 30 percent of people who have experienced at least one panic attack develop chronic panic disorder? What role might cognitive interpretation of symptoms contribute to the likelihood that one will develop the disorder?

3. Generalized Anxiety Disorder (GAD)

4. Obsessive—Compulsive Disorder

What behavior is reinforced, and what is the reinforcer, when one feels less anxious after taking a shower? What principle of operant conditioning is in effect when each shower reduces anxiety?

B. Somatoform Disorders

   1. Hypochondriasis

   2. Somatization Disorder

   3. Conversion Disorder

C. Dissociative Disorders

   1. Dissociative Amnesia and Dissociative Fugue

How would the medical model account for Ed's amnesia concerning the accident? How would that explanation differ from one from the psychodynamic model?

2. Dissociative Identity Disorder

Develop a chart to summarize anxiety, somatoform, and dissociative disorders. Be sure to define each within your chart.

IV. Mood Disorders

    A. Depression

        1. Symptoms

        2. Prevalence and Course

        3. Suicide

Do people who are likely to commit suicide typically give signals concerning their intentions? Read the Myth or Science segment on pages 528 and 529 to learn more about the issue.

    B. Bipolar Disorder

C. Causes of Mood Disorders

    1. Biological Explanations

    2. The Psychodynamic Explanation

    3. Cognitive and Behavioral Explanations

    4. Multiple Causes

V. Schizophrenia

    A. Symptoms of Schizophrenia

        1. Positive Symptoms

        2. Negative Symptoms

    B. Subtypes of Schizophrenia

Develop visual representations that will help you remember each of the five types of schizophrenia.

C. Causes of Schizophrenia

   1. Genetic Factors

What can research with groups of twins, some reared together and some reared apart, tell researchers about the causes of schizophrenia?

   2. Brain Abnormalities

   3. Neurotransmitters

   4. Environmental Causes

   5. Multiple Causes

VI. Personality and Sexual Disorders

   A. Personality Disorders

How could a researcher measure physiological arousal? Design an experiment to study whether low levels of physiological arousal are related to antisocial behavior.

B. Sexual Disorders

    1. Gender Identity Disorder

    2. Paraphilias

    3. Fetishism

Write summaries, one paragraph each, to describe the material on personality and sexual disorders.

Learning Objectives

After you have studied the chapter, you should be able to respond to the following statements and questions to convey your understanding of the material.

1. What criteria must behavior meet in order to be considered abnormal?

2. What tools, methods, and techniques are available to diagnose and determine the prevalence of psychological disorders?

3. Discuss characteristics of anxiety disorders. How are they related to one another?

4. Describe the causes of mood disorders as they were presented in your textbook.

5. The word *schizophrenia* is widely known, but the disorder is not well understood. Why is it difficult to understand schizophrenia? What causes the disorder?

6. How can one use principles of learning (especially classical and operant conditioning) to understand personality disorders and sexual disorders?

Key Word Exercise

Fill in the blanks in the following statements with key words and terms from the textbook. Answer as many as you can without referring to your notes or to the book. If you have blanks after thinking about each item, try using your book. The answers are presented after the practice test.

1. The _____ _____ criterion for determining whether behavior is abnormal involves determining whether the peoples' behaviors are upsetting, distracting, or confusing to themselves.

2. According to the _____ _____, psychological disorders are learned and follow the principles of classical and operant conditioning.

3. _____ _____ _____ involves a chronically high level of anxiety that is not associated with a particular stimulus.

4. _____ is the number or percentage of newly diagnosed cases of a particular disorder in a given population.

5. In some cases major depression and _____ _____ occur together in a condition that is referred to as double depression.

6. What was once called multiple personality disorder is now known as _____ _____.

7. _____ _____ is the belief that one cannot control outcomes through one's actions.

8. A(n) _____ _____ is a conclusion that is drawn in the absence of supporting information.

9. Believing you are Santa Claus would be an example of a(n) _____.

10. An experiment involved MRI scanning of the brains of 'normal' people and persons with schizophrenia. Results indicated that the *thalamus* and surrounding regions in schizophrenic patients were significantly _____ than the same regions in 'normal' brains.

Practice Test

Circle the letter that corresponds to the **best** alternative for each of the following items. Read each alternative carefully. The answers are presented at the end of this study guide chapter. Be sure to learn *why* each correct alternative is better than the others.

1. The criteria for abnormality, as presented in your textbook, include all but which of the following?
    a. statistical rarity
    b. deviance from social norms
    c. interference with normal functioning
    d. adherence to rules for alternative fashion

2. Which example fits best the description of a *dysfunctional* family?
    a. The head of the household rarely functions before noon.
    b. Maids, gardeners, and cooks do all the work for the family.
    c. Typical familial interactions adversely affect the family's functioning.
    d. Both husband and wife get along well, but there are no children or pets.

3. Social norms are:
    a. guys named Norman that like to go to parties.
    b. behaviors such as keeping one's house well organized.
    c. difficult to follow for most people because of their elusive nature.
    d. guidelines (that are usually unwritten) that define the acceptability of behavior.

4. The U.S. public believes felony indictments involve the insanity plea ___ percent of the time, and that ___ percent of those pleas result in acquittal. Actually only about 1 % of cases involve the plea, and less than 1/4 of 1 percent are successful.
    a. 10; 80
    b. 50; 75
    c. 37; 44
    d. 89; 14

5. Psychological models for explaining abnormal behavior emphasize:
    a. the probability that underlying organic causes are at play.
    b. the likelihood that mental illness results from possession by demons.
    c. mental functioning, social experiences, and learning histories as having important causal links.
    d. all of the above.

6. Sociocultural variables apparently influence the likelihood that one will have a psychological disorder. For example, poverty is related to the prevalence of psychological disorders, and rates of psychological disorders are influenced by socioeconomic status. Another (category of) disorder that seems related to cultural variables is:
    a. bipolar disorder.
    b. phobic disorders.
    c. anorexia nervosa.
    d. obsessive-compulsive disorder.

7. A major reason people are diagnosed is:
    a. to be able to make predictions.
    b. so labels can be assigned to them.
    c. so that insurance companies can reimburse diagnosticians.
    d. to determine whether they were insane when they committed their crimes.

8. In the Rosenhan study in which 'normal' people entered hospitals and reported hearing voices:
   a. the people were admitted for an average of 19 days and were administered over 2,000 pills.
   b. while the people were taken seriously, they were not diagnosed as having any type of illness.
   c. the people were referred to a hearing specialist as it was determined their problem was not psychologically based.
   d. it was determined that the diagnostic criteria were very effective at discriminating 'normal' from those with mental illness.

9. The most frequently used diagnostic system for classifying mental disorders was developed by:
   a. Rosenhan and his colleagues.
   b. the American Psychiatric Association.
   c. the American Psychological Association.
   d. members of the American Psychiatric Association and members of the American Psychological association, under the leadership of Rosenhan.

10. An epidemiologist:
    a. is someone who study the bugs that cause mental disorders.
    b. is handy to have around if one experiences an epidemio infestation.
    c. studies the distribution and causes of accidents, diseases, and psychological disorders.
    d. has to have several years of training in brain scanning (e.g., MRI) in order to work effectively.

11. A *comorbid* psychological disorder is:
    a. one that develops initially with symptoms that one has died.
    b. a disorder that co-occurs with one or more other psychological disorders.
    c. a disorder that develops just as the symptoms of another disorder come under control.
    d. all of the above.

12. Phobias are:
    a. innate fears (not related to environment or experience).
    b. excessive fears that are categorized under anxiety disorders.
    c. more prevalent in third world than in highly industrialized countries.
    d. fears that develop as a result of eating diets that are proportionately high in saturated fats.

13. The most severe anxiety disorder(s) is (are):
    a. panic disorder.
    b. simple phobias.
    c. generalized anxiety disorder.
    d. obsessive-compulsive disorder.

14. Obsessions are to ___ as compulsions are to ___.
    a. OCD; GAD
    b. acts; thoughts
    c. thoughts; acts
    d. early onset; chronic syndromes

15. Somatoform disorders involve:
    a. physical symptoms with no known medical cause.
    b. the irrational repetitive creation (forming) of somas (bodies).
    c. medical symptoms that are known to result from psychological issues.
    d. peculiar behaviors that are targeted at reducing anxiety about repetitive thoughts.

16. Sally is forever going to the doctor and consulting pharmacists about what she can do to address a constellation of symptoms that most people would ignore. Sally probably has:
    a. OCD.
    b. cancer.
    c. hypochondriasis.
    d. anterior-lateral sclerosis.

17. A truck driver recently picked up Hans while he was walking toward town after crashing his car. Hans had absolutely no idea where he was, or for that matter where he had come from. After some careful investigative work, officials were able to determine that Hans had rented a car after flying to the U.S. from Europe. However, Hans could recall nothing of his adventure or the events leading up to it. Hans is likely suffering from:
    a. dissociative fugue.
    b. retrograde amnesia.
    c. conversion disorder.
    d. comorbid hypochondriasis.

18. Surveys of people in the U.S., Western Europe, the Middle East, Asia, and the Pacific Rim regarding depression have revealed which of the following?
    a. Depression is beginning at an earlier age with each successive generation.
    b. Rates of depression have risen steadily for each successive generation since 1915.
    c. Both a. and b., above, are true.
    d. Neither a. nor b. is true; depression is becoming decidedly less common world-wide.

19. The most serious complication of severe depression is:
    a. comorbidity.
    b. the possibility of suicide.
    c. that slowed heart rate can least to cardiac rest.
    d. that people with substance abuse disorders often also are depressed.

20. Bipolar disorder involves alternating cycles of ___ and___.
    a. OCD; GAD
    b. wash; rinse
    c. depression; mania
    d. somatoform disorder; conversion disorder

21. The *concordance rate* is:
    a. a measure of treatment efficacy for mental disorders.
    b. the percentage of twin pairs in which both twins have a disorder.
    c. an index of the proportion of the population that has a given disorder.
    d. usually 7/1 Os of a percentage point behind the 30-year mortgage rate.

22. Schizophrenia is a psychotic disorder. That is, it:
    a. involves the symptom of the afflicted person losing contact with reality.
    b. is most effectively treated with psychotherapies rather than drug therapies.
    c. inevitably results in a slow, painful death in which the individual is tormented by peers.
    d. is a violent disorder. As a result many people with schizophrenia have to be incarcerated.

23. Flattened affect is to hallucination as ___ is to ___.
    a. neurosis; psychosis
    b. psychosis; neurosis
    c. positive symptom; negative symptom
    d. negative symptom; positive symptom

24. Someone with antisocial personality disorder is:
    a. outcast, and transforms feelings of rejection into positive feedback.
    b. typically in late adulthood before symptoms develop sufficiently for diagnosis.
    c. characterized as deceitful, impulsive, and reckless and feels no remorse for her or his behavior.
    d. fun to be with at parties because even though others do not treat them well, they have what Freud referred to as strong unconscious needs to enrich the lives of others.

25. Transsexualism:
    a. is a particular form of paraphilia.
    b. is another name for homosexuality.
    c. is approximately three times more common in males than females.
    d. involves thinking like one gender, and acting like the other gender.

Answers to Key Word Exercise

1. personal distress	2. behavioral model	3. Generalized anxiety disorder
4. Incidence	5. dysthymic disorder	6. dissociative identity disorder
7. Learned helplessness	8. arbitrary inference	9. delusion
10. smaller		

Practice Test Answers and Explanations

1. d. Adherence to rules for alternative fashion is not a criterion for abnormality.
2. c. *Dysfunctional* is a term used to describe behaviors that adversely affect functioning.
3. d. *Social norms* are guidelines for what is acceptable and what is unacceptable for a particular group.
4. c. Surveys have demonstrated that people grossly overestimate the frequency with which the insanity plea is used, and the likelihood that people who use it will be successful.
5. c. Psychological models reflect perspectives on behavioral issues. Medical models focus on organic causes (as they do with physical illnesses).
6. c. Anorexia nervosa occurs mainly in Western cultures where thinness is considered a sign of beauty.
7. a. Diagnosis is used primarily to make predictions about patterns in people's behaviors.
8. a. People acting as if they had experienced hallucinations were diagnosed and treated as if they had mental illness.
9. b. The American *Psychiatric* Association developed the Diagnostic and Statistical Manual of Mental Disorders (DSM). The DSM is in its fourth edition (DSM-N).
10. c. Epidemiologists estimate the distributions and causes of maladies, accidents, and problems.
11. b. Comorbid disorders are disorders that co-occur; often people who experience symptoms of one disorder also experience symptoms of additional disorders.
12. b. Phobias are fears, often stemming from experiences that comprise a specific category of anxiety disorder.
13. a. Panic disorder is considered the most severe anxiety disorder.
14. c. Obsessions are repetitive thoughts; compulsions are acts (often targeted at allaying obsessions).
15. a. Somatoform disorders involve physical symptoms with no known medical cause.
16. c. Hypochondriasis involves the interpretation of normal bodily symptoms as indices that one is contracting dreaded disease.
17. a. The symptoms of dissociative fugue include amnesia, flight from the workplace or home, and establishing a new identity.
18. c. More people seem to be developing depression at earlier ages.
19. b. People with severe depression are at great risk for suicide.
20. c. People with bipolar disorder show symptoms of depression and mania, in alternation.
21. b. Concordance refers to the percentage of twin pairs in which both twins have a disorder.
22. a. Psychosis is any disorder in which a severely disturbed individual loses contact with reality.
23. d. Negative symptoms are reductions in functioning, such as failing to show appropriate emotional responses. Positive symptoms are excesses or distortions in normal functioning, as with hallucinations.

24. c.   Antisocial personality disorder is characterized by deceitful, impulsive, and reckless activity for which one feels no remorse.

25. c.   Transsexualism is approximately three times more common in males than females.

Key Vocabulary Terms

Use the following list to write definitions *in your own words* for each of the key terms from the chapter. Translating the terms into language that is comfortable and familiar for you will facilitate your learning. For further study of these terms, go to the companion website for the textbook where you will find electronic flash cards that you may use to test your vocabulary.

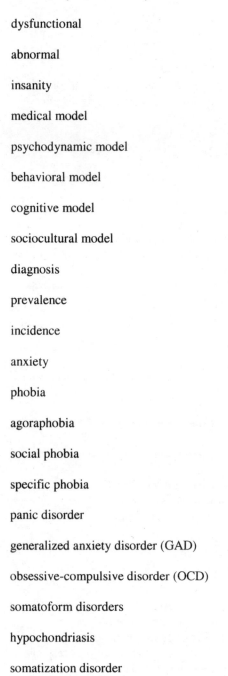

dysfunctional

abnormal

insanity

medical model

psychodynamic model

behavioral model

cognitive model

sociocultural model

diagnosis

prevalence

incidence

anxiety

phobia

agoraphobia

social phobia

specific phobia

panic disorder

generalized anxiety disorder (GAD)

obsessive-compulsive disorder (OCD)

somatoform disorders

hypochondriasis

somatization disorder

conversion disorder

dissociative disorders

dissociative amnesia

dissociative fugue

dissociative identity disorder (multiple personality)

depression

mania

bipolar disorder

concordance rate

learned helplessness

arbitrary inference

schizophrenia

psychosis

delusion

hallucinations

personality disorders

antisocial personality disorder

gender identity disorder (transsexualism)

paraphilia

fetishism

Tip for Success: The Psychology Major

Psychology is a popular major at both the undergraduate and graduate levels. The diversity of psychology means that it holds something of interest for many students. Students who take an introductory psychology course are sometimes surprised when they realize that the discipline has implications for so many other academic areas, as well as for a range of career opportunities.

This last *Tip* section addresses some common questions and concerns for students considering a major in psychology. After reviewing this section, you may wish to make an appointment with a professor from your school's psychology department to pursue additional questions. The career services office, library, and the Internet are other places you can look for answers about a potential major in psychology.

Finally, a recently developed resource that provides a thorough review of issues surrounding psychology, including academic issues and career possibilities and considerations, may be of interest to you. The book is called *The Psychology Major: Career Options and Strategies for Success,* and was written by R. Eric Landrum and Stephen F. Davis (Dr. Davis is one of the authors of your textbook, so if you find the writing style in your textbook to be appealing, you will likely also appreciate *The Psychology Major*).

The following items may be of interest to you:

1. Psychology beyond the Introductory Course. The psychology curriculum varies from school to school. The courses offered in most psychology departments may be considered as extensions of the chapters from your introductory textbook. Here is a list of common courses:

a. Methodology: an introduction to the tools and techniques used by psychologists in their research. This course goes by various names, including Experimental Psychology, Psychological Methods, Psychological Research Methods, and so on. The methodology course is usually required for majors, and is considered an important part of the curriculum by graduate school admissions committees.

b. Statistics: topics include sampling, distributions, probability, descriptive, and inferential statistics. This course may be taught in the psychology department or in the math department at your school. It is usually required as a prerequisite for much of the upper-division psychology curriculum.

c. Developmental Psychology: a study of the physical, cognitive, and psychosocial processes of development. Some schools offer a lifespan development course; others offer separate courses that are based on age ranges.

d. Social Psychology: a study of how people think about, influence, and relate to one another. This class covers a range of interesting topics including altruism, group influences, and prejudice.

e. Abnormal Psychology: a survey of psychological disorders, their characteristics, and their origins. This course represents the aspect of psychology with which lay people are most familiar.

f. Cognitive Psychology: a study of cognitive and memory processes. Topics covered in this course may range from artificial intelligence to biologically based theories of memory formation.

g. Learning: an examination of theories, ranging from the classic to the contemporary, that have been developed to explain learning and related phenomena. The data that support theories in this area are typically from nonhuman animals.

h. Physiological Psychology: an introduction to the nervous system and its relationship to behavior and experience. Students of biology and physiology often take this course as well.

i. Psychological Testing: an introduction to theory underlying test construction, evaluation, and interpretation. This is an important course for those students who may be interested in working in school systems or with clinical populations. This course is sometimes called *Assessment* or *Tests and Measurement*.

j. Personality: a survey of psychological theories and research in the study of personality. Some instructors for this course emphasize theoretical issues; others focus more on research.

k. History and Systems: a study of the development of psychology. This course usually surveys psychology's historical roots in philosophy and the natural sciences. It is a senior-level, capstone course in many programs.

Compare this list with the course offerings in your school catalog. What additional classes are available at your school? Which courses are you interested in taking?

_____

_____

2. Getting Involved in Research. Most academic psychologists have research interests that are accessible to undergraduate students. If you convey your interest in helping with research, you may get an opportunity to become involved. Participating in research is arguably the best way for you to demonstrate initiative and commitment to your career. Establish a goal of presenting findings from a research project at a psychology convention. Attending and presenting data at conventions is a great way to meet others who share an interest in psychology, to get research ideas, and to learn about the latest developments in the field.

What topic(s) are you most interested in researching?

_____

_____

3. Getting an Internship. In addition to participating in research, you may want to do a psychology internship at a clinic, laboratory, school, or business in your town. Internships can be helpful in determining whether you should pursue a given line of study in psychology, and may even open up job opportunities if you decide to seek employment after graduation. If you are interested in doing an internship, consult a professor from your psychology department who can share with you the department's policies and procedures regarding student internships.

What careers in psychology would you like to learn more about?

_____

_____

4. Careers with a Bachelor's Degree in Psychology. People with academic training in psychology hold a wide variety of positions. Often, psychology-related careers require some level of graduate training, but there are many jobs that one can get with bachelor's level training in psychology. The following list indicates areas in which people who studied psychology at the bachelor's level have found meaningful employment.

a. Education and Teaching

      b. Consulting and Statistics

      c. Administration/Clerical

      d. Professional Services

      e. Sales

      f. Health and Related Services

      g. Research and Development

5. Careers with Graduate Degrees in Psychology. After completing your bachelor's degree, you may choose to pursue graduate education in psychology. There are a several options to consider if you are interested in graduate training. Are your interests in applied careers (e.g., industrial and organizational psychology, school psychology, counseling)? Are you interested in doing basic research in psychology or a related discipline (e.g., neuroscience)? Would you enjoy teaching as part of your career? The answers to these questions will have some bearing on your decision about whether to pursue graduate training.

Depending on which career(s) you are interested in, you may plan to complete a master's degree or a doctoral degree. Some undergraduate psychology majors attend professional schools (e.g., medical school, law school) after finishing their undergraduate work. Master's degrees and professional degrees are usually preparation for applied work, whereas a doctorate is required if one is interested in teaching at the college level and in some career fields (e.g., clinical psychology).

Will additional schooling be required for you given your present career interests? If so, how will you begin learning about graduate programs to suit your needs? If not, what can you do as an undergraduate student to improve your chances of getting the job you are interested in?

6. Identifying a Role Model or Mentor. Many of the most successful people gained their success by working with, or otherwise modeling themselves after, other successful people. Find someone who has the career in which you are interested. Ask that person if you can make an appointment to interview her or him in order that you can learn more about everything the job entails. Assuming you are able to get an appointment, plan your questions ahead of time and take notes during the meeting. The following are some items you may wish to address:

      a. Educational Background. Where did the person attend school? What subject(s) did he or she study? What were critical steps and turning points that helped her or him get the job? How long has he or she been in the position?

      b. Job Characteristics. What kinds of things constitute the person's daily responsibilities and activities? How much time does the person spend on career-related work each week? What are the advantages and disadvantages of that career as that person perceives them?

      c. Is There Anything You Can Do? Make certain to communicate your interest in learning outside the classroom. Indicate that you would like to participate in research, read and discuss journal articles, help out with filing, or anything else the person might suggest. Initially you may have less than glamorous responsibilities, but if you do good work and are reliable, you will gain greater opportunities. This may be the beginning of an instructive and mutually beneficial relationship.

CHAPTER 13

Therapy

Do You Know?

Do you know that treating psychological disorders is as complicated as diagnosing them? Many people consider the causes of psychological disorders to be some form of biochemical imbalance in the person's nervous system. According to this notion, having disrupted nervous system chemistry leads to malfunctioning of the nervous system, and the malfunctioning manifests itself in behavioral abnormalities. Because different portions of the nervous system rely chiefly on different neurotransmitters and related substances, the behavioral abnormalities associated with problems in one part of the brain are different than those associated with another part of the brain.

As a result of this thinking, the medical model for treating psychological disorders has tended to be associated with pharmacological, or drug treatment in order to eliminate unwanted behavioral symptoms. While the logic of using biomedical treatment to address problems that stem from chemical imbalances, it is important to note that the origin of imbalance is not presented in this model. Thus, although drug therapies are commonly effective for many disorders, they are rarely enough to help the person of interest return to normal living. Typically behavioral therapies are prescribed to accompany drug therapies.

The increased success of treatment when biotherapies are combined with behavioral therapies underscore the importance for psychology in what might otherwise appear as an area that could be addressed entirely via medicine. Indeed, it may well be that the origins of any chemical disturbances have to do with patterns of behavior that disrupt normal activity in the brain. Just as there is good rationale for treating chemical deficiencies with drugs, so, too, it is logical to consider an appropriate treatment for a behavioral problem with behavioral therapy. Using two or more therapeutic approaches in concert complicates treatment, but then when one considers the complexities of human behavior, it may be too simplistic to think that one therapeutic domain can handle what are likely to be multifaceted problems.

Notes from Class and the Textbook

Use the space provided in this outline to record notes from the textbook as well as from class lectures and discussion. Questions related to the *Psychological Detective, Hands On, Myth or Science* and *Study Tip* sections in the text have been presented in the outline; use the associated space to respond to the questions and to record your own comments about the issues.

I. Therapy Through the Ages

        A. The History of Therapy

                1. Asylums and Hospitals

                2. Moral Therapy

                3. State Mental Hospitals

                4. New Forms of Treatment

5. Deinstitutionalization

6. The Community Mental Health Movement

Construct a timeline of the history of therapy from ancient Greek times to the present. Briefly describe each era in your timeline.

B. Therapy and Therapists

1. Types of Therapists

II. Psychologically–Based Therapies

A. Psychoanalytic Therapy

1. Free Association

2. Dream Interpretation

3. Resistance

4. Transference

5. Evaluation of Psychoanalysis

Draw a cartoon to illustrate each of the four processes of psychoanalytic therapy that are discussed in your textbook.

B. Humanistic Therapies

1. Client-Centered Therapy

2. Gestalt Therapy

C. Cognitive Therapies

1. Rational-Emotive Behavior Therapy (REBT)

2. Beck's Cognitive Therapy

Think of an example when someone might have overgeneralized something about your behavior based on an isolated incident, such as low performance on an exam. Describe what inferences they may have made about you as well as how you might convince them that the inferences do not fit your person.

Take the Assertiveness Questionnaire on pages 566 and 567 in your textbook. Total your score and compare it with others from your class or study group.

3. Stress Inoculation Training

Form an even-numbered group of student pairs. Follow the directions on page 567 to study the humanistic and cognitive therapies that are covered in the textbook.

D. Behavior Therapies

1. Systematic Desensitization

Describe a procedure for combining progressive relaxation with scenes related to a particular phobia to reduce fear. Why might this technique be effective?

2. Aversion Therapy

3. Modeling

4. Extinction

What can one do to extinguish the undesired behavior of others? What can one expect to happen during the early stages of the extinction process?

5. Punishment

6. Token Economy

What are some advantages of using tokens to reward behavior? What steps can be taken to ensure that tokens have value?

E. Group Therapies

1. Marital and Family Therapy

F. Self-Help

III. The Effectiveness of Psychotherapy

    A. Characteristics of Effective Psychotherapy

    B. Psychotherapy and the Needs of Diversity

    C. When to Begin Psychotherapy and What to Expect

IV. Biomedical Therapies

    A. Drug Therapy

        1. Antianxiety Drugs

        2. Antidepressant Drugs

        3. Mood Stabilizers

        4. Antipsychotic Drugs

        5. Variations in Drug Response Related to Ethnicity and Sex

Develop a written device to help you remember the different types of drugs used in drug therapy, their functions, and examples of each. Try writing a song or poem, creating an acronym, or making up a story.

B. Electroconvulsive Therapy

What effect would ECT have on a patient immediately after treatment? What psychological processes would be affected?

ECT involves inducing a seizure in a patient as a form of therapy. Proponents of the technique describe its benefits for some patients, while opponents cite claims of impaired brain functioning. Read the paragraph that begins on page 588 in your textbook to learn how MRI may be used to assess whether ECT brings about brain damage.

C. Psychosurgery

Learning Objectives

After you have studied the chapter, you should be able to respond to the following statements and questions to convey your understanding of the material.

1. Discuss the history of treatment approaches for the mentally ill.

2. What are key differentiating elements of psychoanalytic therapy, humanistic therapy, cognitive therapy, behavior therapy, and group therapy?

3. What are some important considerations when evaluating the effectiveness of psychotherapy?

4. Compare and contrast biomedical therapies (drug therapy, ECT, and psychosurgery).

Key Word Exercise

Fill in the blanks in the following statements with key words and terms from the textbook. Answer as many as you can without referring to your notes or to the book. If you have blanks after thinking about each item, try using your book. The answers are presented after the practice test.

1. _____ convinced many states to build institutions to treat people suffering from mental disorders.

2. The policy of discharging mentally ill patients from institutions on the assumption that they can be cared for in their communities is called _____.

3. A feature of *extinction* as a form of therapy is that the frequency of the undesirable response often _____ initially.

4. Andy gets a coin for every nice thing he says or does during a day, and loses four coins every time he is mean. Andy is on a _____.

5. Jayme is suffering from _____ _____ as a result of taking antipsychotic drugs. Her symptoms include involuntary motor symptoms.

6. Research with people from different cultures who have various disorders has revealed that Asians   require _____ doses of some drugs (e.g., tricyclic antidepressants, lithium) than Caucasians.

7. Freud called _____ "the royal road to the unconscious". They presumably consist of manifest and latent content.

8. A form of therapy in which therapists may frustrate and challenge clients to lead them toward self-acceptance is called _____ _____.

9. One of the most effective techniques for treating phobias is _____.

10. A guiding principle for _____-_____ groups is that compassion and understanding do not require advanced degrees.

Practice Test

Circle the letter that corresponds to the *best* alternative for each of the following items. Read each alternative carefully. The answers are presented at the end of this study guide chapter. Be sure to learn *why* each correct alternative is better than the others.

1. *Bedlam* is a term used to describe disorganized, unorganized conditions. The term came from:
   a. the Greek word for chaos.
   b. a contraction of Bethlehem.
   c. the first letters in each ancient, pre-Hippocrates form of psychological treatment.
   d. the mid-1950s when psychotherapeutic drugs were first being administered to patients.

2. Philippe Pinel, Jean-Baptiste Pussin, and Benjamin Rush had in common:
   a. that they all recovered from mental illness.
   b. that they all advocated moral/humane treatment of mental patients.
   c. ancestry in Dorothea Dix, a leader in the mental health movement.
   d. a view that people with psychological disorders were possessed by demons.

3. The first antipsychotic drug was available in:
   a. 1945.
   b. 1950.
   c. 1955.
   d. 1960.

4. ___ prevention is designed to reduce the damage caused by disorders for both the patients and society.
   a. Drug
   b. Primary
   c. Tertiary
   d. Secondary

5. Biomedical therapies include all but which of the following?
   a. drug therapy
   b. psychotherapy
   c. psychosurgery
   d. electroconvulsive therapy

6. People with master's degrees who have job titles such as *psychotherapist* and *counselor* are accountable to licensing boards:
   a. but are not necessarily regulated by state or federal agencies.
   b. but are called *psychologists* by the American Psychological Association.
   c. and are therefore to be trusted with one's problems and confidential concerns.
   d. ironing boards, surf boards, pegboards, running boards, and many other types of boards.

7. Free association is:
   a. the original name for state-supported in-patient mental institutions.
   b. the name for reinforced trials in a classical conditioning experiment.
   c. a psychoanalytic technique in which the patient reports whatever comes to mind.
   d. far more expensive than the name implies because of taxes imposed by federal legislation.

8. Researchers of psychoanalytic therapy face all but which of the following?
   a. hypothetical constructs that are hard to define and measure
   b. knowing when the essential elements of treatment are present
   c. the difficulty of defining the essential elements of the treatment
   d. Sigmund Freud as they lie on his couch and report on their experiences

9. Carl Rogers is to ___ as Aaron Beck is to ___.
   a. humanistic therapy; cognitive therapy
   b. cognitive therapy; humanistic therapy
   c. behavior therapy; Gestalt therapy
   d. Gestalt therapy; behavior therapy

10. Stress inoculation training:
    a. is required of all emergency room physicians for licensure.
    b. helps clients interpret events and develop self-talk that reduces stress levels.
    c. involves learning to give one's self shots to combat the stresses of daily living.
    d. all of the above

11. Hank employed *systematic desensitization* to overcome his fear of entering libraries. This technique:
    a. probably involved a good deal of reading.
    b. is based on principles from classical conditioning.
    c. was pioneered by Freud as a means of dealing with repression.
    d. was developed by cognitive therapists in response to symptoms that eventually led to depression.

12. Some alcoholics have used a drug called Antabuse (disulfiram) when trying to stop drinking. This approach to therapy fits with which of the following categories?
    a. aversion therapy
    b. inoculation training
    c. maltreatment of insects
    d. systematic desensitization

13. Which of the following was *not* identified in the textbook as an advantage of group therapy?
    a. anonymity
    b. social support
    c. opportunities to receive feedback
    d. opportunities to practice coping skills

14. *Spontaneous remission* is:
    a. analogous to psychological recidivism.
    b. a term used to describe improvement without treatment.
    c. an index of severe psychosis, usually undifferentiated type.
    d. an early symptom of depression and can be treated successfully with psychotherapy.

15. Antianxiety drugs:
    a. are also known as minor tranquilizers.
    b. can reduce the severity of physiological symptoms (e.g., heart rate).
    c. increase the ability of GABA to bind to receptor sites at synapses in the brain.
    d. all of the above

16. Which is *not* one of the three major classes of antidepressant drugs?
    a. major tranquilizers
    b. tricyclic antidepressants
    c. monoamine oxidase inhibitors
    d. selective serotonin reuptake inhibitors

17. A therapeutic technique that involves inducing seizures and has been effective with some depressed patients is:
    a. ECT.
    b. drug therapy.
    c. psychosurgery.
    d. all of the above

18. When patients have received ECT as a treatment for a psychological illness, they often report confusion and a lack of memory for the experience. This is because:
    a. they are administered drugs that block their memories.
    b. they are hypnotized prior to undergoing the therapy session.
    c. people with psychological illnesses have impaired memories.
    d. electric shock seems to disrupt the memory consolidation process.

19. Today, psychosurgery is:
    a. less common than it was in the 1930s.
    b. more common than it was in the 1930s.
    c. limited to an experimental procedure for treating schizophrenia.
    d. being studied in hundreds of labs as people strive for the ultimate treatment for anxiety.

20. The natural mineral salt *lithium* is used:
    a. to treat tardive dyskinesia.
    b. to treat symptoms of bipolar disorder.
    c. recreationally by many substance abusers.
    d. in place of sodium chloride for people who use psychotherapeutic drugs.

Answers to Key Word Exercise

1. Dorothea Dix	2. deinstitutionalization	3. increases
4. token economy	5. tardive dyskinesia	6. lower
7. dreams	8. Gestalt therapy	9. modeling
10. self-help		

PRACTICE TEST ANSWERS AND EXPLANATIONS

1. b. Bedlam is a contraction of Bethlehem, as in the St. Mary of Bethlehem Hospital in London.
2. b. Though they worked on different continents, and with different interpretations of what is humane, all three were interested in employing therapeutic techniques that were morally based.
3. c. The first antipsychotic drug was available for use in 1955.
4. c. An example of tertiary prevention is an after-care program for patients living in a mental hospital.
5. b. Psychotherapy is an example of a psychological, rather than a biomedical, therapy.
6. a. It is important to choose mental health professionals carefully as many are not regulated by government agencies.
7. c. Free association is a psychoanalytic technique in which the patient reports whatever comes to mind.
8. d. Sigmund Freud is dead. The problems with researching psychoanalytic therapy have to do with the nature of the definitions and the fact that psychoanalytic theory does not lend itself to testing.
9. a. Rogers was a humanistic psychologist who practiced *client-centered* therapy; Beck is a cognitive therapist and has focused much of his work on depression.
10. b. Stress inoculation training helps clients learn to interpret and respond to stress differently.
11. b. Systematic desensitization is a technique that represents an application of classical conditioning.
12. a. Inasmuch as Antabuse causes one to become nauseous when it is present in the body with alcohol, this is a form of aversion therapy.
13. a. Anonymity is not a feature of group therapy as comments are shared with everyone present.
14. b. Spontaneous remission is a term used to describe improvement without treatment.
15. d. All of these are true of antianxiety drugs.
16. a. Major tranquilizers are used to treat psychoses, not depression.
17. a. ECT is effective, for reasons that are not well understood, in treating some people with depression.
18. d. ECT disrupts memory consolidation.
19. a. Psychosurgery was performed on untold numbers of people in the 1930s. Today, psychosurgery is rare and only considered as a last resort.
20. b. Lithium is used to stabilize the moods of people suffering from bipolar disorder.

Key Vocabulary Terms

Use the following list to write definitions *in your own words* for each of the key terms from the chapter. Translating the terms into language that is comfortable and familiar for you will facilitate your learning. For further study of these terms, go to the companion website for the textbook where you will find electronic flash cards that you may use to test your vocabulary.

deinstitutionalization

biomedical therapies

psychological therapies

psychotherapy

psychoanalytic therapy

free association

resistance

transference

humanistic therapies

client-centered therapy

gestalt therapy

cognitive therapies

rational-emotive behavior therapy (REBT)

stress inoculation training

systematic desensitization

aversion therapy

token economy

group therapy

antianxiety drugs

antipsychotic drugs

tardive dyskinesia

electroconvulsive therapy (ECT)

psychotherapy

CHAPTER 14

Health Psychology

Do You Know?

Do you know that the nervous system, the endocrine system, and the immune system are intimately connected to one another? Is some ways these systems have to be related, so it may seem obvious to state that their relationship is significant. However, only recently have scientists begun to discover the extent to which the activity in one of these systems influences the other systems. For example, when one experiences stress, the cognitive appraisal of stressful circumstances results in the endocrine system's release of hormones into the bloodstream to help combat the stressful situation. In the short run, this response is very adaptive. However, when exposure to stressful circumstances is prolonged, the extended presence of hormones, including the body's own steroids, epinephrine and norepinephrine, negatively influences immune system functioning. Thus, as a consequence of continued exposure to stressful events and situations, one becomes more susceptible to diseases because foreign matter such as bacteria and viruses can more easily attack one's body when immune system functioning is compromised.

The good news is that there are positive as well as negative effects of the close relationships of these important systems. That is, while the thinking that results in the experience of stress may lead to detrimental effects on the body, it is also possible to engage in thinking that leads to improved health. Indeed, much of the challenge of researchers working in the field of psychoneuroimmunology is to determine to what extent thought can influence endocrine and immune system functioning and how best to apply such understanding. References to the power of positive thinking as illustrated in stories such as *The Little Engine that Could*, and the song about the ant wishing to move a rubber tree plant seem to be consistent with the nature of influence that the brain is able to exert over the body.

Notes from Class and the Textbook

Use the space provided in this outline to record notes from the textbook as well as from class lectures and discussion. Questions related to the *Psychological Detective, Hands On, Myth or Science,* and *Study Tip* sections in the text have been presented in the outline; use the associated space to respond to the questions and to record your own comments about the issues.

I. Health Psychology: An Overview

II. Stress and Illness

Point your Web browser at the textbook's Web page to see Live!Psych module 14.1.

    A. The General Adaptation Syndrome

        1. Alarm Stage

2. Resistance Stage

What relationship, if any, exists between the stress one experiences and one's vulnerability to colds and other illnesses? Read the Myth or Science paragraph on page 597 to learn more.

3. Exhaustion Stage

B. Sources of Stress

1. Catastrophes

2. Major Life Events

Why is there variation among people with respect to the physical and psychological symptoms they develop in response to stress?

3. Acculturative Stress

4. Posttraumatic Stress Disorder

5. Everyday Hassles

C. What Makes Events Stressful?

D. How Stress and Disease May Be Related

Point your Web browser at the textbook's Web page to see Live!Psych module 14.2.

1. Psychoneuroimmunology

III. Lifestyle Influences on Disease Risk

A. Smoking

1. Who Smokes and Why?

What factors can account for the trend that the number of smokers has declined over the past decade?

2. Quitting the Smoking Habit

B. Heart Disease

    1. The Toxic Component of Type A Behavior

Take the Are You a Hostile Person? questionnaire on page 611 in your textbook. Instructions for scoring your responses are presented on page 612.

    2. Reducing the Risk of Heart Disease

C. Acquired Immunodeficiency Syndrome (AIDS)

    1. HIV: A Global Perspective

D. Stress in the Workplace

    1. Burnout

    2. Stress and Women in the Workplace

How would you account for the difference between stress levels of people who work in nonprofit versus for-profit workplaces?

IV. Coping With Stress

    A. Psychological Moderators of Stress

        1. Hardiness

        2. Explanatory Style

        3. Distraction

        4. Social Support

        5. Sense of Humor

With four other people, consider each of the five psychological moderators of stress. Each person should provide a brief overview of one of the moderators, then the group could brainstorm for examples.

    B. Reducing Arousal with Relaxation and Physical Activity

        1. Relaxation Techniques

        2. Physical Activity

        3. Does Physical Activity Reduce Stress?

What are some of the difficulties researchers face in trying to demonstrate the effects of physical activity on stress reactions?

Write a brief evaluation of your own mind-body connection in light of material from the textbook's chapter on health. Identify both positive and negative effects of your behaviors on your health. What mechanisms do you employ to cope with stress?

Learning Objectives

After you have studied the chapter, you should be able to respond to the following statements and questions to convey your understanding of the material.

1. Describe the General Adaptation Syndroms (GAS).

2. Identify several common sources of stress.

3. Differentiate between risk factors for heart disease that can and cannot be modified.

4. What is the role of nutrition and eating in stress and stress-related issues?

5. What are several steps one can take to cope effectively with stress?

Key Word Exercise

Fill in the blanks in the following statements with key words and terms from the textbook. Answer as many as you can without referring to your notes or to the book. If you have blanks after thinking about each item, try using your book. The answers are presented after the practice test.

1. A(n) _____ is anything that causes one to adjust and display the nonspecific stress response.

2. When a stressful situation continues beyond the alarm stage, the body moves into the second stage of the general adaptation syndrome, known as the _____ stage.

3. Unpredictable catastrophes, such as fires and hurricanes, are _____ _____ _____.

4. In an _____ - _____ conflict, the goal's positive values attract us while its negative features repulse us.

5. _____ is the study of how psychological and physical factors interact to influence the immune system.

6. Reductions in recurring heart attacks are more likely with counseling to reduce _____ _____ behavior or personality in comparison to counseling related to heart disease only.

7. _____ _____ _____ is a numerical index calculated from a person's height and weight that is used to indicate health status and disease risk.

8. The three Cs—commitment, control, and challenge—seem to make the _____ individuals more resistant to the negative effects of stressors.

9. _____ support can play a role in reducing the possible negative side-effects of major life events.

Practice Test

Circle the letter that corresponds to the ***best*** alternative for each of the following items. Read each alternative carefully. The answers are presented at the end of this study guide chapter. Be sure to learn *why* each correct alternative is better than the others.

1. Deaths owing to infectious diseases have increased 58 percent from 1980 to 1992. Much of that increase was the result of:
    a. AIDS.
    b. glucocorticoids.
    c. general adaptation syndrome (GAS).
    d. posttraumatic stress disorder (PTSD).

2. Another name for the well-known fight-or-flight response is:
    a. anxiety.
    b. alarm stage.
    c. resistance stage.
    d. primitive fear response.

3. When demands for adjustment exceed the body's ability to respond, the body enters the:
    a. twilight zone.
    b. posttraumatic syndrome.
    c. exhaustion stage of the GAS.
    d. fight-or-flight response stage.

4. A set of symptoms that may follow deeply disturbing events is called:
    a. nerve-wracking.
    b. adaptation stage.
    c. psychophysiological fear.
    d. posttraumatic stress disorder.

5. Slow-moving traffic, long lines at the supermarket, and lost keys are examples of:
    a. hassles.
    b. annoying habits.
    c. newsworthy events.
    d. symptoms of stress.

6. Determining whether an event is a threat is to ___ as deciding how to deal with the stress-producing situation is to ___.
    a. primary appraisal; secondary appraisal
    b. secondary appraisal; primary appraisal
    c. implementation stage; evaluation stage
    d. decision-action stage; recuperation stage

7. The substances that trigger an immune response are:
    a. illegal.
    b. called antigens.
    c. released by the stressor(s).
    d. hard to identity, but easy to deal with.

8. About ___ percent of smokers smoked their first cigarette before the age of 18.
    a. 13
    b. 50
    c. 76
    d. 90

9. Although someone in the U.S. dies of heart disease about every 34 seconds, many of those deaths can be prevented. Which of the following risk factors *cannot* be modified?
    a. stress
    b. obesity
    c. hypertension
    d. increasing age

10. Hypertension varies as a function of one's:
    a. race.
    b. gender.
    c. lifestyle.
    d. all of the above

11. HDL is to LDL as ___ is to___.
    a. hypertension; hypothermia
    b. hypothermia; Harpo Marx
    c. "good cholesterol"; "bad cholesterol"
    d. risk for hypertension; risk for glucocorticoids

12. Type A behavior is:
    a. healthy for promoting HDL.
    b. negatively correlated with risk of heart disease.
    c. associated with competitiveness, aggressiveness, and achievement drive.
    d. the first behavior that is shown by humans; by adulthood, humans usually exhibit Type R (R is for risk) behavior.

13. ___ accounts for most of the cases of HIV in sub-Sahara, Africa.
   a. Incest
   b. Homosexual sex
   c. Intravenous drug use
   d. Unprotected heterosexual sex

14. Which group of subjects experienced the least pain while submerging their arms in a tank of ice cold water?
   a. the group that imagined scenes such as riding on a merry-go-round at a carnival (distraction group)
   b. the group that imagined they were in a hot desert on a very hot day (reinterpretation group)
   c. the group that reinterpreted the sensation as refreshing by imagining they were hot and tired
   d. All groups showed comparable reduction in pain.

15. Which of the following statements is true?
   a. While a sense of humor can be fun it does not seem to buffer stress.
   b. Even a little sense of humor can be helpful in buffering the effects of stressors.
   c. These was a significant difference between people with "average" and "high" senses of humor with respect to incidence of depression as a function of *average* levels of negative life stressors.
   d. These was a significant difference between people with "average" and "high" senses of humor with respect to incidence of depression as a function of *high* levels of negative life stressors.

16. There is converging evidence from correlational and experimental research to indicate that:
   a. exercise aids in dealing with stress.
   b. anaerobic and aerobic exercise are equally helpful in dealing with stress.
   c. exercise is negatively correlated with stress reduction, as was indicated in experimental research.
   d. one must dedicate time exclusively for exercising in order to reap any benefits with respect to stress reduction through exercise.

Answers to Key Word Exercise

1. stressor	2. resistance	3. sources of stress
4. approach-avoidance	5. Psychoneuroimmunology	6. Type A
7. Body mass index (BMI)	8. hardy	10. Social

Practice Test Answers and Explanations

1. a.　Acquired immunodeficiency syndrome was responsible for much of the increase.
2. b.　The alarm stage of the general adaptation syndrome is the same as the fight-or flight response.
3. c.　The exhaustion stage of the GAS is the third phase of the typical biological response to stressors.
4. d.　Posttraumatic (PTSD) stress disorder is characterized by symptoms that may follow deeply disturbing events.
5. a.　Hassles are minor everyday occurrences that are distressing, frustrating, and irritating.
6. a.　One has to determine whether something is a stress before deciding what to do about it.
7. b.　Antigens (e.g., bacteria, fungi, parasites, viruses) are the substances that trigger immune responses.
8. d.　About 90 percent of smokers began smoking by age 18. Consequently, more effort is directed toward preventing smoking by people in this age group.
9. d.　Age, gender, and heredity cannot be modified. However, many of the significant risk factors for heart disease can be modified.
10. d.　All of the above are related differentially to hypertension.
11. c.　High levels of HDL (high-density lipoprotein) cholesterol are desirable, whereas one does not want high levels of LDL (low-density lipoprotein) cholesterol.
12. c.　Type A behavior is associated with competitiveness, aggressiveness, and achievement drive.
13. d.　Unprotected heterosexual sex is most closely linked with HIV in sub-Sahara, Africa.
14. d.　The three groups (imagination, reinterpretation, and distraction) responded comparably.
15. b.　Even a little sense of humor can be helpful in buffering the effects of stressors.

16. a.   Exercise aids in dealing with stress.

Key Vocabulary Terms

Use the following list to write definitions *in your own words* for each of the key terms from the chapter. Translating the terms into language that is comfortable and familiar for you will facilitate your learning. For further study of these terms, go to the companion website for the textbook where you will find electronic flash cards that you may use to test your vocabulary.

health psychology

stress

stressor

general adaptation syndrome (GAS)

acculturative stress

posttraumatic stress disorder (PTSD)

conflict

primary appraisal

secondary appraisal

immune system

antigens

type A behavior

human immunodeficiency virus (HIV)

acquired immunodeficiency syndrome (AIDS)

burnout

coping

hardiness

social support

progressive relaxation

relaxation response

biofeedback

CHAPTER 15

Social Psychology: The Individual in Society

Do You Know?

Do you know that the concepts of conformity and compliance extend into daily living of people who are well beyond the years that are typically considered to be most closely associated with peer influence? Social psychologists define conformity as initiating or changing behavior in response to indirect social pressures, whereas compliance is initiating or changing a behavior in response to a request. While it might seem that circumstances that lead to compliance would likely always be obvious, people often find themselves behaving in ways that they later call into question as a result of phenomena and effects that social psychologists study.

One interesting compliance phenomenon is the foot-in-the-door effect. Did you ever notice that telemarketers and other sales people, particularly those who make 'cold' contact such as in door-to-door sales, begin with small questions to get you engaged in conversation? Once you have begun dialog, the impact of the effect has it that it is more difficult for you to terminate the conversation than if you had denied it at the outset. It is important to know that if you realize you are falling prey to the foot-in-the-door effect, you recognize also that just because you were agreeable initially, you need not continue. Understanding that it is okay to discontinue a series of behavioral decisions that is leading in an undesirable direction may save you time and money.

Alternatively, if you understand how the effect works, it is also possible for you to use it to your own benefit. I once received a parking ticket for backing into a parking place on state property (something that I had no idea was against the law). Rather disturbed by having received the ticket, and armed with a good understanding of the foot-in-the-door effect, I set about to fight the ticket. My line of reasoning began with some very simple questions with which the judge could not disagree—these questions addressed concerns of safety, whether he had witnessed the vehicle and pedestrian traffic at the time of day that I parked (about 6:00 a.m.) and at the time of day I usually left (about 4:00 p.m.). Having gotten him to answer several consecutive questions affirmatively, I began developing my plea to have him drop the charges using language that would capitalize on the pattern of affirmative responding. When I got to my plea, he realized what I had been doing, smiled, and tore up the ticket. Now, I do not for a minute believe that the foot-in-the-door effect would have worked to get me off of many other charges, but it was quite effective in addressing a situation that I imagine would have otherwise cost me a significant amount of money.

Notes from Class and the Textbook

Use the space provided in this outline to record notes from the textbook as well as from class lectures and discussion. Questions related to the *Psychological Detective, Hands On, Myth or Science,* and *Study Tip* sections in the text have been presented in the outline; use the associated space to respond to the questions and to record your own comments about the issues.

I. Social Psychology and Culture

II. How We View Others and Their Behavior

    A. Impression Formation

        1. Aspects of the Perceiver

Why do stereotypes persist in spite of the fact that individuals in a given category do not share the same personality traits?

      2. Aspects of the Actor

         a. Appearance

         b. Speech

         c. Nonverbal Communication

Complete the 25 item Self-Monitoring Scale that is presented on pages 631 and 632 in your textbook. Scoring instructions and interpretative comments for the true-false questionnaire are given on page 667 in your textbook.

         d. Prior Information

      3. Stereotype Activation

    B. Social Judgments: Attributing Causes to Behavior

      1. Internal versus External Causes

Use this space to record the attributions you assign to the three events presented in the Psychological Detective section on page 633 in your textbook.

    a. Distinctiveness

    b. Consistency

    c. Consensus

    d. Attributional Biases

Why do people sometimes possess illusions of control over chance circumstances? Read the paragraph beginning on page 633 in your textbook for insight into this issue.

    e. The Fundamental Attribution Error

Consider the attribution that quizmasters are always rated as smarter than contestants. Write down a few possible situational factors that may not be taken into account when one makes this attribution.

      f. The Actor-Perceiver Bias

Read the Study Tip suggestion from page 634 in your textbook. Use the tip to develop your understanding of actor-perceiver bias.

Record your attributions concerning the hypothetical situations presented on page 635 in your textbook.

    C. Attitudes

Point your Web browser at the textbook's Web page to see Live!Psych module 15.1.

III. Interpersonal Relations

    A. Attitudes

        1. Components of Attitudes: Affect, Cognition, and Behavior

        2. Functions of Attitudes

            a. Ego Defense

            b. Adjustment

            c. Knowledge

Create a mnemonic device to help you remember the components and functions of attitudes.

        3. Measuring Attitudes

            a. Likert Scales

            b. Behavioral Measures

4. How Are Attitudes Formed?

    a. Learning

    b. Cognitive Dissonance

B. Attraction

    1. Proximity

    2. Affect and Emotions

    3. Reinforcement

    4. Similarity

C. Friendship

    1. Self-Disclosure

D. Love

    1. Sex Roles

2. Marital Satisfaction and Dissatisfaction

What are some reasons that abused women (or men) stay in relationships with their abusive spouses?

E. Prosocial Behavior: Helping Others

    1. Situational and Personal Influences on Helping Behavior

D. Aggression

    1. Biological Views of Aggression

    2. Environmental Conditions and Aggression

How do situational variables impact the likelihood that a given experience will be frustrating?

    3. Sexual Aggression

IV. Social Influences on Behavior

    A. Persuasion

        1. Source Factors

           a. Expertise

           b. Attractiveness

Design an experiment to evaluate the role of attractiveness in persuasion. How is the experimental design similar to or different from one that looks into the role of expertise in attraction?

           c. Trustworthiness

        2. Message Factors

           a. Attention

           b. Drawing Conclusions

           c. Message Acceptance

What factors involved in persuasion are used by the advertising industry? List several examples?

d. Primacy and Recency Effects

3. Channel Factors

Is persuasion more effective in group or one-on-one situations?

4. Audience Factors

a. What We Attend to: The Central and Peripheral Routes of Persuasion

Create a mind map or think link for the section on persuasion. Utilize different colors for the different components of your organizer.

B. Obedience

C. Conformity and Compliance

What experimental control condition(s) were necessary for Asch to support his claim about conformity in the line experiment?

Point your web browser at the textbook's web page to see Live!Psych module 15.2.

V. THE INDIVIDUAL AS PART OF A SOCIAL GROUP

    A. Social Facilitation

    B. Social Loafing

    C. Audiences and Coactors

        1. Deindividuation

    D. Group Interactions and Group Decisions

        1. Good Formation and Effectiveness

        2. Brainstorming

Why are fewer ideas generated in group brainstorming sessions than when people work alone?

3. Groupthink

E. Prejudice and Discrimination

1. Prejudice

Where do prejudice-related comments and behaviors come given that most prejudices are general in nature?

2. Discrimination

3. Sources and Functions of Prejudice

a. Social Function

b. Emotional Function

4. How to Reduce Prejudice

LEARNING OBJECTIVES

After you have studied the chapter, you should be able to respond to the following statements and questions to convey your understanding of the material.

1. How does the presence of others, or being part of a group, influence individuals' behavior?

2. Discuss several factors contributing to patterns of social judgment or attributions.

3. What variables are important in developing and maintaining interpersonal relationships?

4. Differentiate between *persuasion, obedience,* and *conformity and compliance* as social influences on behavior.

5. Compare and contrast social facilitation and social loafing.

6. How do groups influence decision-making?

7. Discuss the development and maintenance of prejudice and discrimination from the perspective of a social psychologist.

KEY WORD EXERCISE

Fill in the blanks in the following statements with key words and terms from the textbook. Answer as many as you can without referring to your notes or to the book. If you have blanks after thinking about each item, try using your book. The answers are presented after the practice test.

1. Research on _____ - _____, the amount of personal information a person is willing to share with others, indicates that the more a person reveals, the more positive others' impressions are.

2. The internal attribution bias that involves attending more closely to a behavior than the context in which it occurs is called the _____ _____ _____.

3. Psychologists define _____ as a form of interpersonal attraction that is governed by an implicit set of rules.

4. _____ stresses the costs and rewards involved in interpersonal relationships.

5. Suzy becomes more aggressive when she is frustrated than when she is not frustrated. This trend supports the _____ - _____ _____.

6. _____ is the use of social influence to cause people to change attitudes or behavior.

7. Milgram's experiment, the Jonestown massacre, and the behaviors of Nazis in Germany all provide examples of people initiating or changing behavior in response to direct commands. This change in behavior is called _____.

8. A mechanic has offered to provide several checks on your vehicle free of charge while it is in the shop for an oil change. This is done in hopes that in exchange for this added service you will _____ and will have anything that shows up from the checks repaired at that shop.

9. The blindfolded tug-of-war experiment revealed what students who have worked on class projects with other students already knew. Both the experiment and real-life experiences reveal that _____ occurs when groups work on a task for which there is no individual evaluation.

10. Scott and Meri tried giving candy to trick-or-treaters last Halloween on the honor system. They put a few bowls of candy on their porch, and went to a friend's house for a party. Much to their chagrin, when they returned the candy and the bowls were gone. The likelihood the bowls were stolen was probably increased as a function of the _____ that occurred when the trick-or-treaters donned their costumes.

PRACTICE TEST

Circle the letter that corresponds to the *best* alternative for each of the following items. Read each alternative carefully. The answers are presented at the end of this study guide chapter. Be sure to learn *why* each correct alternative is better than the others.

1. Jean studies *impression formation.* In other words, she is interested in:
    a. how people present themselves.
    b. how people form impressions about others.
    c. various techniques that are used in embossing paper.
    d. why people resist forming impressions on their first exposure to others.

2. A stereotype is:
    a. a brand of hi-fidelity equipment.
    b. a set of beliefs about members of a particular group.
    c. an individual's decision to share personal information.
    d. a bias toward members of one's group (i.e., the ingroup).

3. Carl and his friends went to watch the comedian-hypnotist at a local theater. The entertainer selected Carl as an "assistant". Soon, Carl was clucking like a chicken on stage, playing the role "the human plank", and being generally entertaining. He had not planned to participate, but when asked to, played the part well. Which of the following was at work in influencing his behavior?
    a. self-disclosure
    b. attribution theory
    c. the self-fulfilling prophecy
    d. the fundamental attribution of hypnotists error

4. In an experiment on ___, students in a class were given descriptions of a visiting lecturer that portrayed him as either *warm* or *cold*. After the lecture, those who had been told he was warm rated his presentation more favorably than those who were told he was cold.
   a. the self-serving bias
   b. cognitive dissonance
   c. the effects of prior information
   d. the fundamental attribution error

5. The tendency to make internal attributions when we are successful and external attributions when we fail is called the:
   a. self-serving bias.
   b. cognitive dissonance.
   c. unconscious motivation.
   d. fundamental attribution error.

6. Which of the following was **not** identified in your textbook as a component of *attitude?*
   a. affect
   b. behavior
   c. cognition
   d. environment

7. You just filled out a questionnaire on which you to rated the degree to which you agreed or disagreed with a variety of statements. The questionnaire employed:
   a. Likert scales.
   b. behavioral measures.
   c. minimum wage workers.
   d. the yes-no response scale.

8. An aversive state produced when an individual has two incompatible thoughts simultaneously is called:
   a. confusion.
   b. attitude clash.
   c. thought distraction.
   d. cognitive dissonance.

9. Proximity to others is ___ to the establishment of friendships.
   a. not related
   b. positively related
   c. negatively related
   d. all of the above

10. Which of the following was **not** identified as a contributing factor in attraction?
    a. IQ
    b. similarity
    c. reinforcement
    d. affect and emotions

11. Strong emotional reactions are to ___ as commitment is to ___.
    a. friendship; love
    b. passionate love; companionate love
    c. companionate love; passionate love
    d. compassionate love; dispassionate love

12. Altruism is one of the most widely studied forms of ___.
    a. prosocial behavior
    b. cognitive dissonance
    c. interpersonal attraction
    d. social influence on behavior

13. The tendency for a group of people to be less likely than an individual to provide assistance to a person in trouble is called:
    a. the bystander effect.
    b. the individual effect.
    c. the bystander intervention effect.
    d. the individual intervention effect.

14. ___ aggression is to the specific intent of harming another as ___ aggression is to harming others in the process of achieving another goal.
    a. Implicit; explicit
    b. Outright; concealed
    c. Instrumental; hostile
    d. Hostile; instrumental

15. Source factors that contribute to one's persuasiveness include all **but** which of the following?
    a. expertise
    b. attractiveness
    c. trustworthiness
    d. all of the above

16. ___ is another name for what is popularly known as "reverse psychology."
    a. Reactance
    b. Unconscious reversing
    c. Subliminal transference
    d. None of the above; psychologists do not describe the constellation of phenomena popularly described as "reverse psychology."

17. The *foot-in-the-door* technique is a good example of persuasion that:
    a. backfires when persuaders say things they should not say.
    b. gets cut off by the audience before the persuader's message has been heard entirely.
    c. is more effective in a face-to-face situation than with one person addressing many people.
    d. is based on another persuasion technique that involves telling lies in order to maintain audience attention.

18. In psychology, the term *confederate* refers to someone:
    a. acting for the experimenter.
    b. who fought for the South in the Civil War.
    c. who attempts to block the federation by subjects in an experiment.
    d. who realizes the goal of an experiment and produces meaningless data.

19. Asch's "line experiment" was designed to provide insight into:
    a. the phenomenon of conformity.
    b. factors contributing to one's persuasiveness.
    c. why subjects in Milgram's experiment acted as they did.
    d. a perceptual phenomenon that was originally studied by Gestalt psychologists.

20. ___ is a phenomenon in which group decision making enhances or amplifies the original opinions of the group's members.
    a. Reciprocity
    b. Risk taking
    c. Deindividuation
    d. Group polarization

21. People will wind fishing line more quickly when they are competing against others at the same task than when they are racing against the clock. This is an illustration of:
    a. social conformity.
    b. social facilitation.
    c. bystander intervention.
    d. a hypothetical construct.

22. The activities of the Ku Klux Klan and lynch mobs reflect ___ in action.
    a. group think
    b. social loafing
    c. outgroup bias
    d. none of the above

23. The free expression of ideas by members of a group to solve a problem is called:
    a. risky-shift.
    b. expressionism.
    c. brainstorming.
    d. free determinism.

24. ___ frequently results in behaviors that adversely affect members of a targeted group.
    a. Altruism
    b. Prejudice
    c. Groupthink
    d. Brainstorming

25. Because the majority of psychological research is conducted in the U.S., many of the results have been seen through ___ eyes.
    a. angry
    b. naked
    c. geocentric
    d. ethnocentric

ANSWERS TO KEY WORD EXERCISE

1. self-disclosure
4. Interdependence theory
7. obedience
10. deindividuation

2. fundamental attribution error
5. frustration-aggression hypothesis
8. reciprocate

3. friendship
6. Persuasion
9. social loafing

PRACTICE TEST ANSWERS AND EXPLANATIONS

1. b. Impression formation is the process of forming an opinion about another person.
2. b. Stereotypes are beliefs about members of particular groups.
3. c. The self-fulfilling prophecy is a phenomenon whereby expectations elicit behaviors in others that confirm those expectations.
4. c. The classic experiment was designed to study the effects of prior information about others.
5. a. The self-serving bias involves crediting one's self for one's successes and blaming circumstances for one's failures.
6. d. Environment was not identified as a component of attitude.
7. a. Likert scales are tools for measuring extent of agreement (e.g., 1 = strongly disagree... 7 = strongly agree).
8. d. *Cognitive dissonance* involves two simultaneous, incompatible thoughts or cognitions.
9. b. Mere proximity to others increases the likelihood that people will become friends.
10. a. Age was not listed among the variables that contribute to interpersonal attraction.
11. b. Passionate love involves strong emotional reactions; companionate love involves lasting commitment.
12. a. Prosocial behavior is that which benefits society or helps others; altruism is prosocial behavior that is done voluntarily with no anticipation of reward.
13. a. The *bystander effect* describes the decreased likelihood of people who are part of groups (as compared to individuals) to come to the assistance others.
14. d. Hostile aggression involves harming others as the primary goal. Instrumental aggression involves harming others when striving to reach a primary goal.
15. d. Each of the items in the list plays a role in determining one's persuasiveness.
16. a. *Reactance* is the tendency to react in the opposite direction to a persuasive message.
17. c. Most forms of persuasion are more effective in face-to-face situations; this is true with the foot-in-the-door technique.
18. a. A confederate is someone who, unbeknownst to the subject(s), acts as a subject in an experiment.
19. a. Asch's experiment provided surprising results regarding conformity.
20. d. Group polarization involves the enhancement or amplification of the original opinions of the group's members.
21. b. Social facilitation involves improved performance in the presence of others.
22. a. The activities of these groups reflect group think. Groupthink is also thought to have been involved in decisions to initiate or escalate wartime strategies (including some well-known poor decisions).
23. c. Brainstorming is the free expression of ideas in a group. However, it is noteworthy that many people are more creative when brainstorming alone.
24. b. Prejudice most frequently involves judging others on the basis of negative stereotypes.
25. d. Ethnocentrism is the belief that one's own country or culture is superior to all other countries or cultures. Failure to consider other cultures when designing research studies is an extension of this.

Key Vocabulary Terms

Use the following list to write definitions *in your own words* for each of the key terms from the chapter. Translating the terms into language that is comfortable and familiar for you will facilitate your learning. For further study of these terms, go to the companion web site for the text book where you will find electronic flash cards that you may use to test your vocabulary.

social psychology

ethnocentrism

individualism

collectivism

impression formation

stereotype

self-fulfilling prophecy

self-disclosure

attribution

fundamental attribution error

self-serving bias

just world belief

attitudes

likert scale

cognitive dissonance

attraction

friendship

passionate love

compassionate love

interdependence theory

comparison level

prosocial behavior

altruism

bystander effect

aggression

hostile aggression

instrumental aggression

frustration-aggression hypothesis

persuasion

sleeper effect

reactance

obedience

conformity

risky-shift phenomenon

group polarization

compliance

foot-in-the-door effect

door-in-the-face technique

reciprocity

social facilitation

social loafing

coactors

deindividuation

brainstorming

groupthink

prejudice

discrimination

CHAPTER 16

Industrial, Organizational, and Other Applications of Psychology

HUMAN RESOURCES PSYCHOLOGY
Personnel Selection
Training
Performance Appraisal

ORGANIZATIONAL PSYCHOLOGY
Motivation
Job Selection

HUMAN-FACTORS PSYCHOLOGY
Human-Machine System
Workplace Design

OTHER APPLICATIONS
Forensic Psychology
Sport Psychology

Do You Know?

Do you know that psychology is a dynamic field with developing sub-areas that have significant implications for many aspects of life? Although the lay public may still struggle to think of psychologists as anything other than practitioners whose clients sit on couches and reflect on feelings, increasingly psychology is making its way into such diverse areas as engineering, forensics, law, sports, and numerous other contexts. Further, the training necessary to have some of the cutting edge careers in psychology does not necessarily have to extend well beyond the bachelor's level.

Perhaps one reason that people with training in psychology are finding employment in so many new areas is that their training, even at the bachelor's level, is diverse and provides many useful skills. Work in the field of psychology requires proficiency with language and communication, as well as with quantitative skills. But, those only mark the beginning. Because behavior is challenging to study, students of psychology must develop good analytical and critical thinking skills. Armed with this mix of verbal, quantitative, and analytic skills, and given a passion for understanding the causal agents that contribute to the complexities of human behavior, it is no surprise that psychologists are finding meaningful, interesting employment in a host of places.

Whether your formal experience with the science of psychology ends with this course or extends through several years of education and into your career, it is certain that you will continue to be exposed to examples of the work of psychologists throughout your life. Psychology is a relatively young field, but despite its youth, it has much to offer for myriad allied fields. Because we are surrounded by behavior, it is hard to think of a domain for which the work of psychologists does not have important implications.

Notes from Class and the Textbook

Use the space provided in this outline to record notes from the textbook as well as from class lectures and discussion. Questions related to the *Psychological Detective, Hands On, Myth or Science* and *Study Tip* sections in the text have been presented in the outline; use the associated space to respond to the questions and to record your own comments about the issues.

I. Human Resources Psychology

    A. Personnel Selection

When selecting workers, what are some reasons that employers continue to use in interviews in spite of their having poor validity? Consider the question from the perspective of a company recruiter.

      1. Using Personality Tests in Selecting Police Officers

B. Training

C. Performance Appraisal

II. Organizational Psychology

    A. Motivation

    B. Job Selection

Summarize the various theories of work motivation. Add a new example or two to illustrate each theory.

III. Human-Factors Psychology

    A. Human-Machine System

Create icons or other visual representations for the criteria for good design in human-machine systems.

B. Workplace Design

    1. Safety

IV. Other Applications

    A. Forensic Psychology

        1. Memory and the Law

        2. Insanity, Competence, and Civil Commitment

    B. Sport Psychology

        1. Enhancing Athletic Performance

        2. Coaching

        3. Fan Violence

Evaluate and outline the key points of forensic and sport psychology. Include brief timelines of the history of each.

Learning Objectives

After you have studied the chapter, you should be able to respond to the following statements and questions to convey your understanding of the material.

1. Compare and contrast the fields of Industrial and Organizational Psychology.

2. Identify the purposes of human resources psychology.

3. How are training and performance appraisal used in employment settings to assure worker efficiency and productivity?

4. What factors contribute to the likelihood that one will be satisfied with one's job?

5. Discuss the variety of topics human factors psychologists study.

6. What is forensic psychology?

7. Discuss the purposes served by sport psychologists.

Key Word Exercise

Fill in the blanks in the following statements with key words and terms from the textbook. Answer as many as you can without referring to your notes or to the book. If you have blanks after thinking about each item, try using your book. The answers are presented after the practice test.

1. _____ _____ involves measurement of human physical characteristics and development of machines to fit those characteristics.

2. The _____ _____ _____ is used in U.S., Canada, and Australia in selecting police officers.

3. The deliberate and planned process by which employees are exposed to learning experiences designed to teach new skills and improve job performance is called _____.

4. Using a red light on a machine to indicate that one should stop doing something is an example of good use of the _____ _____ _____.

5. The U.S. Army's M-1 Abrams tank was used to illustrate poor _____ _____.

Practice Test

Circle the letter that corresponds to the *best* alternative for each of the following items. Read each alternative carefully. The answers are presented at the end of this study guide chapter. Be sure to learn *why* each correct alternative is better than the others.

1. *Army Alpha* is to *Army Beta* as ___ is to ___.
   a. soldier; officer
   b. literate; illiterate
   c. boot camp; retirement
   d. 1st Battalion; 2nd Battalion

2. A key responsibility of personnel psychologists is to determine which of the following?
   a. skills
   b. abilities
   c. knowledge
   d. all of the above

3. The best interviews are:
   a. structured.
   b. situational.
   c. both a. and b.
   d. neither a. nor b.

4. Employers screen prospective employees for drug use because:
   a. drug use correlates with absenteeism and turnover.
   b. most state governments mandate that the employers do so.
   c. the federal government mandates that all employers do so.
   d. None of the above are true.

5. According to the textbook, which of the following types of measures is *not* used in evaluating a training program?
   a. Reaction Measures
   b. Learning Measures
   c. Behavior Measures
   d. Perception Measures

6. Samantha has been with her employer for six months. She has just been handed feedback ratings from her boss on a series of criteria. This is part of the process of:
   a. training.
   b. applicant screening.
   c. performance appraisal.
   d. a formal exit interview.

7. Clive studies labor unions, including rules and benefits of membership, as well as the social dynamics of them. Clive is a(n):
   a. personnel psychologist.
   b. industrial psychologist.
   c. organizational psychologist.
   d. human-factors psychologist.

8. Expectancy suggests employees are concerned with *valance, instrumentality, and expectancy*. This combination means:
   a. the average employee is not smart enough to know what they want.
   b. workers will be motivated if they believe they have the means and opportunity to succeed.
   c. that employees are bound to be dissatisfied with their jobs because one cannot have all three.
   d. that worker motivation is equivalent to a given employee's desirability by another employer.

9. The most widely researched work attitude in organizational psychology is:
   a. job satisfaction.
   b. employer loyalty.
   c. employee benefits appreciation.
   d. worker efficiency (expressed as a ratio of worker cost to worker productivity).

10. Greg's patio door baffles most of his houseguests. For some reason, everyone tries to get it to open out, when actually it was made to open into his house. The designers of the door should:
   a. consult human-factors psychologists.
   b. carefully consider using a more effective training program.
   c. go to Greg's house and see whether it was installed properly.
   d. approach the labor union for the company that made the door and consult about plant conditions.

11. Some psychologists are concerned with distinguishing workplace accidents that occur as the result of unsafe conditions from those that occur as the result of unsafe acts. Reducing the likelihood of accidents by modifying some aspects of work conditions, by redesigning tools and machines is:
   a. the ergonomic approach.
   b. more effective than prohibiting unsafe acts.
   c. not worth the trade-off when one considers efficiency.
   d. usually done at the expense of workers' wages and benefits.

Answers to Key Word Exercise

1. Engineering anthropometry
2. California Psychological Inventory (CPI)
3. training
4. principle of compatibility
5. workplace design

Practice Test Answers and Explanations

1. b.   The *Army Alpha* was the first large-scale group intelligence test; the *Army Beta* was developed subsequently for testing illiterate and non-English-speaking soldiers.
2. d.   Personnel psychologists try to determine the knowledge, skills, and abilities of job applicants.
3. c.   To be effective interviews should be structured (every candidate gets asked the same questions) and situational (providing job-related questions that require candidates to "think on their feet").
4. a.   Though it is controversial many employers screen applicants for drug use because it is useful in predicting absenteeism and employee turnover.
5. d.   The fourth type of measure of training programs is *results measures.*
6. c.   Performance appraisal involves evaluation of a person's functioning on job-related tasks.
7. c.   Organizational psychology is a blend of work-related psychology, social psychology, human relations, and business.
8. b.   Workers need to have the means and opportunities to succeed in pursuit of a desired outcome.
9. a.   Job satisfaction is the most widely studied attitude in organizational psychology.
10. a.   Human-factors psychologists focus on the designing of equipment and machines for human use.
11. a.   The ergonomic approach involves focusing on the fit and design of tools, machines, and instruments with which humans interact.

Key Vocabulary Terms

Use the following list to write definitions *in your own words* for each of the key terms from the chapter. Translating the terms into language that is comfortable and familiar for you will facilitate your learning. For further study of these terms, go to the companion website for the textbook where you will find electronic flash cards that you may use to test your vocabulary.

industrial/organizational (I/O) psychology

human resources psychology

training

performance appraisal

organizational psychology

human-factors psychology

engineering anthropometry

forensic psychologist

sport psychologist